Shoki Coe

Shoki Coe

An Ecumenical Life in Context

台灣人的先覺 -黃彰輝

Author: Tiuⁿ Sūi-hîong
張瑞雄

Translator: Siau Chheng-hun
蕭清芬

WCC Publications
Geneva

Foreword

It is my distinct honour and joy to pen this Preface to *Shoki Coe: An Ecumenical Life in Context*. The original title as published in Taiwanese and Japanese, which translated as "Prophetic Taiwanese Pioneer," expresses in three words the context for Shoki's life and work as he was prophetic, a pioneer and Taiwanese throughout.

Shoki Coe was first and foremost Taiwanese. In spite of the difficult and tumultuous period into which he was born and in which he gained his theological formation, his love and passion for the land and people of Taiwan remained steadfast. Although he spent much of his formative years abroad, first in Japan and then in England, he eventually returned to Taiwan and served for 18 years as the principal of Tainan Theological College. He returned to face a changing and challenging context in which the church was called to give prophetic voice and priestly ministry. The various revolutionary changes that were enveloping Taiwan, as well as other countries in Asia and elsewhere in the world, informed his theological analysis of the situation and contributed to the development of "contextualization" as a new method of Christian engagement with the world and particularly of theology and theological education. In spite of his "good works" within Taiwan, he experienced the pain of betrayal and distrust because of his participation in the Self-Determination Movement of Taiwan and because he spoke out on behalf of many who were not being heard. Although such a stance eventually led to a virtual exile, separating him from the land and people he loved so much, he did not let this period of suffering detract from his pride in identity nor his self-awareness as a Taiwanese.

It may be safe to say that this exiled existence further honed his prophetic voice. It was during this period of estrangement from the land and people of Taiwan that Shoki Coe joined the Theological Education Fund (TEF) of the International Missionary Council, which was created in Achimota in 1958, integrated into WCC in 1961 and later in 1977 became the Programme on Theological Education (PTE). In this capacity he was able further to develop and elaborate the analytical tools of "contextualization" at a global level. His contribution to the universal church was much more than simply presenting a "term" for defining what must be done for Christianity to be relevant to the world in which it was called to bear witness. He presented the church with both a conceptual and procedural tool for formulating a method of authentic witness that held in creative tension the scriptures (text) and the dynamic changes in the society (context) in which it was read, interpreted and applied. Coe's contribution not only revolutionized the ecumenical movement's approach to mission and mission theology, his approach revolutionized the understanding of theological education which is valid for many streams of contextual theologies, for regional associations of theological education in Asia and the WCC from that time until today. It would make inroads into the evangelical and even the Roman Catholic perspectives on mission. This is surely evidence of the prophetic nature of Shoki Coe's theology.

In many ways Shoki Coe represented the pioneering spirit of the ecumenical movement. His work in relation to the missiological concept of "contextualization" not only extended the horizons of mission theology but opened up a new avenue for exploring the interrelatedness of the Christian message and the world in which the church is called to witness. His understanding of *kairos*, the entrance of Jesus Christ into time (*chronos*), as the ultimate example of contextualization provides a fundamental theological foundation which intimately connects the church with the context in which it lives.

The transformative power of Christ's incarnation as the "contextualization" of God's message to the world was also a source of identity for the church as it took up its responsibility of being the prophetic voice affecting social transformation. In putting forward his theology of contextualization this pioneer ecumenist argued staunchly for the catholicity of the gospel. He adamantly believed that contextualization was the authentic way for achieving a vital catholicity. For Coe, contextualization was not simply about painting the gospel message of Christ (text) in different colors to fit in with the environment (context). Rather, it was holding these two in tension in a critical assessment of the context enacted in light of the *missio Dei*. His creative and forward-looking approach provided insight into how the church's authentic acts of mission could embody the missological work of God in today's world. This vision revealed a new horizon in which individuals could be both true to the transformative power of the gospel and free to transform society without being above, beyond or estranged from it. It also set the stage for the development of an Asian theology by successive theologians, such as C. S. Song, Kosuke Koyama and Aloysius Pieris.

The life and work of Shoki Coe exemplify for us what it means to be honest and faithful—to the gospel of Christ, to one's own ethnic and social reality, and also to the spirit of ecumenism and its quest of mission in unity and unity in mission. I am confident that this volume will enrich, empower and energize us to "take home the good news" in ever creative and contextual ways, being mutually accountable for our texts in our contexts.

Rev. Dr Olav Fykse Tveit
WCC General Secretary

Tributes

Shoki Coe and the Theological Education Fund

I came to 13 London Road, Bromley, Kent in England in 1972, when I was appointed associate director for the Theological Education Fund (TEF) of the World Council of Churches Commission on World Mission and Evangelism (CWME). I had returned home to South Africa to teach in a theological seminary in accordance with the TEF scholarship grant. The last thing I ever expected was an invitation to join the staff as successor to the quietly efficient Dr Walter Cason, who had been associate director of the TEF with area responsibility for sub-Saharan Africa. I knew very little about this organization except that it was doing innovative and exciting work, particularly in the area of staff development, theological teachers' associations and the encouragement of indigenous theological thinking and writing.

We were not certain that the South African government would allow me to take up the post. The WCC was like a red rag to the South African apartheid government because of the grants its Programme to Combat Racism had made to the ANC and PAC, banned organizations which the South African government deemed to be terrorist organizations. As it happened I was granted the rare privilege, for a black South African at the time, of a passport, and so began a very important phase in my life.

We formed a team of four associate directors plus the director, Shoki Coe. We each had different area responsibilities. So, for instance, Aharon Sapsezian, a Brazilian Armenian, had area responsibility for the Middle East and Latin America. James Berquist (the only Caucasian) from the United States looked after India. Shoki and Ivy Chou divided the rest of Asia between them. We were operating under a Third Mandate from the WCC and were especially given the task of promoting contextualization in so-called third-world theological institutions and churches. This meant that we were supposed to encourage and support efforts in the different regions at making Christianity, and therefore theological education, more native, more indigenous, more at home in those contexts and not the alien product that it so often seemed to be.

We were as diverse as you could ever hope to be racially, nationally and ecumenically. Shoki was Presbyterian, Ivy Methodist, Jim Lutheran and I was Anglican. I think Aharon was Methodist. English was the first language of only one of us, but it was the language of our organization. We were diverse in our life experiences as well. Ivy had been born on mainland China but grew up in Singapore; Jim was a US citizen who had taught in India for quite a while; Aharon came with all the memory of the Armenian genocide and the radicalness of Latin American liberation theology. Shoki was a refugee, an exile from his native Formosa, now Taiwan, and I came from the injustices and restrictions of apartheid South Africa. And we all were representing in addition the diverse needs and complex problems of poverty, corruption, exploitation and misgovernment in our various areas of responsibility.

We each had to convince our colleagues in our regular staff meetings of the vital importance of our particular projects be it a scholarship for staff development in a college or university in our area, or library development, and so on. Our meetings were raucous and bruising in a way because each sought to carry the day and our colleagues were rigorous in their examination of each project. Shoki was quite wonderful in his ability to remain calm and serene amidst the cacophony, and we always ended still friends despite the sharp criticisms we had given and received. I doubt that anyone else could have kept us as a team despite our different temperaments and interests. He believed fervently in our theological enterprise and had the skills to herd this particular collection of cats.

I was always impressed by his capacity to hold us together, and yet he suffered deeply being an exile from his beloved motherland. He used to say, "My homeland was the fourth world ignored by almost all." But he never indulged in self-pity. It just made him more sensitive to the plight of others.

I am so privileged to have had him as my boss and friend. He made a difference in my life and in that of the many he touched. I learned a great deal about leadership and about the power of gentleness in an abrasive, competitive world. I am a better person for having been touched by Shoki and I give thanks to God for him. He must have heard his Lord and Master say, "Well done, good and faithful servant."

Archbishop Emeritus Desmond M. Tutu

My Guru Shoki

Above the door to the library of Tainan Theological Seminary, a photo with the face of Shoki Coe greets every student who enters. For many years he was the principal of this seminary. Later, when he became one of the directors of the Theological Education Fund of the World Council of Churches, he regularly visited theological seminaries in Southeast Asia. I remember numerous wonderful occasions of free and relaxed theological discussion, often ending in serious reflective moments. He was genuinely happy to be with us "younger theologians" as he visited Singapore, Djakarta, Hong Kong or Manila. He was quite naturally, with grace and charm, dialogical. For him, to be educational was dialogical. Our dialogue inspired the mood of prayer together, affirming the ecumenical presence of Christ in Southeast Asia and beyond. We "younger theologians" were privileged to enjoy those many hours to be spiritually and theologically near "Shoki," as we called him. He was the *guru* to many of our generation, certainly to me.

He authored the word "contextualization." Contextualization, he told me, is another name for the church's constant need of reforming itself—*ecclesia semper reformanda*. This thought is foundational for the church, the beloved community. The church cannot "settle down" in some fixed religious ideology or even with theological theses. The Head of the Church had "no place to lay his head" (Luke 9:58). For the Church of the Crucified and Risen Lord, contextualization is a serious matter. The gospel creates moments of reformation, reconstruction and resurrection, not just once but constantly. In accordance with the spirit of *ecclesia semper reformanda*, Shoki insisted upon the expression "contextualizing theology," not "contextual theology" or "contextualized theology." It must be understood in the present progressive mood. Contextualization is inspired by the urgency of the *here and now* power of the gospel. It is, in the words of Toyohiko Kagawa, to imitate God who is "the awesome power that uplifts us."

Contextualization is more than a cultural adjustment. It engages in a prophetic critique of the given context itself and the creation of a new context *here and now*. Such spiritual energy originates from the church's engagement in the struggle for social justice as demonstrated, for instance, by the 1934 Barmen Declaration against Hitler's idolatrous use of power or by the Dalits's open protest against the 2002 Anti-Conversion Legislation in Tamil Nadu. "Act justly one with another" says Jeremiah (7:5-7). "Yes, you are the keeper of your brothers/sisters!" (Gen. 4:9).

"You shall not kill," says the Biblical commandment. This uncompromising commandment must be publicly contextualized. It must be mobilized and articulated. In the words of Article Nine [Renunciation of War] of the Postwar Constitution of Japan (1946) this commandment was historically contextualized:

> Aspiring sincerely to an international peace based on justice and order, the Japanese people forever renounce war as a sovereign right of the nation and the threat or use of force as means of settling international disputes.
>
> In order to accomplish the aim of the preceding paragraph, land, sea, and air forces, as well as other war potential, will never be maintained. The right of belligerency of the state will not be recognized.

My dear guru, Shoki, with millions of people in Japan and beyond, I am convinced that this contextualization is for the life and death of humanity upon the earth today. Lord Jesus bless us in this critical moment of contextualization as we struggle against the deceptive power aiming to abolish this Article! I remember our last time together in your home in southern England. I saw the tranquil afternoon sea over the window, and I listened to your concern for the future of humankind.

Kosuke Koyama (小山晃佑)
Professor Emeritus, Union Theological Seminary, New York

Translator's Notes

The original writing assumes readers have some knowledge of the background and the historical and social setting of the main character of the book. For English readers who may not be familiar with the background, I have placed additional footnotes to clarify the usage of some words or nomenclature. All these footnotes are clearly indicated as "Translator's note"; other footnotes are the author's.

With the consent of the author, all the Taiwanese names, persons and places—except Shoki Coe—are put in romanized Taiwanese. But occasionally, additional or optional pronunciations in Chinese Mandarin are given. For the references to old documentation used by the author, I have kept the names in Chinese Mandarin transliteration.

The name "Formosa" was commonly used in the Western world to refer to what today is called "Taiwan." Both names are used in this translation, as determined by the occasion. For instance, the Foreign Missions of the Presbyterian Church of England called its mission in Taiwan "Formosa Mission," and the official English name of the Presbyterian Church in Taiwan was at one time the "Presbyterian Church of Formosa." In the original text there was no distinction between Formosa and Taiwan.

Some international and local church agencies or organizations have changed their names in the course of their history. Although the original text uses the same nomenclature, the translator has tried to name them to match the historical setting.

Ching-fen Hsiao

Introduction

Like the man himself, the name Shoki Coe is a blend of global cultural influences, with its Japanese pronunciation (Ko) and English spelling for the Taiwanese surname Ṅg. Born in 1914, he lived exactly half of his 74 years away from his home in Taiwan. By the time he turned 51, when he left Taiwan for what turned out essentially to be the last time, he had already been abroad 14 years: four years studying in Japan and ten years in England, where he had gone to study and then been stranded at the outbreak of World War II. From 1965 until his death in England in 1988, his career was dedicated to the theological education and ministerial training of younger churches through the Theological Education Fund (TEF) and beyond.

Those who called him Teacher or heard him speak marvelled at his ethnically grounded perspective, intellect and behaviour as an authentic Taiwanese "everyman." His state of mind and outlook on life were described by Nobel Laureate and Archbishop Emeritus of Cape Town, Desmond Tutu, as "a man without country" and by the Dean of Southeast Asian Graduate School of Theology, Kosuke Koyama, as "a homeless guru." People who came to understand him were impressed by his deeply rooted Taiwanese identity, yet he was a well-seasoned international and interdenominational leader, a thorough ecumenist. Such a person is truly a "contextual thinker," characterized by a "life lived contextually." In words he first coined in the "third-world" setting, his theology is now widely known as "contextual theology."

His 14-year tenure with the World Council of Churches (WCC) began in 1965 until his retirement in 1979. However, his involvement with the ecumenical movement started in 1939 when he attended the World Conference of Christian Youth in Amsterdam as a Japanese delegate. Shoki was invited to Geneva in 1951 to participate in planning the WCC's second assembly in Evanston in 1954, which he attended as an official delegate of the Presbyterian Church in Taiwan; he was then forty years old. As a theologian from the Third World, he was invited to participate in the 1958 creation of the Theological Education Fund as part of the International Missionary Council. As the director of the Theological Education Fund, he advocated, assisted and guided the seminaries and ministerial training projects of the younger churches in the third world. In this role he was involved firsthand in defending and protesting the imprisonment and deportation of seminary professors by the dictatorial regime in South Korea. Even if he could not participate in the struggle for human rights and freedom of religion in his homeland, he could apply his considerable energy and influence to struggles in other countries. In the basement of the WCC library, I was astonished to read handwritten volumes of notes taken by then–Associate Director Desmond Tutu for reports to the director Shoki Coe of the seminaries he visited. The TEF staff team thus touched many trainers and trainees of the gospel of Jesus Christ throughout the world.

As I look back on the germination of Shoki Coe's biography, I cannot help but point to a divine call and providence. As his student, I was not one of those chosen by Shoki to succeed in the task of engaging in theology and educating the future church workers at Tainan Theological College. Was I angry? Certainly. So I decided to run away from Shoki and his Presbyterian Church in Taiwan (PCT). Like the prophet Jonah, I went my own way in 1962. After a few years of study, I chose to stay in the United States and accepted the opportunity to serve a Japanese American church in the United Methodist denomination. I thought I had escaped the gravitational pull of Shoki and the Presbyterians. But through our common concern for the future of Taiwan and commitment to the Christian mission and ministry, God led us to seek each other and work together.

It was during a critical time of Shoki's leadership in the world movement for Taiwanese self-determination that he discovered God had prepared an "indispensable friend" for Taiwan and its Presbyterian Church within the United States and in the United Methodist Church. In 1976, Rev. Dr Tracy Jones, General Secretary of the Board of Global Ministries of the United Methodist Church, drafted a resolution for the board to adopt. His resolution consisted of two main points: (1) the US should normalize its diplomatic relationship with the People's Republic of China; and (2) as diplomatic negotiations take place, the United Methodist Church should support Taiwan as *an integral part of China*. The latter phrase was poison to the Taiwanese self-determination struggle. As a full voting member of the Board, I was led by the Holy Spirit to amend the second part, which was then approved by the Board. The amended resolution read that "the United Methodist people support the idea of 'self-determination' and respect human rights for the Taiwanese people."

Since 1945, at the end of World War II, Taiwan was ruled by the Nationalist Chinese Party, or Kuomingtang (KMT) regime. The colonialists from China, headed by Chiang Kai-shek, exploited the island and its people. As the exploitation deepened, the leaders of the Presbyterian Church in Taiwan—many of them Shoki's students—stood up for the people of Taiwan. Not surprisingly, as a result the entire church was subjected to severe persecution. From 1972 to 1980, the leaders of the church issued three declarations as the regime watched for their chance to arrest the Presbyterian leaders. Finally, in December of 1979 many PCT leaders were arrested. With the April 18, 1980, arrest of Rev. Dr Chun-Ming Kao, general secretary of the Presbyterian Church in Taiwan, the church fell under surveillance, if not outright captivity, by the KMT. I took part in the strategy session summoned by Shoki in Geneva; we tried to reach out to all possible church leaders to appeal to their national leaders to work towards the release of imprisoned PCT leaders and ask Chiang Ching-Kuo—Chiang Kai-Shek's son and successor—to stop persecuting the church. Aside from our business matters, Shoki and I shared a hotel room, ate and walked together on Geneva streets for three days. They were memorable days of friendship, bonded by staunch commitment to a common cause.

After Shoki's death in 1988, his *Recollections and Reflections*[1] was published. I was deeply moved and realized that I could trace the outlines of his life. When I was stationed in Japan from 1991 to 1999, I realized I was in a position to collect data, to verify and back up his stories from partly faded memories. But my real search began in earnest only from the time I retired from my active duties in 1999. Making use of my free (retired) time and with my slow pace, I started to trace Shoki's shadow in Taiwan, Japan, England, Switzerland and the United States. Everywhere I searched, I found surprise rewards of photographs and documents; and in several cases, I arrived barely in time to obtain valuable pictures before the contributors passed away.

I am not a gifted writer, but I believe that the stories of a prominent ecumenist will attract readers. So I felt bold in getting the Taiwanese version completed and published in 2004. Within about a year the Taiwanese edition sold out. Then I recruited a well-known Japanese church leader, Rev. Dr Hiroshi Ohmiya, to help translate and edit in Japanese, and the Japanese edition was published in 2007. For this edition, Rev. Dr Ching-Fen Hsiao, a prominent Taiwanese theologian, took on the task of translating the book into English. The Presbyterian Church in Taiwan has accepted the book as its property and is ready to publish the English edition under its auspices. I am indebted to Ching-Fen for his efforts in translating, for which he took three months leave from his pastorate to complete. I am grateful to the Presbyterian Church in Taiwan for lifting the financial burden of this project from my shoulders and for negotiating the partnership with WCC for publication of this book.

I sincerely pray that people of the world will be inspired to join the movement of peace and mutual respect and to realize the inherent *imago Dei* (image of God) in the human race, as Shoki used to preach and pray with his students.

1
Country and Family
A History of Struggle and Faith

Taiwan: Conquest and Identity

The island of Taiwan is located on the west end of the Pacific Ocean, off the continent of Asia. In the sixteenth century, Portuguese seafarers upon their first sighting shouted, "Ihla Formosa," and so the name Formosa was given and commonly used by Europeans since then.

Taiwan possesses a long shoreline that allows traders, pirates, refugees, adventurers—even military conquerors and political authorities from abroad—to enter easily. When, during the early seventeenth century, Dutch and Spanish commercial colonialists occupied the southern and northern parts of the island, for 38 years and 17 years respectively, very few ethnic Chinese inhabited the island. The majority of residents were from Pên-po˙ ("plains," Mandarin pronunciation is *Ping-pu*) tribal groups. These people were gentle, tolerant, peace-loving and trusting people. They got along well and mingled with the colonizers. Taiwanese today still demonstrate these roots in their personality. At that time the cultures of these Pên-po˙ and their neighboring mountain aboriginal tribal groups did not depend on written language. There were enough natural resources for them to rely on simple hunting and food gathering for the sparsely populated land. Their social structure and life were primarily self-contained and did not require self-promotion and advancement. The intruders and colonizers from outside took advantage of them, regarding them as uncivilized barbarians.[1]

To promote high profits from trade, the Dutch colonizers, who developed sugar cane cultivation, created various sizes of plantations—large, medium and small *Kiat* (Chieh, "parcels")— hired local people and imported indentured farm workers from the mainland (China). This changed a multiethnic society into a racial and ethnic mixture and created a community where hunters and food-gatherers coexisted with settled plantation farmers. As the number of Chinese increased, the colonizers recognized the advantages of the language, skills and tools introduced by the farm labourers and accorded them special privileges and better living conditions. However, the labourers, being mostly single men, began to marry the local women, often polygamously. They were indigenized and identified themselves as Formosan.

In 1662, when the Dutch surrendered to Koxinga, the Pên-po˙ population in Taiwan was estimated to be about forty thousand. This was the number provided by Iân-pêng Kūn-ông/Yenping Chun-wang (Koxinga's official title). The number reflects only those under his rule or people with whom he was dealing. Twelve years earlier, in 1650, the Pê^n-po˙ population was estimated to be about seventy thousand. It is not likely that the population was slaughtered so rapidly that it was reduced by 30% in fifteen years. Most likely, the native population fled the persecution by both the Dutch and Chinese (Han people).[2] Furthermore, according to Chen Shaohsing's estimate, towards the end of the Dutch occupation there were as many as twenty-five thousand Chinese (Han) living in Taiwan.[3] This number, although smaller than that of the original inhabitants of Taiwan, was gradually catching up.

In 1680, under the rule of the so-called Kingdom of Yenping Chunwang, the population of Taiwan was estimated to be 120,000. In 1830, 150 years later, it had grown to about two million. As an immigrant country this increase could be seen as natural. However, for 75 years, half of the 150 years of the Ching Dynasty's relations with Taiwan, the official Ching Imperial Court forbade people to immigrate to the island, referring to it as "a lump of clay overseas."[4] In effect, the Ching Court regarded Taiwan as a place for outlaws and rascals. However, for single men it was a new land of frontier adventure, and in marrying women from the mainstream Pê^n-po˙ matriarchal society,[5] a new unique Taiwanese people and culture were born. The conquered, in some sense, became the conquerors of their oppressors.

However, under its leader, Koxinga, the Kingdom of Yenping Chunwang forced on the people of Taiwan the culture of the Chinese people and with it the Chinese language. Having obtained imperial authority, the Kingdom used it to exert its control over all of Taiwan. The Pê^n-po˙ and the mountain tribal people were considered uncivilized barbarians. The Han culture was used to unify the land and to implement the imperial government system based on Confucian ethics. Around 1758–1759, one hundred years after Koxinga occupied Taiwan, the Ching Emperor, through his officials, began the process of "granting family names" to the Pê^n-po˙. This process led to the "Hanization" (assimilation by the Han) of the Pê^n-po˙ people. Thus, although the people of Taiwan carry the Pê^n-po˙ and tribal genes in their heritage, they identify culturally with the Han.

Three Generations of Christians
The First Generation
Shoki Coe's grandfather, born in 1852, was named Ñg Lêng-kiat, also known as Chì-sêng. He was born during the Ching Dynasty, an extension of the Kingdom of Yenping Chunwang, in the village of Ku-î, Tang-káng in southern Taiwan. The ancestors of the Ñg family immigrated to Taiwan from Kim-mñg

(Quymoy/Kinmen). Ng Lêng-kiàt's family settled in Taiwan during the 1600s. He was born about two hundred years later into the seventh generation. Thus the Ngs were early residents in Taiwan, part of the Taiwanese people and culturally indigenized.

Ng Lêng-kiàt was known to local residents as a Taoist priest who was affiliated chiefly with Tong-liông Keng Temple[6] to provide services to those who lacked peace of mind and physical health. All these people felt the need for religious healing. He believed that he was cleverer than others and was able to attract the attention of a great number of people. Thus, he could make people believe that the deity he served was more powerful and effective than others. He learned special shamanist techniques, one of which was unique and of which he was most proud. It was to make an egg climb up to the top of a bamboo pole. He later admitted that he did preparation before he performed this shamanist "miracle." To make it happen he placed a spider web thread on the bamboo pole and then threaded the web inside the eggshell. The shamanistic technique he established included the healing of water buffalo by supplementing their diet with herbal medicine.

Due to his specialty and effectiveness, his family's livelihood was quite comfortable. Nevertheless, deep in his heart he felt a certain emptiness. On the one hand, he made up his mind to be a good counselor to others, for which his conscience constantly demanded that he be honest in speaking and diligent in work. He maintained one principle: his charge was consistent with the degree of helpfulness of his prescriptions and of the counsel he gave. On the other hand, he and his wife suffered pain over the premature death of their own children. Consequently, he earnestly searched for truth and reliable help.

The efforts and influence of foreign missionaries most probably impacted Ng Lêng-kiàt, although we do not know if he had any direct contact with them. In 1865, when the British missionary Dr James Maxwell arrived in Taiwan, Lêng-kiàt was only twelve years old but was already a priest. Led by his desire to have both male and female offspring,[7] he must have made his first contact with Christianity in 1873 when he was about twenty years old. According to the records, in 1885 he enrolled in the Gospel College (now Tainan Theological College and Seminary) when he was 32 years old and Maxwell had been in Taiwan for twenty years. Lêng-kiàt had been a religious person and had ethical and moral principles to follow. His study at the college increased his literary abilities and laid a high-quality foundation for his knowledge. When Maxwell began his evangelistic mission, he set his base in Tainan. However, due to resistance and opposition, he soon had to move to Kî-āu, Ko-hiông (Kaohsiung)[8] to carry on his medical and evangelistic mission. Across from

Kî-āu, on the hill of Tá^n-káu, was the British Consulate. Shortly afterward, when the disposition of the people toward foreign medical doctors improved, Maxwell was able to move back to the capital city (Tainan) to carry on his mission. According to the history of Tang-káng Church, in 1867, the third year after his arrival in Taiwan, Maxwell, accompanied by the Rev. Hugh Ritchie, came to Tang-káng to carry on missionary work. Ritchie arrived in Taiwan in 1867 and died there in 1879. After his first visit Ritchie continued to come to Tang-káng to conduct worship services. With the help of believers, he was able to rent a straw hut as a chapel for worship and a place to conduct evangelism.

In 1871 another missionary, the Rev. William Campbell, came to Taiwan. He befriended Taiwanese throughout the southern part of Taiwan and conducted his evangelistic work. In 1878 two American merchant ships appeared near the coast of Hêng-chhun county, a place south of Tang-káng. The captain of one of the ships intended to sink his vessel. The Taiwanese, seeing this, invited Campbell, the British missionary, to come watch. This was an era when European and American powers possessed extraterritorial concessions of judicial powers that prevented the Ching government from exercising judicial authority over them. The American ship captain falsely reported to the British Consulate in Tá^n-káu that the Taiwanese had sunk his ship in order to claim insurance from the insurance company. At the court hearing, Campbell, assisting the county magistrate and Taiwanese people, presented himself as an interpreter and witness. The American captain lost his case. This incident ocurred very close to Ńg Lêng-kiàt's hometown, when he was 23 years old. As a young intellectual at that time, he must have had the opportunity to obtain information about this incident. Along the shores of Taiwan, the Taiwanese had significant contact and involvement with people from Europe and America.

For the forty years from his graduation in 1887 from Tainan Gospel College to his death in 1927, Ńg Lêng-kiàt engaged in church ministry. When he was still a student at Tainan Gospel College,[9] he was sent by the Tainan Mission, with William Campbell as its representative, to Pescadores to carry out evangelism. Ńg Lêng-kiàt was assigned to ministerial work in the Pecadores, Tek-á-kha, Hōng-soa^n, Lâm-chú and Tá^n-káu churches. His ordination service was held in Lâm-á-khe^n (Lâm-chú) on December 28, 1903. The photograph of the event is now deposited and preserved in the Presbyterian General Assembly Archives. Lâm-á-khe^n Church was established by the work of Ńg Lêng-kiàt, his spouse, and their son, Sū-bēng.

In his memoir[10] Shoki Coe remembers his grandmother Iû^n Giâm-hân as an important senior member of the family. According to a verbal report by Shoki's mother, his grandfather's decision to convert to Christianity was greatly encouraged by the grandmother. And Grandmother had a very unique role in educating her son.

When in 1887 Giâm-hân and their only son, Iok-se, accompanied Lêng-kiåt to the Pescadores, they encountered a great storm in the strait. The young son lost his life. When Iok-se was about to drown, instead of panicking, Giâm-hân spoke words of consolation and encouragement to her panicked fellow passengers. She told them that the Lord was coming to receive the boy. Three years after Ng Lêng-kiåt's ministry in the Pescadores, in 1890, Mrs. Ng bore their second son,[11] Ng Sū-bēng, Shoki's father.[12] About 13 years later, in 1903, the family started the church in Lâm-á-khe^n (Lâm-chú, Kaohsiung). The boy Sū-bēng, although only 13, already showed great potential as a future church leader. Unfortunately, his mother, Giâm-hân, died shortly after the church was established.

Giâm-hân, in addition to performing the tasks of a pastor and evangelist, served the village as a well-respected midwife. She never hesitated in rendering assistance to families with newborn babies or in giving a hand to sick women. In his memoir Shoki reports that his mother told him that when Giâm-hân died, the villagers, whether Christians or not, mourned her for one month and erected a monument ten meters high facing the main street of the village in memory of her.[13] Ng Lêng-kiåt's preaching touched the hearts of villagers in Lâm-á-khe^n. Giâm-hân's manifestation of Christian living moved and inspired the entire community. She was indeed a person of faith.

Because he possessed ample financial resources, Ng Lêng-kiåt was able to resign from his position at Lâm-á-khe^n and move to Kî-āu to become a freelance, unpaid evangelist. His resources also allowed him to pay for the education of his children. According to his third son, Ng Kî-chhiong, Ng Lêng-kiåt owned a house in Kaohsiung that generated income. Lêng-kiåt's grandson, Ng Teng-hui, also has shared that before World War I, Lêng-kiåt had some family farmland properties that were leased out to tenant farmers.

If one looks back a century in Taiwan's history, one sees that young men of excellent ability, but without the resources processed by landowners or government officials, had no choice but to become religious professionals. A religious professional was simultaneously an educator; a medical practitioner; a conductor of coming-of-age, weddings, and funeral ceremonies; a psychoanalyst; a fortune-teller and a geomantist. The long shoreline of Taiwan provided ample room for nurturing the Taiwanese spirit in the inquisitive mind of Ng Lêng-kiåt. But after accepting the Christian faith and his vocation as a Western religious professional, his eyes were opened wider. He pondered more deeply a variety of issues in his society and even participated in their reform.

In his memoir, Shoki Coe recalls that his grandfather was his first theological teacher. When he was about ten years old, his grandfather was about seventy years old and served as the pastor at the Kî-āu Church, in Ko-hiông/Kaohsiung. Every year Shoki's father, the Rev. Ŋg Sū-bēng, and his family spent about a month's summer vacation at his grandfather's place. For two summers, grandson Shoki was the sole student of the grandfather. At the tip of the Kî-āu peninsula stood a hill and on top of it a lighthouse. Leading up to the lighthouse, there were about three hundred stone steps. About halfway up on the left side of the steps was an old temple. On the right side of the temple stood an old church his grandfather used to serve. The church could accommodate about eighty to one hundred worshippers. Adjacent to the church was the manse. Next to the church building was a two-story, Western-style building, which used to be the summer retreat for British missionaries. The house had a wide porch from which one could view the beautiful scenery across the shore, particularly when the lights of the Kaohsiung Harbor began to come on. When a light breeze blew, there could be no better classroom.

Grandfather was an expert storyteller, easily attracting the attention of his grandson. The story usually began in this way: Once upon a time there was a young man who was naughty until one day he met another man called Jesus and his life was changed. The story was black and white and might have become monotonous, but in fact it never did so. The young man was a magician and knew an endless variety of tricks. Each time the grandfather told his grandson about a new trick that this young man performed. For instance, he could make an egg climb up to the top of a bamboo pole. Every time there was something new and fascinating to hear about. In fact, it was something of an anticlimax when Jesus appeared. But being a person of faith with a life centered on Jesus, and being so creative, Ŋg Lêng-kiảt's story never became cut and dried but was always entertaining and full of inspiration.

The grandfather, Ŋg Lêng-kiảt, taught the little theological student the difference between a Taoist religious professional and a follower of Christ. The former relied on his knowledge and technical performance, the latter sought after the truth about the universe and the mystery of the creator God with the whole of his heart, mind and spirit in order to serve people with a sincere heart.

Self-narrated Biography of the Rev. Ñg Lêng-kiat

Ñg Leng-kiat's original home was in Chúi-thâu Village of Kim-mîng, Tâng-oaⁿ County, Chôan-chiu Hú, Hokkien Province of the Nation of Chheng (or Ching). He was born 12 September 1854 in Ku-î Chng, Tiong Lí, Tang-káng, Hōng-soaⁿ Koān. When he was 14, for eight months he studied under Master Au-iông Hui in Lāi Koan-tè Chng to learn Taoist Scriptures. At 17, he studied under Master Ñg Chài-lâi to learn shamanist techniques. When 19, he studied under the tutorage of Master Tân O'-bóe, who had just come to the Township of Tang-káng from Chìn-kang County in Hokkien Province to learn more and deeper Taoist shamanist techniques. But when he was 26 years old, he heard that there was a Westerner in the village preaching the Christian message. Having been attracted to this message, he received guidance and instruction from an evangelist, Tiō Chiok-siông.[14] He was converted and embraced the Christian faith. On 16 January 1881, at the age of 27, he was baptized by the Rev. Dr Thomas Barclay, a missionary from the United Kingdom. Five years later, at the age of 32, he entered the "English University" in the Provincial Capital City, Tainan, which later became Tainan Theological College. In December 1886, at age 33, he was assigned to be an evangelist at Má-keng Church in Pescadores Islands. At age 36, he was reassigned to the Church in Hōng-soaⁿ, at 37 to the Church in Lâm-á-kheⁿ Town, and at 38 to the Tek-á-kha Church in Tiong-lí, Tang-káng. At 42, he was commissioned to take responsibility for the Church in Lâm-á-kheⁿ again. At age 46, with enthusiastic support of the people at the church in Lâm-á-kheⁿ, he was elected "Elder of the Holy Religion of Jesus."[15] On December 28, 1903, he was ordained at the Lâm-á-kheⁿ Church. He was then 49 years of age.[16]

The Story of a Taoist Priest's Conversion to Christ

When Shoki Coe was in England, he wrote the following article to tell the people in the Presbyterian Church of England the story of his grandparents as Christian testimony.[17]

I have been asked to put into words a rather personal story about my grandfather which I have told to some of our churches. It was related to brothers and me when we were still boys. Will you imagine an old church built on the side of a steep cliff overlooking the sea? Nearby there was a building which had once served as our Mission hospital, but now only used by my grandfather's family or by our missionaries in holiday time. The house was much worn, but it commanded a beautiful view. It had a wide balcony overlooking the harbour, and here in the cool of evening we used to gather together. Picture to yourselves, then, a group of boys (including my cousins) sitting around their old grandfather in the moonlight listening to fascinating stories about the earlier days of Formosa, meanwhile watching the junks and sampans going in and out of the harbour.

Suddenly my grandfather asked us boys if we knew what he used to be before he became a Christian. We were perplexed to hear that our grandfather was once not a Christian, and we gazed at him with curious expectation. After a little while he began this story.

A World of Fears
Well, boys, I was once a magician serving in a heathen shrine. I was feared by all the people because they thought I could call upon good or bad spirits as I wished. They feared me terribly, and they hated me because I used to threaten them with evil curses, so they had to appease me with money or presents. I lived by their fears. For instance, I used to tell them that on a certain night an evil spirit would visit them unless they paid me some money to appease it. When some of them refused to do so I would perform a terrifying fraud, and they believed that the evil spirit would really visit them on the night which I specified. I would go to their house during the night and stick fish scales onto the doorknocker. When the moonlight shone, the fish scales would be brightened with a peculiar light and then the bats (abundant in Formosa) would come and attack it, making eerie sounds by flapping themselves against the knocker and causing it to rattle against the door. The people inside the house trembled, thinking that evil spirits were molesting them. This is the way I got my living, a living made by other people's fear and by wicked fraud.

But I had fear also—deeper in a sense, because I knew that evil spirits were only my own imagination, and the people might find out some day. And if so, what should I do? By my own wickedness and their fear of me alone, I was separated from my fellow men and tormented by a dark mysterious unknown. I tried to forget by absorbing myself in the pleasures of sin. Living as in the wilderness, I went from bad to worse, and was cut off from the fellowship of those who should be nearest to me because I lived in deception of others as well as of myself.

The Call of Christ
One day I heard that a peculiar-looking man from a foreign country had come to our village telling the people a curious story about one called Jesus,

and to my anger and indignation some of the villagers stopped coming to my shrine and went after him. I determined to go to interfere with their open-air meeting held in the bamboo surrounded village. I listened for a little while, amusing myself with the strange appearance and unfamiliar eyes of the foreigner. To my surprise I found myself listening to what he was saying. It was the old, old story of the prodigal son, and I suddenly felt my anger melt away and my heart mysteriously touched. I went away with a wound and a conflict and a defeat in my heart. I heard on the one hand, a wild voice shouting to me, "You mustn't listen to this pagan teaching!" On the other hand, a new and gentle voice appealingly saying, "Come back to me." I lived a few days in new agony, but the more I resisted the more I was attracted to this soft, gentle voice.

I went several times to the preaching hall in secret. One day I heard the same story of the prodigal son and his loving father. I could bear it no longer. I stole away with tears in my eyes, repeating the words I had just heard, "I have sinned against thee and am no longer worthy to be called thy son." I said it over and over again on my way back. They seemed burnt into my heart. From that moment I felt that a new life had been born in me. In spite of old sins still piercing my heart, somehow I felt that He called me His son. I was comforted by new comfort. I went to the preaching hall every Sunday and stopped going to the shrine.

It became known to my family and to the villagers that I was a follower of the pagan teaching. The villagers who had feared me before, now openly scorned me and ridiculed me, and those who had hated me now despised me. My brother threatened to expel me from the family if I did not stop going to the preaching hall. He even planned to kill me once on the way to church, but I escaped by accident—no, by Providence—as I had promised to take a friend with me, so had walked by another road. In spite of all this persecution no one could deprive me of my new life. Since then, boys, I have learned more and more of the truth, now I know that reconciliation with God is the foundation of reconciliation with them.

Suddenly my grandfather stopped and, after a pause, he added pensively, "I wish your grandmother were still alive to tell you what happened to her." But he never continued her story, and not long after, he died.

A Changed Home

One day, when I was an older lad, my father was discussing with me my future career. He talked again of my grandfather, and more especially of my grandmother, saying that they both, along with himself and my dear mother who had recently died, had greatly desired me to enter the ministry if I so decided. Then he continued with the story of my grandmother which my grandfather had left untold.

"Before your grandfather became a Christian, he used to ill-treat your grandmother. But one day," my father went on, "your grandmother noticed that something had happened to her usually cruel husband. He stayed at home all the time, stopped going to the shrine and was absorbed in reading a little book day after day. She wondered and wondered, but did not dare to ask what he was reading. Besides this, she received unusual and rather shy, kind words from her husband.

One night she could no longer resist the desire to see what he was reading. She got up quietly at midnight when everyone was asleep, went and opened the little book with trembling fear, and began to read it. (It was the first separate translation of St. Matthew.) She was moved at the story therein. After this she continually got up at midnight to read the book, always with fear in her heart lest some of the family might discover what she was doing. Till one night, as she was reading, she suddenly realized that her husband was standing behind her. She was terribly frightened."

My father stopped speaking and looked intently at me, and I looked at my father with equal intensity. After a little while I asked my father in a faint voice what happened to them. He said, "They wept and were reconciled, and dedicated themselves to God."

Not long afterwards my grandparents were compelled to move away from their family because of persecution, both from within and without, but they were full of joy with their new fellowship as husband and wife. They began telling people all around the story of the One who had given them this new life. My grandfather became a preacher, and later became a minister (one of the five earliest in Formosa), serving in many churches for more than forty years, and preaching the good tidings until two weeks before he was called back to the Lord.

Before I came to England I went to visit some of my relatives in my grandfather's old village. I saw the old shrine, and I saw another magician there burning incense, and uttering threatening and unintelligible words to frighten women and children. I recollected with wonder and amazement that my grandfather, and consequently the whole family, was like that, and I remembered with joy that, by grace of God and by self-sacrificing love of missionaries, we were transported into a new life; at the same time I ask myself, "Is it not my privilege and task?"

The Second Generation

The Rev. Ńg Sū-bēng was born on 3 March 1890, five years before the Ching Nation was defeated by Japan in the Sino-Japanese War and Taiwan became a colony of Japan. Since Ńg Lêng-kiåt and Giâm-hân's eldest son died on the shore of Phêⁿ-ô˙ (Pescadores Islands), and the Japanese initiated a domicile registration system in Taiwan in 1900, Ńg Lêng-kiåt registered Ńg Sū-bēng as "the eldest son." Since his birth, he experienced the life of the ministerial work of the Ńgs at the church in Tek-á-kha and then in Hōng-soaⁿ. When Ńg Lêng-kiåt was ordained in 1903, Sū-bēng was 13 and still a primary school pupil. According to records, he helped his father establish and build up the church in Lâm-á-kheⁿ. On 17 June 1903 he was confirmed as an adult member of the church by the Rev. Duncan Ferguson. When he graduated from Lâm-á-kheⁿ Public School in 1906, he entered the Presbyterian Middle School (Tióng Tiong)[18] and graduated three years later.

Before Ńg Sū-bēng had graduated from Tióng Tiong (Presbyterian Middle School), he passed the entrance examination of Taihoku (Taipei) Medical School. But his father, Pastor Lêng-kiåt, persuaded him to go to the "tāi-håk (university)" in Tainan—the theological college. Pastor Lêng-kiåt encouraged this decision because of a solemn vow he had made when he was converted to Christ, to dedicate his eldest son to the holy ministry of God. Of course there were great struggles in Sū-bēng's heart. After sincere prayers, he decided to take this difficult road of the cross for his life. From then on, whenever he encountered difficulties or obstacles—particularly when he was forced to resign from his teaching position at the Presbyterian Boys Middle School and when he was forced out of the East Gate Church in Tainan, which he built up—that initial decision in 1909 always came to his mind. He repeatedly told his son, Shoki, that he did not regret that he had given up the opportunity to take up the medical profession in order to walk on this path of Christian ministry. In 1909 he entered Tainan Theological College. At that time in Taiwan, other than the theological college, which was then known as the "university," there was no other "higher" school that would be able to provide education in liberal arts, humanities, philosophy or history. He graduated four years later in 1913.

The Presbyterian Church put great emphasis on educational ministry from early on in its history; the Mission set up divisions of evangelism, education, medical ministry and women's ministry. When a church or a preaching station was established, on Sundays there were worship services, but on weekdays there were primary schools and middle schools affiliated with that church or preaching station. The purpose of middle schools was to train teachers for the primary schools. Both the primary and the middle schools would be under the supervision of the same director. However, by 1914 when Edward Band took over the directorship of school education, only the schools in Tainan and Chiong-hòa remained open. After 18 years of rule in Taiwan, the Japanese had established public schools all over the major cities and towns in Taiwan, and the limited resources of the church schools were in no way comparable to the government's public schools and were therefore not viable. Thus the 1913 graduate of the "university" in Tainan, N̂g Sū-bēng, was sent to teach at the Chiong-hòa Church-Affiliated Primary School and the preparatory school for Tainan Presbyterian Middle School.

For two years after Sū-bēng's graduation, he taught at the Chiong-hòa Church-Affiliated Primary School. During his second year, on 20 August 1914, Shoki was born. In naming their eldest son, n̂g Sū-bēng and Lîm Kim decided that their sons would have a name with the word "hui."[19] Since he was born in Chiong-hòa, their eldest son was named "Chiong-hui" (Shoki).

From Chiong-hòa, n̂g Sū-bēng was reassigned to pastoral duties in the Kiâm-chúi-káng Church. However, after only one year, Edward Band called him to join the teaching staff of the Presbyterian Boys Middle School to teach Bible and Han Language and Literature[20] and be the warden of the student dormitory. When Band took over the school as its head, there were a total of sixty students; all had to live in the school dormitory. So after the pastoral duties at a local church, n̂g Sū-bēng now had to pastor the school and its students. He was only 26 years old, while Band, the headmaster, was only 28. He stayed on at this school for 18 years, from 1916–1934.

In his book *The History of Tióng-êng Middle School*, Band commended Sū-bēng's contributions to the school:

> During his 18 years of tenure as the Chaplain of the School, he had led 334 students to become Christians. At the time when he left the school in 1934, 133 of them were either still at school or had gone on to receive higher education; the profession or occupation of 65 of them were unclear (most likely engaged in agriculture or business); 41 of them became ministers; 37 medical doctors and 14 dentists, 23 entrepreneurs, 15 in public service and clerical positions, 7 teachers, and 9 had passed away.

Headmaster Band recalled that Chaplain n̂g often felt sorry when students broke rules. He took initiative to help students resolve their problems, even sought out students to discuss their problems, staying with them until midnight. He worked hard to help and meet their needs. He would punish students if necessary, but most of the time, he gave careful and thoughtful guidance to students, and prayed with them as well. Band described his and Ng's role at the school as like the "head (the Headmaster) and the heart (the Chaplain) of the same body." Headmaster Band was very pleased to have Chaplain Ng and two other young men's cooperation, Tēⁿ Khe-phòan and Phoaⁿ Tō-êng, so that the school was able to hold an island-wide Sunday School Teachers Training Conference, giving guidance for composing curriculum and applications. They were also able to let the students go out to help give Christian education and spiritual nurture in local churches.

Lîm Kim, Ng Sū-bēng's wife and Shoki's mother, was to Shoki a good teacher of theological interpretation. Every time Shoki had any question about the stories of Grandpa, or description of events, he would ask her. For a ten-year-old boy, she was like an encyclopedia and an interpreter. Being the wife of the dormitory warden, she was in practical terms a dormitory mother. She had to take note of and care about students' health, clothing, eating and behaviour. When Shoki and his brother Éng-hui, who was a year younger than he, began to acquire memories, what they could remember was the life in the warden's quarters just next to the dormitory. The living quarter was like a glass house, which was always open and visible to all students. Later, every time when Shoki pondered the roots of his identity with Taiwanese Christians, the memories of his mother's interpretation of world events and society in Taiwan, and her insightful comments on family and church life, always returned to him vividly.

During the time when Ng Sū-bēng was serving as a teacher and warden at the Presbyterian Boys Middle School, he also took on the pastoral responsibilities of the East Gate Church in Tainan. At that time he was granted the status of a "qualified candidate for ministry" awaiting to be called and ordained by the then "Presbytery of South Taiwan" of the Taiwan Presbyterian Church. Due to the fact that the East Gate Church, geographically speaking, was closest to both the Boys School and the Girls School, and that he believed that students from both schools should attend Sunday worship service at a church, he worked hard to solicit funds to build a church that would accommodate one thousand persons for worship. The building was completed and dedicated in 1927. For long years of faithful and diligent ministry, he was called and ordained in that church on 12 May 1927.

However, at the school Sū-bēng ran into difficulties with the forceful demand of the Japanese authorities that all educational institutions must be "Japanized." At the same time a movement to make everyone a Japanese "imperial subject" was on the rise. The schools were not allowed to employ teachers who did not use Japanese to teach. The language Sū-bēng used for instruction was Taiwanese Hoklo, and the written forms were both in Han ideographs and a romanized form of Taiwanese. He had earlier passed the entrance examination to the medical school; that definitely included an ability to use Japanese. However, after years of studying theology and ministering to Taiwanese-speaking people, he did not have much time to improve his Japanese. Because the Japanese authorities would not permit Taiwanese to use their mother tongue to instruct or receive education, Sū-bēng was eventually forced to resign his teaching position at the middle school early in 1934.

When he left the Boys School, he became the full-time pastor of the East Gate Church. He also continued to take an interest in municipal policy, so for two years, 1933–1935, he was elected to be a council member representing the East Gate neighborhood (Tang-mn̂g Teng), similar to what is today a city or township council member. An historian of Taiwan Church, the Rev. Iûⁿ Sū-ióng said of the Rev. N̂g Sū-bēng, "His spiritual life was rich, his sermons so powerful that they moved people to the inner core of life."[21]

However, when N̂g Sū-bēng was forced out of the teaching position at the Presbyterian Middle School, he also began to encounter problems at the East Gate Church. Around August–September 1934, because of financial constraints due to overstaffing and assumptions that something was "wrong" with Rev. N̂g being ousted from the school, the young associate pastor and the Japanese-speaking people of the church decided to run the church in the Japanese way. Rev. N̂g therefore left the church in early October.

Even at this difficult time, he was able to manage the living expenses of the family, including the education costs of Shoki and other children. The daily expenses of maintaining a family, of transportation and education were considered to be rather expensive. The "imperial universities" did not provide any scholarship assistance to students and the local churches did not have enough resources to support their ministers' children's education. The first generation ministers normally served at a "self-support church" ("tông-hōe"). Unless the church could support a minister, they were not allowed to call a minister, and the Mission would not ordain a minister unless he was called by a church. However, as the compensation usually stayed at the minimum required, the Mission paid for the children's fees and expenses if they attended the Presbyterian Boys Middle School, Girls Middle School or theological college. No records have been found of the Mission providing scholarship assistance for Shoki's education at Taiwan High School or Tokyo Imperial University. It was probable that Shoki's family paid for all the costs, including fees, transportation and other expenses. It was likely because of this family background that

Shoki was not intimidated by Japanese or Westerners, dared to express his free will and behaved just like the son of a well-to-do family.

With no job, Rev. Nĝ Sū-bēng paid his own way in 1935 to go to Tokyo to spend over one month with his eldest son, Shoki. He stayed in the guest room of the Tokyo University YMCA Student Hostel. During that time, he joined the students' Bible study about the book of Job and was greatly inspired by the Scriptures and encouragement from his son, Shoki.

Upon returning to Taiwan on 1 April 1935, the Rev. Nĝ Sū-bēng took on the pastoral charge of Tōa-tō˙ Church in central Taiwan. His whole family moved with him to this village. During his pastorate at the church, a great earthquake destroyed its manse. He and his family moved to another village, Liông-chíⁿ. As a result he ministered both at Tōa-tō˙ and Liông-chíⁿ. At the same time, his children's education placed heavy financial burdens upon him. His oldest daughter, Siok-êng, graduated from the Girls' High School and contemplated going to Japan for further education. His third son, Bêng-hui, transferred from Tainan Second Middle School to Taichung First Middle School. His fourth son, An-hui, passed an exam to enter Taichung First Middle School. And Shoki completed his university education and planned to go for further education in England. Because the stipend from small village churches was barely enough for basic sustenance, this burden of education was indeed heavy. Even though the Nĝs had other resources, such as farmland, it was the kind of burden that could easily lead to financial disaster.

For four hundred years Taiwanese who had lived under various colonial rule did not have the opportunity to participate in island-wide politics. Under the rule of foreign powers, important positions were all occupied by the privileged—such as Japanese. Fortunately, within Christian organizations, particularly the Presbyterian system, Taiwanese had opportunities to learn democratic process and politics. Religious personalities had their opportunities, upon organizing "presbyteries" and "synods." If elected moderator, the jurisdiction covered all the territories involved. So if elected as moderator of the Synod, the person would be the leader of the whole island.

Between April 1937 and April 1938, the Rev. Nĝ Sū-bēng served as the vice-moderator of the South Synod of the Presbyterian Church and also served as the Chaplain to the Chiong-hòa Christian Hospital of the Presbyterian Church of Southern Formosa. It was in this year when Shoki graduated from Tokyo University and left Taiwan for England and that Shoki's brother Nĝ Bêng-hui graduated from Taichung First Middle School. In April 1938 the Rev. Nĝ Sū-bēng was called to be the pastor of Ôan-lîm Church where he remained until the end of World War II.

On 21 April 1939, Ng Sū-bēng was elected Moderator of the South Synod of Taiwan. It was just about one and a half years before the Second World War broke out; his eldest son Shoki had already left for England to study for one year and eight months. The Japanese authorities had increased their pressure on the Christian Church. Headmaster Edward Band had to close the English Presbyterian Mission Station in Taiwan and left to go back to England in November that year. Thus Rev. Ng led the Presbyterian Church in Taiwan at a time when all missionaries departed and the church was under harsh persecution by Japanese authorities.

This second generation of the persons of faith in the Ng family, Ng Sū-bēng, though living under a "hand-tied" and very limited situation, was able to carry out his teaching and nurturing tasks for the younger generation. Throughout his life, he struggled with foreign colonial policy to spread the gospel and teach Christian ideas among the local Taiwanese people. He was willing to go through hardship to live a life of hard work and thrift, but those whom he taught enjoyed abundant and meaningful life. He was indeed a true practitioner of Christian religion. As a minister, he was a model for pastors to learn and as a teacher he inspired and changed youngsters for a better life, and thus also was a model for all teachers. He was, among Taiwanese, like a prophet who received the spirit from above as the source of his power, and his life was the utmost expression of Taiwanese spirit.

Shoki Coe considered his father Ng Sū-bēng to be his second theological teacher. His roles of father, teacher and pastor formed a perfect model of a person who practiced all what he believed.

The Third Generation

Over his lifetime Shoki Coe had four different ways to officially pronounce and spell his name. In his native Taiwanese tongue, his name was Ng Chiong-hui, although among church people, friends, schoolmates or his students, he was known as "Ng Bók-su" (Pastor Ng). During the Japanese occupation of Taiwan, in schools or on official occasions, the same name was pronounced Shoki Ko. During the entire period when he was in schools for formal education, he was called Ko Shoki. During the rule of Chiang Kai-sek, in which the official language was Mandarin Chinese, his name was officially changed to Chang-hui Hwang (commonly called C. H. Hwang) to comply with the new pronunciation. In 1965, when he left Tainan Theological College and took up residence in England, and subsequently was naturalized as a British citizen, he used Shoki Coe as his legal name.

Shoki Coe also used three different passports with three kinds of spelling of the same name in Han ideograph. He often said sadly, "I have so many names, and used passports issued by different countries. This fact does not give a Taiwanese any glory, but only to show the sad history of Taiwanese under generations of foreign oppression."

In order to prepare himself to be a third-generation pastor in the family, he graduated from Tokyo Imperial University, majoring in philosophy in 1937, and then went on to study theology at Westminster College, Cambridge, England. His father did his best to let Shoki learn the roots of his family, their religious background before converting to the Christian faith, their cultural background and ethic of family life. So before he left for England to study, he was sent to his "family hometown" of Tang-káng to visit a "patriarch" of the family, Kūn Chek-kong (Grand Uncle Kūn).

Kūn Chek-kong was the youngest first cousin of Shoki's grandfather Nĝ Lêng-kiảt. He was only ten years older than Shoki's father and over thirty years older than Shoki. He was rather well-to-do. Shoki stayed with his family for three days. Kūn Chek-kong's eldest son Thian-tek, who was about one or two years older than Shoki, acted as his guide. One evening he took him to see the temple where his grandfather had practiced as a Taoist priest (or magus) before he was converted to the Christian faith. At first Shoki was rather curious and wanted to go forward to see more, but soon he was struck with panic and fear and felt ill. There was a mixture of joy and excitement with anxiety, as he was able to have an opportunity to glimpse "Egypt" in the family religion in the old hometown, and to have a sense of a pilgrim's journey of "Exodus."

The third generation of the Nĝs as persons of religion, Shoki Coe was a person with higher education. When Shoki returned from England to Taiwan in 1947, he was a Taiwanese person in a religious profession with the highest formal education. Like his father, he taught at the Tióng-êng Middle School. After two years of teaching there, at the age of 35, he was ordained as a minister[22] of the church and appointed the Principal of Tainan Theological College. He was the first Taiwanese to head an educational institution of university level. The theological college itself was the first institution of higher learning in Taiwan designated as a college or university. At that time in 1949, he was likely the youngest head of a higher education institution.

Shoki Coe was not only the principal of a theological college, he was also a professor of systematic theology. His influence extended to the whole Presbyterian Church in Taiwan because he taught about the connected relations and interactions between and among God, humans, society and the entire world.

To him theology must be involved with science, politics, economics, health care and other knowledge and all the ethical issues thereof. Therefore, he was of the opinion that theology must be a constant "search and reflection" of living human beings in the real societal situation.

Later on in his life, Shoki Coe considered himself a "theological educator." In this we can see his intention to be a "pastor-theologian." He gave all his energies to "reflections," "enlightening," "influencing through persuasion" and "nurturing." Yet he also had to take care of "personnel issues," "management," "operation" and the problems related to constructing the "hardware" of the college. His pastoral duties included not only overseeing students' daily class work but everything from their living condition to their physical health. I remember one particular case: the year I started college, a student fell ill and was hospitalized at Tainan Hospital and in need of a blood transfusion; Shoki gave his own blood to the student.

He "encouraged," "urged" and "recommended" many faculty members to go for further studies overseas. During his 16 years as principal, the ministers, elders and the churches with whom he was in contact were from all over Taiwan. He often reminded the churches in Taiwan, "to preach good news of Christianity is not something to be done alone. There are people of the same mind and colleagues all around and in every corner of the world who are concerned about our work and praying for us; in like manner they also need our support in concerns and prayers."

During his years as principal of Tainan Theological College, he was supported and, without precedent, elected two times (1957 and 1965) as moderator of the General Assembly of the Presbyterian Church in Taiwan. During his era, as a Taiwanese there was no way for him to be a top political leader, yet he was able to be the top church leader, to consolidate different existing movements, programmes and organizations, and to express the concerns of the church to the common society and political organizations. Furthermore, he was able to bear the duties of church leadership in the world community, to participate in interchurch and international cooperative tasks which led to furthering of harmony and peace in the world.

In 1965 after he had resigned from his position as principal of Tainan Theological College, Shoki Coe went on to engage in full-time work in the World Council of Churches to promote and develop theological education for the world. He served as responsible staff of the Theological Education Fund, and its continuing agency, Programmes for Theological Education. His staff colleagues included a theologian from Africa, Dr Desmond Tutu, as well as an Asian theologian who had been the principal of a theological college, Dr Ivy Chou.

Tutu came from South Africa where people of colour were suffering under the apartheid policy. Although Tutu was in London working for a world-wide agency, he always thought about his home country and his own people who were being oppressed and discriminated against. In 1975, he was the first black person to be chosen to take the position of the Dean of St. Mary's Cathedral in Johannesburg, yet he was not quite sure what to do. He brought the issue to his supervising colleague Shoki Coe for his suggestion. Shoki encouraged Tutu to go back "to share the bitterness and sweetness" of his own people. He did, and the next year, 1976, Tutu was elected the Bishop of Lesotho. In October 1984, Desmond Tutu was awarded the Nobel Peace Prize for his leadership in a non-violent way to struggle against the discriminatory policy of apartheid.

Shoki Coe set foot on all continents of the world. His responsibilities were especially to give assistance to churches and theological educational institutions in developing countries to train their pastors. He also spoke on behalf of churches in third world nations when they could not be present in the activities of the European and North American churches. He stayed in this position at the WCC for 14 years until he retired in 1981.

During Shoki Coe's tenure at the WCC, his former students began to take positions of leadership in the Presbyterian Church in Taiwan. They began to let the church speak out for the mind of all Taiwanese, for all inhabitants of Taiwan. They made statements of their conviction, that the future of Taiwan must be determined by the people. Led by the general secretary of the General Assembly, the Standing Executive Committee of the General Assembly that was composed of the moderator plus leaders of institutions and commissions, made three courageous statements: "On our National Fate" (1971), "Our Appeal" (1975) and "Human Rights Declaration" (16 August 1977).

The Kuomintang regime twisted and misinterpreted these statements that were based on religious convictions. As a result the church and its leaders were persecuted as if they were great enemies to be suppressed. Shoki Coe, being outside the country, tried to help, but his name was on the black list and he was not allowed to enter the country; he could come only as far as Northeast Asian or Southeast Asian countries. On 25 December 1975, he took the opportunity of one of his visits to New York to join with three other Taiwanese Christian leaders in North America in issuing the "Declaration of Taiwanese for Self-Determination" and initiating the "Taiwanese for Self-Determination" movement. This movement had now turned religious activities from within Taiwan into actions taken up by global and international religious personalities. In this manner, in order to deal with four hundred years of foreign political authorities, the religious leaders, relying on God's gift of spirit and power, attempted to reform the system of oppression and privileged politics and to replace it with new democracy. This kind of effort resulted in a new and creative initiative in the history of religion in Taiwan and was the legacy and model that Shoki Coe left for his students and subsequent generations.

2
Early Years (1916–1937)
Education against the Odds

Awakening at a Tender Age

In the spring of 1916, the warden of the Presbyterian Middle School Dormitory, the Rev. Ńg Sū-bēng and his family moved to the new quarters next to the newly completed Chu-se House (Chu-se-liâu) for students just outside the East Gate of Tainan. Shoki was two when the family moved into these small quarters.

Shoki, in sharing his early memories, recalled having a good playmate, Éng-hui, his brother, who was a year younger than he. He also recalled first experiencing what the Taiwanese speak of as "tender mother" (Chû-bó) and "stern father" (Giâm-hū).

Two other early memories stayed with Shoki. On one hot summer day, with hardly anything on, Shoki lay on the ground. Suddenly a biplane flew by very low just above him. He had not seen this kind of monster before, so huge and flying so close above him that he could see the "Rising Sun" insignia clearly on its wings and fuselage. He was shocked, horrified, and ran into the house, shuddering, wondering what on earth was that monster in the sky that looked down on him. There would be no place for him to escape and to hide; his laziness was surely the cause of what happened.

He also remembered the wedding of his father's younger brother, Tiâu–siông, held at the Chu-se House: "For the first time I was able to taste what was called a splendid wedding feast." Both he and his brother, Éng-hui, had to dress up for the occasion. Both put on the new and fashionable clothes their new Auntie had given them. As they looked at their reflections in the mirror, they were surprised to see how smartly they had dressed and how handsome they were, so that they almost thought they were other persons. They had to remain dressed though the whole series of ceremonies, including the "bride's tea ceremony" until everything was over, and all the guests were gone. At that time they felt a sense of relief. As Shoki reflected on this "uncomfortable" dressed-up experience, he said, "Was I sensing already that so-called 'culture' and 'civilization' were beginning to invade my 'natural' and 'innocent' existence?"[1]

After four years of living at Chu-se House, in 1920, the Ńg family moved to a house built for the school staff near the East Gate Church, with the official address of East Gate 4–70. Shoki's family stayed in this place for seven and a half years. The last five of them he attended the "model public primary school" affiliated with Tainan Normal School (College). He and his younger brother were in the same class. In his memoir Shoki describes that he and his younger brother were one year and four months different in age; as the older one, he was shorter, thin and sickly, with a large head, and always suffered headaches. Thus, he acquired a nickname, "big head." His younger brother was robust and a couple of inches taller than Shoki.

Shoki and his brother Éng-hui were good playmates, and perfect partners in Sunday school children's programs. Shoki well remembered how they were pupils in the same class, enjoyed going to school and coming home together. He recalled the happiest occasion they were together, that also turned out to be their last partnership. During the Christmas season in 1925, they went to visit their paternal Aunt N̂g Í-lī and her husband Âng Tiâo-Thiu's home and church. They had a very good time. But on the day they were to come home, Éng-hui suddenly fell sick. When they reached home, he had a very high fever. On 9 February 1926, he died. His death cast a grim shadow on the family, particularly on Shoki. This event marked the beginning of Shoki's pessimism and anxiety about public primary school education.

After the death of Éng-hui, Lîm Kim, Shoki's mother, also became weaker every day. Although her heath steadily declined, she never stopped carrying out her daily busy chores and caring for her children. But on 24 September 1926, just over seven months since the death of Éng-hui, she departed from this world. She left behind three sons and one daughter, with the oldest one, Shoki, aged twelve, a younger sister Siok-êng, younger brother Bêng-hui, and an infant boy An-hui.

No sooner than the troubled and tragic year of 1926 was over, another sad event happened in the N̂g family, the death of Grandpa, Lêng-kiat. He had lived to the mature age of 75. At that time in Taiwan, 75 was considered to be a blessed long life. He had extraordinary experiences in his life; he had observed many events of the world. From the world of a Taoist priest, he led his family to break through a cocoon to taste the experience of the other shore, and the reality of international exchanges. Throughout his ministry, he was himself in touch with—and had enlightened, comforted and led many on the path to—truth, peace and hope. Therefore his death was indeed a victorious return to a heavenly home. His funeral was a big celebration of his triumphant life. Nevertheless, his death placed an inerasable scar on the young heart of Shoki.

In April 1927, soon after Shoki became a fifth grader at the primary school, he and about ten other school children were on their way home from school when they encountered about a dozen Japanese schoolchildren. The Japanese children taunted them with abusing words—"Chiang-ko-lo," "cowards," "morons," "we dare you"—and began to fight the Taiwanese children. Shoki and all the kids were involved in this fight. He came home with bruises and wounds on his face and other parts of his body. His father sent him back to school the next day and told him to tell the truth to the school authorities. The principal, who had already heard about the fight, was ready to punish Shoki and his party. But although Shoki was only in the fifth grade, he was brave and eloquent enough to act as spokesperson for his group. He told the principal exactly what happened: the fight was initiated by the Japanese children who first verbally abused them and called them "Chiang-ko-lo" and then fought them. The Taiwanese children had to defend themselves. The principal ruled that the Taiwanese kids were not at fault and dismissed them to go home to rest for a week. After the explanation by Shoki's father, he came to the realization that the meaning of "Chiang-ko-lo" was more detrimental than he thought. The words mean "the slaves of the Chings" (a "second-class nation" built by Manchurians). This meant that Taiwanese were looked down on as even less than second-class citizens—they were third class.

Shoki and his Taiwanese compatriots showed strong moral principles and a fighting spirit. When they grew up they would demonstrate great achievements in academics and other areas. But fate still dictated that, when these young people came of age, they would continue to be oppressed by another totalitarian colonial power—this time the Chinese.

Growing Up Fast

In 1927 Shoki successfully passed the entrance examination for the Presbyterian Middle School, even though he had just finished fifth grade. Now he did not have to return to the public primary school that had caused him so much anxiety. However, he also had no certificate of graduation, just like students who avoided class or were kicked out of primary school. Because the middle school officials worried that academically he might not measure up with other students who had finished all six grades, he was placed with another student on "probation" (or preparatory) class. However, after one school term, Shoki proved to be quite a good student worthy to be placed with other regular students and treated with equal status.

To comply with the school policy of the Presbyterian Middle School, Shoki moved into a dormitory called East Hall. Both East Hall and West Hall dormitories had their own dormitory warden, and the Rev. Edward Band, the headmaster, appointed himself to be the chief warden to supervise dormitory life. It might well have been the well-regulated and disciplined dormitory life that helped Shoki's physical condition to improve greatly. He became healthy and strong. No one called him "big head" any more. He even joined the school soccer team. He was known to be a fast runner, a good kicker and an energetic player.

Shoki excelled in Han Literature[2] class, and several of his compositions appeared in the school journal. His family was a "typical Taiwanese family." There were daily family worship services every morning and evening at the home of the Rev. Ng̍ Sū-bēng. There were times for Bible reading and Han Literature class. For Bible readings, the romanized Taiwanese Bible version translated by Thomas Barclay was used. The romanized Taiwanese language was a useful tool in learning Han literature as it gives each word an exact pronunciation designated by one of the eight tones possible with each sound. But later, when the Chinese Kuomintang regime came into power, it claimed that, "romanized Taiwanese is harmful to the policy of the Party and the Nation." Like other colonial regimes, a "single-language" policy was adopted to ensure that the colonized or conquered will abide by the rules and policies established by their regimes. What such regimes never seem to understand is that the oppressed know well both the languages of the oppressors and the oppressed, while the colonial regime may know only their own language.

At the middle school, Shoki studied Bible, Moral Discipline, Speaking and Reading Japanese, Japanese Grammar, Composition, Calligraphy, Han Literature, Reading and Translating English, English Grammar, English Composition, English Calligraphy, History of Japan, History of the East, Geography of Japan, Geography of the World, Mathematics, Algebra, Geometry, Botany, Biology, Health and Hygiene, Physics, Chemistry, Arts, Singing, Physical Education and Taiwanese Language.

There were not many schools that offered the kind of multi-language programme that included Japanese, English, Taiwanese and Han Literature. The Presbyterian Church in Taiwan, and the Presbyterian Middle School, did what they deemed necessary in language education under the oppressive conditions. They also recognized the value of interracial, intercultural and international experience as well as awareness of native culture. In his first year, Shoki's grades ranked him thirty-third in a class of 56. By his third year, when he left the school, he was ranked second. He excelled in Bible, Reading and Translating English, English Grammar, Algebra, Geometry, Health and Hygiene.

On Saturday afternoon, students were allowed out of the school grounds. However, they first had to scrub their dormitory rooms spotlessly clean and take care of the allotted flowerbeds. Headmaster Band would make a round of inspection, and if anything had not been done properly, the students would be "punished" by remaining on the school grounds to do chores, such as trimming the grass of the athletic field. All the students looked forward to being released from their prison-like dormitory. They could walk out to the city streets and proudly show that they were students at the prestigious Presbyterian School and go to the food stands to get some of their favourite food. Or they could go to the Presbyterian Girls Middle School to meet up with their sisters, who were also released from their "prisons" at the same time.

On Sundays the students were allowed out in groups, both morning and afternoon, lined up two abreast in rows, to go to worship at East Gate Church. This was required of all students except for those who had been assigned to assist with Sunday school teaching in nearby churches.

The First Secondary Educational Institution in Taiwan[3]

The Tióng-êng (or Changjung) Middle School in Tainan was the first Western-style secondary educational institution in Taiwan. In 1883, 18 years after the arrival of English Presbyterian missionaries in southern Taiwan, the idea of establishing a secondary school was conceived. After two years of preparation, the school was established in Tainan on the grounds of what is known today as the Blind and Deaf School. It was named the Presbyterian Middle School. When the Japanese colonial occupation forces arrived in Tainan, seven classes had graduated from the school and other students had been attending for three years.

On 30 June 1906, eleven years after the beginning of Japanese colonial rule, the school received accreditation from the Office of the Governor of Taiwan as the Tainan Cho-ei Presbyterian Koto Gakko (Tainan Tióng-êng/Changjung Presbyterian High School). At that time a high school was considered to be a tertiary educational institution, the graduates of which were qualified to teach at a middle school. According to Edward Band, earlier that year a Japanese police officer, while doing his routine inspection around the East Gate district, accidentally came upon the school and was greatly impressed. After speaking with the staff, he realized that this school was a high-level, English-style school. Consequently, he filed a report with the Governor's office. The school was then granted the status of Koto Gakko (high school). Most of the Koto Gakkos of the time were soon promoted to college status. As time passed, however, the Japanese placed more and more restrictions on allowing Taiwanese to receive higher education. As a result, Changjung was later demoted to middle school status and thus again called Presbyterian Middle School.

One of the most outstanding figures in the history of the Presbyterian Middle School was Edward Band. At the age of 26 in 1912, Edward Band was sent to Taiwan by the Overseas Mission Committee of the Presbyterian Church of England as an educational missionary in response to the call of the Presbyterian Mission in Taiwan. At that time he had graduated from Queens College Cambridge, majoring in mathematics. He had also completed his theological studies at Westminster College Cambridge and one year of teaching at the prep school from which he had graduated. Because he would be engaged in education in a Japanese colony, before he began his duties he was sent to Tokyo to study Japanese for two years.

In 1914 he began serving at the Presbyterian Middle School. For 21 of the 25 years he was at the school, Band was headmaster. When he took over the leadership of the school, it had just moved to its present location. His great achievements include raising the quality of education in the areas of spiritual life, academics, athletic performance and moral character. There was, however, one problem beyond his control. During his tenure, the Japanese authorities removed the school's accreditation as a regular educational institution. As a result, its graduates were denied the opportunity to take entrance examinations into what was known as a high school or prep school to prepare for university education.

According to Band, in 1930 he received a notice from Commissioner Sugimoto of the education department of the Taiwan governor's office stating that, although the school met all the requirements in regard to buildings and facilities, operational funds, and qualification of teaching staff, the school would not be given accreditation unless the school directed its students to participate in the religious ritual at the Japanese Jinja (Shinto Shrine) in Tainan. The Military Colonial Government's official explanation of the worship at the Shinto Shrine was that it was not a religious act but part of Japanese national education. After careful consideration the board of directors of the school refused to accept this demand. To participate in Shinto shrine worship would amount to contradicting the Christian faith and also denying freedom of religion. The Southern Synod of the Taiwan Presbyterian Church also agreed with the board on not compromising with this demand. The Association of Christian Schools in Japan and the Council of Christian Churches in Japan at the time were very sympathetic with the position taken by the school. At that time the Ministry of Education of the Japanese government did not place the same kind of demands on the Christian schools in Japan itself. Unfortunately, the two organizations in Japan did not speak out for the school in Taiwan. In the following year in Japan, the civilian government of Minseito collapsed, a militaristic government took its place, and Tióng-êng Middle School lost all of its channels and possibilities for appeal for accreditation.

In 1933, while Edward Band was on home assignment in England, the media focused an attack on the school.[4] Not only would the school not be accredited, the demands increased to a total "Japanization" of its education.

Taking advantage of Edward Band's absence from the school, and against the wishes of the acting headmaster and the board chair, a Japanese teacher surreptitiously took the student body to the Tainan Shinto Shrine. Although Band hurried back to Tainan at the end of the year, the situation was beyond his control. Although the school and the church in Taiwan yielded a few steps to accommodate demands, pressure continually increased to produce absolute loyal subjects of the Emperor. These demands included appointing a Japanese to be headmaster and the chair of the Board, requiring more than half the Board members, teachers and staff, as well as all the dormitory wardens, to be Japanese, ending Bible and religious instruction, and including military training. As a result, the school chaplain Nḡ Sū-bēng and the chair of the school board, Dr Lîm, both resigned.

Headmaster Band, who had an MA from Cambridge University and had received proper training in Japanese language in Japan, was indeed a qualified leader. The chair of the shool board, Dr Lîm Bō͘-seng, was not only a graduate from one of the best universities in Japan—Tokyo Imperial University—but also in 1929 received a PhD from the world-class Columbia University in New York City. No one could dismiss his academic credentials. Nevertheless, under Japanese colonial rule, they were totally ignored. In later times, the Chinese Kuomintang colonial policy was no less cruel than the Japanese. In 1947 Dr Lîm was executed by the Chiang Kai-sek regime.

The board elected the Rev. Kami Yoichiro—a minister of the Presbyterian Church of Japan who was residing in Taiwan as its chair—and also contacted the Presbyterian Church of Japan for assistance in finding a Japanese headmaster. At the general assembly of the Presbyterian Church of Japan in October 1934, a retired Japanese Navy Admiral, Kato Choichiro, was selected. And in February 1935, the new headmaster came to Tainan to assume his position. After the appointment of Kato as headmaster, the dedicated educator Edward Band remained to serve the school as a teacher of mathematics and advisor to student life (as a kind of chaplain). Thus "the school was effectively taken out of Taiwanese control."[5]

Even after the change of headmaster, the Japanese continued to make things difficult for the school for six more years, until finally on 21 June 1939, the school was granted accreditation. Accreditation was also granted to the

Presbyterian Girls Middle School on the same date. These were the very last schools to be given accreditation by the Japanese colonial authorities. It was ironic that the oldest school was the very last to receive accreditation.

A Young Student Abroad

After three years of study at the Presbyterian Middle School, Shoki had already deeply experienced the discriminatory policy of the Japanese toward Taiwanese. He would not be allowed to pursue further formal education in Taiwan. Thus in February 1930, at the young age of fifteen, Shoki left the beloved school, bid goodbye to all his friends and family, and went to Japan to enroll as a fourth-year student at the Middle School Division of Aoyama Gakuin in Tokyo.

Aoyama Gakuin was established by the American Methodist Episcopal Mission in 1874, eight years before the Presbyterian Middle School was founded. By 1920 Aoyama Gakuin was well established with five Divisions: the Main Division (college), Theology Division, High School Division, Middle School Division and Women's High School Division. At the time Shoki enrolled in that school, it already had 57 years of history.

When Ñg Sū-bēng was considering sending his son Shoki to Japan to obtain proper school credentials, the headmaster of the Middle School Division of Aoyama Gakuin was the Rev. Yoshimune Abe. In the summer of 1929, Rev. Abe was invited to be a speaker at the summer youth conference sponsored by the Presbyterian Church in North Taiwan. Abe's itinerary included a visit to Tainan Presbyterian Middle School in the South. Upon his return to Japan, he wrote an article about his visit in the Aoyama School Journal that included the following statement: "In Tainan, there are more than ten students of Aoyama Middle School Division. On that day, August 6, I met the following students: Lí Bo̍k-ek, Gô Thian-chù, Gô Lâi-sêng, Png Ek-chhoan, Iûⁿ Chàn-hun, Lîm Sin-chín, Ñg Hiàn-chiong, and Ñg Chiong-hui. These young people's homes are all in the South Country, and they were blessed with good health and love of their families; they all enjoyed happily their vacation in their home environment of beautiful and natural mountains and rivers. They all gave me a sense of great satisfaction."

Both Gô Lâi-sêng and Ñg Chiong-hui (Shoki) were included on this list of students, even though they had not yet started at Aoyama Middle School when Abe visited them. But Abe's article was written in the academic year of 1930, and thus he thought that it was appropriate to include two new students from that year. According to Shoki, Abe[6] had personally promised both father and son Ñg to admit Taiwanese students in the fourth year of Aoyama

Middle School without taking qualifying examinations. This promise allowed the Presbyterian Middle School to send these two to Aoyama.

During the cold early March days in 1930, Shoki and Gô˙ Lâi-sêng boarded a postal ship from Keelung heading for Japan. In those days there were two major shipping companies that served the route between Keelung and Kobe, Japan: Kinkai Post Line and Osaka Mercantile Shipping Line. It took more than three days for a one-way journey. Upon arrival in Kobe, it was necessary to take a train ride that lasted almost a whole day. This was the first time that Shoki had to leave his home country and sail across the "salted seas." Later, Shoki could remember only being on board the ship but nothing about the train ride from Kobe to Tokyo. He had little interest in being a tourist in Japan. Fortunately, in Tokyo Mr Tiō Thian-chû, whom Shoki addressed as "Tâng-nî-pa" (literally "the same year father"),[7] came to the train station to meet both students.

Shoki was much encouraged in having the care of Mr Tiō when he arrived in Tokyo. However, on the day of their arrival, both young students received a notice from the school authorities that in ten days they were to take qualifying examinations as fourth year students. They also heard that there were 25 applicants out of which there was room for only four or at most five. They were not well prepared and felt frustrated. Of course they both failed miserably. According to his memoir, Shoki lost all his self-confidence and even thought of committing suicide.

After intensive negotiation by Mr Tiō with the school, they were given a grace period as "probation students" for one school term with special instruction and notice emphasizing "one term only" and, if not successful, they were to be dismissed and returned home. During that term Shoki worked hard, thinking that this was the only chance to win glory and honour for himself, for his alma mater (Presbyterian Middle School), and for his own homeland Taiwan. As a result both he and Gô˙ ranked within twenty out of more than two hundred classmates at the end of that term. Their effort was rewarded. Each of them was then assigned a home class, and each was later ranked within the top five. Thus they overcame the discrimination faced by Taiwanese students in receiving such short notice of the exam and were able to compete successfully with native Japanese in Japan.

The newly constructed buildings for the Middle School and the High School Divisions of Aoyama had just been completed and dedicated in 1929.[8] For the first time in his life, Shoki was able to study in a reinforced concrete structure. Shoki lived with a group of about thirty students in a dormitory at Aoyama. They were looked after by two or three other older students from the Theology

Division. It was there that Shoki met a boy by the name of Toshimichi Suzuki, who became a close friend. It was he who turned up so unexpectedly and miraculously, five years later, as an officer on the Kashima-maru which Shoki took to go to England. It was in that year at Aoyama that Shoki saw in Suzuki and in others the human side of the Japanese in their own homeland.

One day, Shoki recollected, a history teacher, Mr Tanaka,[9] broke off his lesson to tell the class that news reports were often not true stories. He stated that the report about the "Manchuria Incident" was fabricated because he lived in Manchuria and had just returned home to Japan. While in Manchuria, he saw the invasion of Japan and pointed out discrepancies from what the official news media had reported in Japan. It was the injunction of the Scriptures, abiding to the ultimate sovereignty of God and the prophetic tradition of respect and love of freedom and justice, that gave a teacher such courage to speak out.

The tension between Christian principles and militarism became more of an issue. The school admission brochure of Aoyama Middle School in 1929 stated two points in the purpose of the school: (1) The Middle School is founded on Christian principles to carry out education on the Middle School Level. (2) It has the privileges and rights equivalent to all public schools to pursue further study and fulfill military duties. The school made the following statement in relation to the introduction of "military instructors" in a school founded on Christian principles: "Not only that there is no conflict of the two, but they complement each other."[10]

Maybe the attempt to use this kind of "complement" idea as "rationalization" had begun to infiltrate Christian schools in Japan. From then on, all Christian denominations were within shooting distance of Japanese militarism. Around 1940 the government started to intervene and imprison many ministers and leaders who refused to cooperate or compromise on the basis of their faith.

During the year at Aoyama, Shoki did his duties as a student, studying hard and trying not to meddle in other activities. He also took advantage of being absorbed in the atmosphere of enlightenment and freedom to clear his mind, to open his eyes and experience those Japanese who upheld justice and loved peace, particularly the witness of Christians.

After the grades of the second term were out, upon consultation with Mr Tiō, Shoki bravely went to see his home-class master, Mr Masao Yasui, to ask whether he could skip over a year to take the high school entrance exam. Mr Yasui agreed and said, "You may well try. Even though you might fail, you would have gained the experience of high school entrance exam." At the end of the fourth year in middle school, he took the high school entrance exams. As a result he was the only one from that school who passed the examination to enter a public (or government) high school, Taiwan Koto Gakko (Taiwan High School).[11] Mr Yasui wrote in the School Journal, "It is indeed very difficult for private middle-school graduates to pass entrance exams for a public high school! There were altogether forty students from Aoyama Middle School (including those who just finished four years) who took the exam that year. I would be happy if 10% of them would pass!"

In the student directory of the Taiwan High School, Shoki is listed as coming from Aoyama Gakuin. It was the only middle school that accorded him acceptable credentials, so he was indeed proud of being an alumnus of Aoyama. Nevertheless, to those close friends of Shoki, his greatest pride was his other alma mater, Tainan Tióng-êng Middle School. It was at the latter that his family and his church converged and where his character was built and nurtured, his wisdom and his knowledge finding their roots. However, his one year of study at Aoyama afforded Shoki's education legitimacy and was a stepping-stone to further education. Thanks be to God that when many doors closed to Shoki because of colonial oppression, this single one remained open.

For nine years, from 1922 to 1931, Shoki went through three different schools without the benefit of receiving a diploma. The road was rough and difficult, but it was something worthy of celebration. It was the road that God led him through to make him a worthy instrument of God.

Testing and Commitment

According to Shoki's memoir, the most important examination that he ever sat, a decisive one for his whole educational process, was the entrance examination for the Wan-Ko (Taiwan High School in Taipei). The educational system at that time required those who aspired to enter university to go through three years of high school. Those who had completed four years of middle school were allowed to take the entrance examination; otherwise they could take another route by attending specialized high schools that focused on normal (teachers') education, commerce, technology or agriculture. Graduates of these special high schools obtained credentials to teach in middle schools, but no academic degree was awarded.

At that time, opportunities for education for Taiwanese were severely limited. The Taiwan High School was the only high school in Taiwan and very competitive. The colonial education policy made it possible for only a very limited number of Taiwanese, about thirty or so, to be admitted every year.

In 1931 Shoki entered the school. The following statistics show the ratio of Japanese students to Taiwanese at the school:

Year	Humanities			Science		
	Japanese	Taiwanese	Total	Japanese	Taiwanese	Total
1927	26	0	26	44	4	48
1928	55	10	65	44	11	55
1929	52	13	65	48	12	60
1930	57	14	71	56	15	71
1931	51	13	64	39	12	51
1932	49	15	64	48	23	71
1933	54	16	70	34	21	55
Total	344	81	425	313	98	411

As a matter of fact, Taiwan High School was not established for Taiwanese but for the colonial Japanese living in Taiwan. Shoki was a member of the Humanities-A category of the seventh graduating class. As he recalled, there were 35 in this category, only six of which were Taiwanese. There were a total of seventy humanities majors in the graduating class, with 16 Taiwanese. There were more Taiwanese among science majors but still two thirds less than the Japanese. On average, less than one third of every graduating class were Taiwanese. According to Shoki's senior schoolmates, about one out of every twenty Taiwanese applicants was chosen. Only one out of every twenty thousand Taiwanese received higher education at that time because of the discriminatory colonial education policy.

According to his memoir, Shoki had to take examinations in four subjects in the entrance exam. He did quite well on three. On the fourth one, Classical Japanese, he had some doubt. There was an essay of 1,500–2,000 words on the subject, "What should the student's attitude be in regard to the present unrest?" The mark would depend not only on the quality of the writing but very much on the attitude of the reader as well. It was a time when Japan was facing the challenge of great political and national tension. Everyone knew that both in this written essay and in the subsequent oral examination, the examiners would look carefully for subversive thinking, and thus all candidates had to be prepared. Shoki wrote: "I read the subject for the essay, I shut my eyes and said a little silent prayer, and suddenly Paul's words in Romans Chapter 5 verses 3–6 flashed into my mind, 'Let us also rejoice in our tribulations, knowing that tribulation worketh patience, and patience, probation; and probation, hope; and hope putteth not to shame; because the love of God hath been shed abroad in our hearts through the Holy Spirit.' I immediately began to write with great speed, determined to end my essay with that quotation, and succeeded in doing so just as the bell rang. I didn't even have time to read through what I had written, though somehow I thought I had not done too badly."[12]

Most likely because of the high scores Shoki made on the first three subjects, in the afternoon of the Classical Japanese exam he was called in for an oral exam. There were five examiners, one of them in military uniform, sitting in a row behind a light. No one smiled. Again, Shoki recalled:

No sooner was I seated than the one in the center, a young, good-looking man, abruptly produced the first question, "You are a Christian, aren't you?" I was a bit taken aback, but answered "Yes." I hoped loudly enough. "What are the basic teachings of Christianity?" I relaxed and answered, "God is love, and we are to love Him and our neighbors." "Then," he paused and gave a slight smile, "then don't you think that Christians are hypocritical, just as Jesus said of the Pharisees, when they plant crosses not only in the churches but in many other places too?" I was puzzled and a bit frightened, but at the same time my "Christian" fighting spirit was roused. "I don't know what you mean. I don't see why putting up a cross, which is the most precious symbol of Christian faith, should have anything to do with 'being hypocritical.' You must have made a mistake or misunderstood," I concluded boldly. "No, I am not mistaken, nor have I misunderstood. Just tell me how you can reconcile your assertion that Christianity is a religion of love with putting up crosses everywhere to remind people that the Jews crucified Jesus nearly two thousand years ago, so shaming them even today, two thousand years later."

Now I was really taken aback. I had never heard anyone talk about the cross in that way before. At the same time, I could no longer contain myself, and almost forgetting that he was the examiner and I the examinee, said quite loudly, "You are quite wrong there. The cross is the symbol of God's love, the extent of the sacrifice he would make for mankind, not even sparing his own son. It is the symbol of Jesus' love too, that he was obedient unto death…" and here I quoted the verses from Philippians. I began to be aware of the amusement on the faces of the other examiners, including the stiff military instructor, and stopped abruptly.

There was a rather strange smile on the face of the handsome examiner too as he said, "Young man, you seem to know your Bible well. But you had better think further about the question I put to you. I have just come back from Germany. There was growing anti-Jewish feeling there, and I think the crosses everywhere may have had something to do with it. Germany is supposed to be a Christian country, isn't it?" He turned to the colleagues on his right and left, asking them whether they had any questions they wanted to put to me, and I was greatly relieved when they all shook their heads, still looking very much amused. Then the examiner said, "Well, you may go now." I got up and began to say, "Sir, I am," but I couldn't finish it and turned and fled, feeling that they were all having a good laugh at me now.

I was very depressed. I knew of course that I had failed. When I at last got back home to Tainan the following evening, I was so quiet and subdued that no one dared ask me anything, thinking, no doubt, that I must have done very badly. But before I went to bed, father took me to his study and asked me gently what had happened. I told him the whole story in sobs and shame. Then, to my great surprise, father pulled me up and embraced me (a thing he had never once done before) saying, "Well done, my son. You delivered your first sermon and did it well. Even if you are to fail, I am very proud of you." I was both surprised and consoled by father's words, but next morning the sense of failure and shame returned. After a day or so, father sent me to go and stay with my favourite aunt A-ko˙ in Kî-āu, only returning on the day the results were to be announced.

I got back late in the evening, filled with the strong foreboding that I was bound to have failed and still shuddering at the recollection of the oral, afraid to face the family. Softly I opened the door and went in. My father, stepmother and sister were all there, and jumped up smiling to welcome me. "You have passed!" father almost shouted. Auntie A-chím had been to the college that morning, seen my name and phoned father straight away. I was overwhelmed, not so much by joy as by incredulity and relief. I was 17 years old and the future was opening for me.

That night father and I had a very serious talk about my life. "My son" he began, "I have refrained from telling you this before, but with your good news today I think it is right to tell you now. When your grandfather was converted, there was a very radical change in his life. And at that time he made a vow...to go into the ministry himself, and not only himself but the firstborn of his family. I did not know this until I heard that I had passed the entrance examination and been awarded a scholarship to go to the newly established medical school in Taipei. When I asked your grandfather for his permission, he said, 'No, you are to go to the theological school in Tainan and become a minister.' I pleaded with your grandfather, but he was adamant. I was very unhappy then, and thought of running away; but now, after more than thirty years have passed, I can honestly say that I have been very happy in the ministry. It has been a very rewarding life. I have no regrets, and am grateful now I finally decided to follow in your grandfather's footsteps, as he wished I would do. You are his first grandson, the 'firstborn' of the next generation. He reminded me several times before his death to tell you about his vow and I promised that I would do so. Now I am fulfilling my promise to him, but you must choose for yourself. Times have changed. In promising your grandfather to let you know about his vow, I have also made up my mind to tell you about two things which I have come to value dearly—freedom and education. God gives us freedom, and we must treasure it as dearly as life itself and exercise it responsibly before Him. Secondly education: each generation must aim to be better educated and equipped than the previous one. God has now granted you a very precious and rare opportunity. Make the very best of it for whatever you decide to do.

Shoki intimated to his father later that he had thought about following his grandfather and father's steps to choose the path of ministry and that was why he chose the humanity (literature) section in his entrance examination, even though mathematics and other science subjects were his favourite. His wish and that of his father's were in harmony, and thus the course of life was set.

Life as a High School Student

Deep in his heart, Shoki felt that passing the high school examination was a "mystery." This feeling of mystery was still there when the school year began. He saw then that on the school public notice board there was an announcement about a student YMCA meeting for new students. On the announced date and time, Shoki showed up for the meeting. He was surprised to see there the oral examiner who had posed that difficult question. The examiner must have spotted him first and was on his way to approach Shoki, so there was no way to avoid him. He was Ishimoto Iwane, a professor of German at the school. He came up to Shoki to introduce himself saying that he was also a Christian and had just returned from several years of study in Germany.

Later, Professor Ishimoto explained to Shoki that the examination team had asked him to be in charge of Shoki's oral exam because they knew that he was a Christian and were interested in finding out how he would handle someone like Shoki who openly declared himself a Christian during such a time of tension, with militarism on the rise. The professor said that the questions about the cross he put to Shoki were very real ones, because at the time, the German Nazi regime was openly using the Christian cross to instigate anti-Jewish feeling in Germany. He felt that Shoki gave a reasonably satisfactory answer, even though he himself was still in search of right answers. He said that he and the other examiners were quite taken aback by the courage and sincerity of Shoki's answers. He said to Shoki, "Well done! Incidentally, your examination results on other subjects were quite good, especially geometry and algebra."

When reflecting on the experience of the entrance examinations, Shoki said "the same old nagging question returned again—was it all just good luck, or was there a hidden guiding hand behind?"[13]

At this time Shoki had passed his sixteenth birthday and had yet to reach his seventeenth. Being a high school student in those days meant a change into a free lifestyle. As indicated earlier, in those days in Taiwan only the best in ten thousand could enroll in a high school, and once in high school there was almost a 99% guarantee of a place in a university. After graduating from a university, a career would be assured. Now he had been set free from the middle-school life of tight discipline and an incessant drive for top of the class.

High school meant freedom, even wild freedom. Society seemed to tolerate this attitude and style. For example, the students used to kick their high school caps along the gutter until they were adequately grubby and ragged. Their clothing was as casual as possible. There were no more big, crowded dormitories with little room for privacy; two or three friends would rent a room together somewhere, coming and going at will, eating whatever they pleased, whether eating out or cooking themselves, and at night they would pick a corner of the tatami room to sleep. Classes were more varied, interesting and enjoyable. One had to exercise one's own freedom and self-control. They spent out-of-class hours on school grounds or on streets with busy traffic.

Shoki used these words to describe his three years of high-school life: "[High School] represented my first taste of real freedom. It was the time of my first cigarette, and my first confrontation with the police. It was a time of physical strength. I was soon enlisted by the football club, and became quite prominent in it."[14]

Was Shoki alienated from the church in those days? Certainly not! The Student Y was very much the center of activities, and he joined discussion groups and seminars. Attending Sunday services and teaching Sunday school were regular parts of his life. He even got a glimpse of church politics. During that time the Northern Synod of the Taiwan Presbyterian Church was on the verge of splitting. The Presbyterian Church in Canada, the sending Mission of the Church in Northern Taiwan, voted to merge with other denominations to form the United Church of Canada. However, some congregations chose to remain separate as a Presbyterian denomination. The missionaries assigned to Taiwan were designated to be under the management of the separated Presbyterian denomination. Those who opted for the union were forced to leave Taiwan. However, the Rev. Hugh MacMillan and his wife, though opting for the union, decided to stay for the sake of their work, which was among students. When they were under attack, students organized a petition to the Canadian Church demanding that they be allowed to stay. Nobody knew how much weight the petition carried, but the MacMillans were allowed to stay.

The year 1932 was unforgettable for Christians in Taiwan. The Rev. Toyohiko Kagawa visited Taiwan. Most of the Presbyterian churches and their pastors got together to organize an island-wide Taiwan Sunday School Assembly, and an all-island Taiwan Christian Youth Alliance was organized. Shoki was at both meetings.

University Life and Learning

Shoki began his studies at the Tokyo Imperial University (To Dai) in April 1934. According to his memoir, the philosophy students at Tokyo Imperial University at the time were allowed to plan their own course of studies. There were very few required courses to take, so it was necessary for a student to spend time outside of class to do his own study and research. Most of the courses taken were of an introductory nature. Professors did not address a particular subject matter or respond to special needs of students.

The top chair as Professor of Philosophy was Genyoku Kuwaki (1874–1946). He was due to retire in 1935, and it was Shoki's great desire to take Kuwaki's course, Introduction to Philosophy, which he did. Along with the courses in his major area of philosophy, which covered Eastern and Western philosophy, Shoki also took courses in Ethics, Religion, Sociology, Pedagogy and English. His thesis was on "Studies on Augustine's Theory of Memory."

Tokyo Imperial University was the oldest, largest and best university in the nation. It was well known for its academic excellence and superior facilities. However, it was not a place for human interaction. There were eight to nine entering philosophy students in the class in 1934 (a total of 21 students in the Department of Philosophy). After a session of "getting to know each other," there was little contact or interaction among students or even classmates until graduation. Shoki said that he did not know what others were doing or where they were heading. All he could remember was one classmate's name.

All students, wearing the same uniform with a "square hat," were swallowed up in this "super university" and lost their direction. Fortunately, Shoki said, he found a true sense of community at the Christian Students' Hostel, where individual opinion and dignity were honored and where Christians carried out actions for what they believed.[15]

Shoki reached Tokyo in March 1934 and moved into the SCM (or "Student Y" or "Student YMCA") Hostel for To-Dai (Tokyo University) students close by the university. When he registered with the university, he put his residence address as Christian Students' Hostel.

The To-Dai Student Y Hostel was located on the right side of the university gate known as "Akamon" ("Red Gate," which was also the nickname for To-Dai), just three minutes' walk from the gate for the College of Humanity and Culture, across from the College of Agriculture, on Oi-wake Cho in Hongo District. It was an ideal location for students of Humanity and Culture.

There were fifty rooms at the hostel with rooms for forty resident students. Each student had his own room. They were divided into six "muras" (villages), and each included students of different classes, as a team. Each team held morning prayers two times every week, during which the members circulated notes and shared common concerns and news. On Sundays the hostel sponsored a Sunday school for about one hundred children from the neighborhood, and each team was responsible for one class of children. According to the Directory of the To-Dai Student YMCA, there were seven programmes, namely, Residential (dormitory), Bible Study, Academic Study (research), Library, Music, Athletics and Sunday School. All students at the hostel took their meals together. The meal times were occasions for dialogue and sharing of common concerns. Morning prayers were also led by the students,[16] even when attended by only a few of the residents. All of these experiences provided an atmosphere of a loving family.

There was a big bathing room provided with a Japanese-style hot bathtub large enough to accommodate twenty persons at a time. Here one could not only enjoy a hot bath but, more invaluable, discuss frankly all issues under the sky, national or international. It was the time after Japan had invaded Manchuria and established a "protectorate" Manshu-Koku (Manshu Nation). Japan was under the military government; "special agents" and "intelligence agents" infiltrated every academic institution and all activities for "witch hunting" the "free thinkers" and "rebels." Shoki indeed enjoyed this "naked" discussion every day. Hostel residents used the opportunity to empty their hearts where they could share whatever news they had and their inner thoughts and feelings.

The hostel had a visiting speaker once a month to lead Bible study or speak on a subject of special interest. A lively discussion would generally follow. Shoki remembered one special occasion when a young pastor by the name of Junichi Asano spoke on the book of Job, which particularly attracted his attention. In 1966, by chance when Shoki visited the Theology Division of Aoyama Gakuin, he met Asano again, who was then a professor there. They reminisced about that first meeting they had over thirty years ago.

The To-Dai Student Y was the center of student movements in Japan, like a processing chip of a computer. It stood at the forefront of studies of Christian social movements and their application in the nation. Within the campus, there was a group of Christian professors and academicians, known to be members of the "Non-Church" movement, who held regular Bible studies that attracted a big crowd of both Christians and non-Christians. The hostel was often used as a venue for public lectures on important issues. It was while Shoki was a resident at the hostel that a very distinguished professor of economics at the university, a specialist on Japanese Imperialism, Tadao Yanaihara, spoke while he was under surveillance by militarist agents. Yanaihara spoke courageously about the Japanese colonial policies and behaviour in Taiwan, Korea and Manchuria. He cited statistical data to prove how Japan had colluded with capitalists to oppress the people and rob the resources of these colonies.[17]

During the years when Shoki was at the To-Dai Y Hostel, the To-Dai Y also sponsored public Christian lectures on the university grounds. They were able to invite an outstanding scholar and speaker, Toyohiko Kagawa. Kagawa was the leader of the Japan Christian Social Movement and a great advocate of labourers' rights in Japan. Shoki was able to attend one of the lectures with a jam-packed audience in a lecture hall accommodating seven to eight hundred. Kagawa infused Shoki with broad social consciousness and deep Christian conscience. Shoki then volunteered to join in the service of the poor. Once every week he was among the group to distribute food and clothing for the slum dwellers. He said that for the first time in his life he saw so many miserable poor people who lived in the capital of Japan and so close to the Imperial Palace grounds.

Among the professors of philosophy, there was an outstanding professor, Seiichi Hatano, whom Shoki highly respected as a scholar and a professor. Hatano was a very interesting professor, and his class lecture audience normally included intellectuals from outside the university.

Shoki had earlier heard that Kagawa had little "academic depth," while Hatano's philosophy was more "secular" and fit for "public taste." In fact it was not so. Both had very deep-rooted philosophical and academic bases and were very eloquent speakers and attractive personalities who would easily entice an audience into the arena of religious faith and philosophy.

The assessment that Shoki gave of the Japanese Christians in those days was that they were "theologically conservative" but socially "liberal" and "activists." All Christian students came from rural and small town churches, but while they were in Tokyo, particularly at To-Dai, their religious activities were not in sync with their own home church life.

The advocates of the "Mukyokai-ism" (non-institutional church) held their weekly Sunday Bible study at the homes of prominent professors and occasionally held Bible study of an "academic nature" in a classroom. These meetings played the role of "worship service" at least on the To-Dai campus, with a high-caliber theological lecture or Bible study type of "worship" service.

A professor like Tadao Yanaihara, a professor of political economics, was also well-versed in Biblical Hebrew and Greek languages and a leader in biblical interpretation. It was a surprise that an academic institution such as a university regarded religion as an academic field worthy of pursuing. There was no such idea as the separation of politics and religion. This benefitted Christians in To-Dai, but it also was twisted to benefit the "Imperial National Shintoism," which could then be interpreted as a "national ideology" and not a "religion."

The To-Dai Y published a quarterly journal called the *Kaiho*. The journal carried reports, news and notice of the To-Dai Y, other Ys in Tokyo and all over Japan, and also news about the churches around the world. It also included the content of the lectures given at the To-Dai Y. Occasionally, it also included some essays written by the Y residents. *Kaiho* No 17,[18] published on 10 November 1935, included an essay written by Shoki on "The Ethical Nature of Restlessness."[19] The translated essay, in part, is as follows:

Just as a gold miner, regardless of the location, be it a wilderness or otherwise, is not yet rewarded with the result of finding gold, but disappointing sighs, yet he does not give up hope. He is exhausted but he perseveres. As a philosopher, who must seek after the truth with passion, repeatedly again and again turning over the waste he has thus far dug out, he persists in looking for the meaning that might have been hidden and unseen. If it were not for the passion for truth, who could ever find it? Failure is bidding one to move forward with greater passion.

Shallow understanding of unrest is caused by having been covered by double layers of veil. One, "unrest" itself, and two, its implication. Only those who are in the situation of unrest deserve the promise of true "peace" of mind; the "peace" of mind without "unrest" is but an escape and self-deception.

To those who do not acknowledge the seriousness of sin, how can one discuss the meaning of "unrest" (restlessness)? Under the looking glass of eternity, restlessness is like the sound of a falling leaf, and like a wave of a vast ocean. O, "the door to happiness," we can only bid you goodbye.

There is no precedent in history like today, a period that makes people restless (anxious). In all areas of life, there is "restlessness," everybody is crying out loud, "Crises!" The new nomenclatures such as restless society, restless thinking, restless theology, restless philosophy seem to be full of magic and magnetism to draw people in. In comparison to the Middle Ages, which we call "Dark Ages," we can call our age the "Age of Restlessness." However, the changes in the objective world may not necessarily create "restlessness." It is all because of the "restlessness" in subjective human beings that creates this crisis.

Of course there are quite a number of scholars who view "restlessness" as merely biological and psychological issues and interpret it as such; one may say that this kind of view is dogmatic. The restlessness we face is not a matter of survival, but a deep-rooted question of "restlessness of human being." The restlessness we speak of is what the existentialists of the world call "existential restlessness." So long as a human being lives, it follows like a shadow. It may not be seen but it is an unavoidable destiny of restlessness. Within the scope of "eternity" it is ever "present" to demand decisive human response. Therefore restlessness is a constant attribute of human existence.

The purpose of this essay is to begin with the definition of restlessness and "angst" as stated above and then to look at its meaning from the attribute of human existence. What is said above is basically similar to what Heidegger has defined as human angst. His basic hold on the idea of human restlessness did not occur suddenly but was an insight gained through the careful deliberation of many religious thinkers. This, however, does not mean that we do not acknowledge Heidegger's contribution in positing this issue to a philosophical plane for further deliberation. On the contrary, his original discussion started from the negative realm of human pathos and thought of it as an interference to the basic Logos and from there on posited it as a core of philosophical theme. This is the greatest contribution of Heidegger. From this point of view we must regard philosophy as a down-to-earth subject, not as many think of it as a subject of "learning for the sake of learning."

It is beneficial for us to learn from the understanding of former thinkers on the issue of "restlessness." Here are examples from Augustine and Pascal. We shall compare them with that of Heidegger.

Augustine: A human being has been created by God but has fallen away, living in a state where he is not able to live independently from God, struggling to be free but not capable, in a situation of tragic magnitude. Moreover, "those who are proud and self-conceited will be judged." Here one may find the very root of human restlessness. As a creature, the human being, created after God and for God, at the moment of rebellion, enters into the status of "negative" relationship with God. Broken humanity in its present state of existence, of course, is restless. The dialectical relationship of God and humanity is exactly where restlessness resides. The moment when a human being pleads to God is the very moment that human being begins to fall away from God. This dreadful restlessness is when God says "No!" to human being. This is the crisis of a rebel's running away in escape. "God is in humanity, and yet humanity stays apart from God. How can humanity expect to have rest? Unless we rest in Thee (God), how can our hearts find rest?" What drove Augustine to the endless journey was indeed this restlessness. What led him back to God was also this restlessness.

Pascal contends that the human being is wandering in an abyss between infinite greatness and the most infinite smallness in the hope of finding the root of restlessness. Restlessness provides the human being with passion in search of God, and at the same time allows him to remain in the abyss of human desires.

The modern existentialist philosopher Heidegger also digs deeply into exploring the meaning of restlessness. As we notice, the subject matter of restlessness is at the core of his philosophical inquiries. We do not intend to go into the details of his philosophical system, but would just like to point out that he does not agree with the above-mentioned two scholars' ideas, and that we would like to see how these differences may enforce the position I take. To Heidegger, restlessness lies in the "open-end-ness" of existence. The "existence here and now" is open, and left open, that is the reason of restlessness. Therefore, restlessness is existential restlessness. As such, it becomes restlessness of "self," and thus it is an *a priori* restlessness. This means that this restlessness is not only in present existence but often also in the potential existence. Therefore, it is indeed restlessness. Restlessness is restlessness about one's own potential (which is ultimately about one's own death). We have to be reminded that in Heidegger's thinking, he often deals with the issue of restlessness in terms of personal restlessness. The starting point of his discourse on restlessness is individual self. The following explanation may prove this observation. Heidegger and other human beings are the same, ordinary human, simply human, and as such he is not fallen from his original self; neither I nor he may be seen as not one of all human beings, yet one of the human beings, not an original self. We often are just "ordinary" persons. The "openness" of restlessness is shown, the potential of this open existence is revealed, resulting from that "non-I" of future potential "I" to our original "I." We must now have knowledge of restlessness, not only in a conceptual way, but also in its positive sense. We must also not forget that what Heidegger speaks of as restlessness is personal and individual. He has defined it in that way right from his starting argument.

The present existence in the world, by nature, is basically concern for one's own individual self, its burden and uniqueness. There are two double-sided layers, first there is the "awareness of existence" and "transcendence," and then there is "existence" and "phenomenon." There is no difference of one from the other, on the contrary they are one and the same, but express themselves from different perspectives. Not one of the whole can be ignored; any one of them will be expressed in any other phenomenon.

In further analysis of Heidegger's concepts, although he insists on present existence, in fact what he speaks of is "borrowed existence." In essence he only speaks of restlessness from an individual self, and extends it to its social dimension. He has not gone beyond the appearance of "individualism." Otherwise, I will attempt to pose the following two questions to him: One, is restlessness only individual and personal? Two, if one agrees that it is, can it be regarded as genuine restlessness? Because the individual "I" is not the original "I." They are "I," but they are two different "I's." Are these two "I's" not in conflict with each other? Can the restlessness that is present in the realm of independent transcendence be regarded as the only genuine restlessness? In other words, in differences of the quantitative realm, restlessness is not to be found, but only in the qualitative realm can restlessness be understood.

Now we may proceed to examine the root of restlessness, and to find its meaning. We begin with our daily affairs. Normally when we say we are in a state of unrest (or feeling uneasy), we are talking about being uneasy about a certain thing or about a certain affair; it is meaningless if we only say we are restless (uneasy). Even if we do not know why we are restless, we just cannot say my emotion is restless. This kind of restlessness is only an indication that we are oblivious of the thing or matter that makes us restless, not that our heart per se is restless. Therefore, restlessness cannot stand by itself, it must be related to some thing or matter. This is one reason why restlessness is individual and personal. We may temporarily call it the "relativity of restlessness." However, we may not identify restlessness with fear. The former is in relation to a human being, while the latter is in relation to a thing. That which is caused by earthquakes, floods, and wild beasts is not "restlessness" but "fear." Restlessness only comes from human being. This does not mean that they are not related. The fear that has been caused by natural phenomena may become a means to turn into restlessness. A person's fear of earthquakes may become restlessness to a particular person due to his knowledge about earthquakes. Although there is a situation of mutual conflict, only when it happens in human relationship, may we call it restlessness. Therefore we can say that restlessness only happens when "I" and "Thou" confront each other. In other words, only on the ground of human relations does restlessness occur. Aside from the "I-Thou" relationship, restlessness amounts to only imaginative restlessness. What is involved may not clearly reveal its existence. A thief who steals someone else's possession is restless not because of the thing he steals or because of his own restlessness, but because of the "hidden" (or unseen) owner of the stolen thing. From an individualistic argument, one may pose a serious contrary point of view, that is the issue of the individual nature of death. A human being constantly bears the burden of the possibility of death in his existence, realizing that death is always ahead of him. Death has the nature of finality, and there is no way to escape from it. It is a destiny that each has to accept. One may temporarily forget about death, after all it is only "temporary." For every human being eventually must drink that cup. "A human being must walk that road of death alone" is what Pascal said. Death is only like the unbroken skeleton of a castle that has been left behind after all its contents have been robbed clean. Death is the restlessness of all restlessnesses. If there is no death there will be no boring weariness and no anxiety (angst). Looking at death from an objective and natural perspective, it is the death of an individual. If considering death as a natural phenomenon, it is just like any other natural phenomena without difference. There are changes within natural phenomenon, but there is no meaning in death itself. From the perspective of natural phenomenon, death is but an "imaginative (or general) death," not a concrete (or specific) death. There is a qualitative difference between death as a form of change in numberless natural phenomena, and the death that evokes a subjective "I" deep sense of fear. For a concrete human being in existence, natural death is something about which he cannot have foreknowledge nor can he predict; death from an objective perspective is only a change in natural phenomenon which does not evoke restlessness.

If death of a human being is not natural, but is the restlessness of all restlessnesses, then who exactly is this subject, "I," who experiences it? There are different "I's" within the one and the same "I," and they are not in conflict with one another. Now we may proceed to examine the reason why we are conscious of the fact that death is the restlessness of all restlessnesses.

If my existence is related to others', why does not my death become restless? Does not a mother with children have more fear and trembling than a mother without any child? The reason that I am who I am is because I am related to others. Apart from others, I will not be what I am, it is then that

death becomes restlessness of all restlessnesses. Death becomes real restlessness in my relationship with others. However it is in its very foundation that
lies the one who is neither I nor you, who is "wholly other," who has the
grip on me. It is through death that we stand face to face with this absolute
and wholly other. This further proves that death is the condemnation of sin.
Because judgment is by evidence of our rebellion, death becomes the very
root of restlessness. Therefore, death is the pronouncement of *Nein* ("no")
of the Absolute and Wholly Other to human being. Therefore, death is the
restlessness when the judged is confronted by the Judge. Thus, death is not
an individual; on the one hand it must face the others with whom he shares
a mutually dependent destiny, and on the other the Absolute Wholly Other,
it is restlessness of all restlessnesses. By nature the former, facing those companions of the mutually dependent, is an ethical issue, while the latter, in the
face of the Absolute Wholly Other, a religious issue. The root of the former
is contingent upon the latter.

According to the records appearing in No. 16 of *Kaiho* (July 1934), Shoki
was officially accepted by the committee meeting of 23 March of the To-Dai
YMCA to be a member and a resident at its hostel. There were five others who
were admitted at the same time.

In September 1935, his younger sister, Siok-êng, his cousin Lîm Sūi-hûn
(maternal uncle's eldest son), and N̂g Ngá-chu (paternal uncle's eldest daughter) all came to Tokyo for further education. Together they moved into a
house that had been bought by Shoki's father, the Rev. N̂g Sū-bēng, in Nakano
of Tokyo. Shoki remained in this house for the rest of his one and a half years
at university.

Shoki's recollection of an incident at the end of this period illumines its
larger context:

An Incident of Unacceptable Injustice[20]

I was on an NYK[21] boat on my way back to Taiwan from Tokyo, where I had
just completed my course at Tokyo Imperial University (To-Dai, also well-
known as Akamon), the most prestigious university in Japan in those days.
I was returning with the only graduation certificate I ever had. Humanly
speaking, I was one of the very few Taiwanese who ever had it so good—
educationally at least. Also, I had ahead of me a further very exciting and
rare opportunity. After a few months' stay in my homeland, I was to leave

again for England to study in Cambridge. I had every reason to be happy and contented, and in fact I was so—until that unforgettable incident that took place, bringing out of me a bitter feeling of "m̄-goān." My brother, A-Bêng, was involved, and on a recent visit to Taiwan I mentioned it to him, and he said he remembered it as vividly as if it only happened yesterday.

A day or two after our boat left Kobe, I was walking along the deck when suddenly and completely unexpectedly I came face to face with my brother, A-Bêng, whom I hadn't seen for three or four years. He had just completed his final year of Middle School in Tâi-tiong, and his class was returning from a tour of Japan (Shiu-gaku Lio-ko), where they had all been taken by the form master (or possibly the military instructor) for a few weeks. You can well imagine that in our excitement and joy we began to talk and chatter loudly together in our mother tongue, Taiwanese, and not in the official Koku-go (the "national language,"—then, of course, Japanese). Soon we were in deep trouble. What was our fault then? We had spoken our mother tongue instead of Japanese. "Ko Mei-ki (my brother's name in Japanese), come here," shouted the form master. I saw my brother suddenly turn pale. He went at once to his master, who took him away. I learnt that he had been taken to the master's cabin and was there with him alone. I couldn't get any news of him for nearly two hours, until I learned from one of his classmates that he was undergoing a "severe disciplining."

I hurried to my bunk and pulled out from my things the best kimono I had, a new one I had bought before leaving Tokyo. I dressed carefully as if for some very special "official" occasion (what the Japanese call Sei-So). I even took my *kaku bo*—my university hat—as a kind of status symbol. Thus in full glory I went off, determined to have a showdown with that master, cost me what it might. I knocked at the cabin door. "Hai-re," came a shout from inside ("enter"—a command from a superior to an inferior). I opened the door and found myself right in front of him as he sat on his heels on the floor in the formal Japanese way.

He was a little taken aback, perhaps not recognizing me dressed in so formal a fashion or perhaps expecting it to be one of his own boys. He even began to stand up. But one glance at where my brother knelt in agony and fear—I could almost feel him trembling—and within a second I had instinctively changed my mind. "Please," I said to the master, "Please don't get up." I was as calm and polite as I could manage. "May I sit down?" He stretched out his hand, palm upward, indicating that I might. Then I too sat down on my heels in the proper Japanese fashion and began to speak. "I have come,"

I said, "to apologize" (quite the opposite of my original intention!). "It was all my fault and not my brother's. We haven't seen each other for nearly four years; so when we suddenly met, I involuntarily began speaking to him in our own dialect (I even avoided saying 'our own language') and he involuntarily responded in the same way. It was all my fault. So please forgive my brother this once —*ko shite owabi shi ma shu.*" As I said this I knelt forward, bowing until my head touched the ground. I even repeated what I had said again—"*Ko shite owabi shi ma shu.*"

The Japanese male is a very strange creature. He can be as brutal as an animal, then all at once transform himself into something very human. He suddenly said to me in a completely different tone of voice, "*Io-ku wa ka ri ma-shi-ta*" ("I now well understand") and, turning to my brother, "*Ko Mei-ki kun, mo it-te io yi*" (using a form of address from teacher to student which is polite and even affectionate, "You may go now").

Yes, I did control my "m̄-goān" that time. I was, and am, glad that I did it for my brother's sake. But I felt the utter humiliation of it all the same. What! For talking with my own brother in our own mother tongue he was severely disciplined and I had to kneel down and bow to the ground to apologize!! No! m̄-goān! I refuse to accept it. A thousand times *no*. One's mother tongue is part and parcel of one's very existence. To try to forbid it, to take it away forcibly, this is nothing less than an attempt to obliterate one's identity as a person. It is almost like treating people as things to be moulded into someone else's shape. At the very best it is treating others as second-class human beings, second-class citizens, even in their own country.

3
England (1937–1947)
A New World for Learning

In early 1937 Shoki was 22, ready to graduate from university and embark on a new future. He had decided when he was in high school that his goal was to study theology. That was why he took philosophy as his major at university. In response to the request of Shoki's father, the Rev. N̂g Sū-bēng, the English Presbyterian Mission in Taiwan, in its meeting on 18 February, decided to grant a scholarship of £400 to assist Shoki to study theology in England. At that time the exchange rate was £134 to ¥1,000. The scholarship was to support Shoki for four years in England. The Mission suggested that he spend the first year at Overdale College, one of the colleges in Selly Oak, and then on to Westminster College, Cambridge.

To provide the financial resources to support Shoki, the Mission obtained about £65 per year from the Burns Scholarship, and the Overseas Mission Committee of the Presbyterian Church of England raised £35 for a total of £100 per year for four years. Shoki was responsible for additional needs. The Taiwan Mission recommended that before he set out on his journey to England he should continue his ministry in Taiwan and also meet and become better acquainted with the church leaders who were active in social issues there. The meeting assigned two missionaries, the Rev. W. E. Montgomery and the Rev. F. G. Healey, to serve as his advisors to prepare for England.

Leaving Taiwan

Between March 1937, when Shoki graduated from university, and August, when he started for England, he visited many churches to familiarize himself with the ministry of the church in Taiwan. At the suggestion of his father, N̂g Sū-bēng, he went to his ancestral town Tang-káng to meet many relatives. Among those visited was a well-to-do, prominent community leader whom he called Great Uncle Kūn. He was a farmer who was responsible for managing the famous local temple Tong Liông Keng[1]. Shoki was able to learn from him more about his family roots. He also especially visited the Rev. N̂g Bú-tong, Dr Lîm Bō·-seng, and Mr. Tiō Thian-chû, a teacher.

In his letter of recommendation to the Rev. Douglas James, Overseas Missions Secretary of the Presbyterian Church of England, the Rev. W. E. Montgomery stated that both Shoki's grandfather and father were among the most respected and active Taiwanese ministers. His father, Ng̊ Sū-bēng, who served for many years with distinction as the warden of the Presbyterian Boys School, made a proposal to the Mission Council to assist his son Shoki to study theology at Westminster College in Cambridge. Members of the Council had known Shoki for many years, and were all very concerned and willing to help him study in England. The letter further stated that Shoki had studied philosophy and English literature at Tokyo Imperial University and that his graduation thesis was on the theological thoughts of St. Augustine. Rev. F. G. Healey particularly emphasized Shoki's academic achievement and his excellent character while he was a student at Tokyo Imperial University. No mention is made about a condition that, upon finishing his study, Shoki would return to work for the church in Taiwan, although it was a common desire among the Council members.

During the 1930s it was quite a feat to make a trip from Tainan to Tokyo. One first took a train from Tainan to Keelung. The railroad in Formosa was operated by the Japanese National Government and managed by the Taiwan Governor's Office. The ride took 14 hours by local train and nine hours by express. Then at the Port of Keelung, one boarded a ship for Kobe, Japan, a journey requiring three days. After disembarking at Kobe one rode a train to Tokyo that took twelve hours. When waiting and transfer time were added on, the entire trip required twelve days. At that time, Taiwan was a part of the Japanese colonial territory, and no traveling documents such as passport or visa were required. But traveling from Taiwan, a Japanese territory, to London was another matter. This was going from one country to another!

According to the official railroad schedule published by the Ministry of Railroads in July 1937, during the months of July and August the Nippon Yusen Kaisha (Japan Postal Shipping Corporation) scheduled one ship about every two weeks from Yokohama to London. The dates for 1937 were 13 and 28 July and 11 and 25 August. One of these ships, the Kashima Maru, embarked from Yokohama on 28 July, making port calls at Nagoya and Osaka of one day each and at Moji for two days before setting sail for Shanghai. The vessel stayed in Shanghai's inner and outer harbors for three days before setting out to make a call on 11 August at Keelung. It left the same day. Since one ship left Keelung for London every two months, it was very likely that Shoki was on board this ship. According to his autobiography, he took a Japanese ship and left around August-September. The Kashima Maru was a steamboat of 9,900 tons. In addition to cargo space, it also provided berths for passengers.

A Taiwanese graduate of a Japanese imperial university at that time had no special privileges. Instead he received special treatment by the Japanese

Special Police—high-level, plain-clothes security officers—who had him on a surveillance list. He was trailed all the time and watched for whom he made contacts with and what he said about the Japanese empire.

Shoki remarked on the harassment he received from the special plain-clothes police in the period between his return from Tokyo in March 1937 and August when he left for England in that year. International tensions were high. Japan was looking for causes to invade China, which actually began with the "incident" on 7 July that year at Marco Polo Bridge near Peking. This incident happened a month before Shoki's departure for England. All Taiwanese with higher education could not avoid the watchful eyes of the special police. Any little idea or opinion that departed from the official lines would cause not only personal danger but also affect the safety of one's family.

On the day when Shoki was at the dock of the Port of Keelung, he sensed that he was being carefully trailed and watched by the special police with the purpose of intimidating him from leaving the country. Then came the most unexpected and extraordinary intervention. When he walked up the gangway of the ship and presented his travel documents to the uniformed ship official, the officer almost jumped in the air with surprise and said, "Aren't you my friend Ko? I had suspected that it might be you, and it is indeed you." He was Toshimichi Suzuki, a classmate at Aoyama Middle School and a roommate in the dormitory. Suzuki, the officer-in-charge that day, became a guardian angel on the journey. He saw the group of people with Shoki, sensed the situation and changed his voice to a more official tone saying, "We will have plenty of time during the long voyage to talk about what we have done during the past six years. We have to leave in an hour or so. I see your parents and friends are here to see you off, but I am afraid that they cannot go beyond this point." With that he picked up Shoki's passport, flicked it open and read out in a louder voice than usual, "Issued by the Ministry of Foreign Affairs on such and such a date, and valid for four years until...yes, yes, everything is in order." He then turned to Shoki's parents and said, "Pardon me, we were at middle school together," and directed Shoki forward. Since everything was in order, there was no reason that the special plainclothes police could go on board to stop him. They looked abashed and seemed to fade away. What a way to resolve the tense situation! On reflection, Shoki asked himself if it was coincidence or providence. He was on board the ship in Keelung, the only passenger joining the ship there, and now beginning a long journey in the next chapter of his life.

Later on during his class lectures on Dogmatics, Principal Coe mentioned that as soon as he went overseas to another country, he encountered the problem of his own identity. Japanese did not kindly look at a young man with a

"Sina" (Chinese) surname "Ko" holding a Japanese passport. The single syllable surname revealed he was not Japanese. For foreigners, it was strange and even unbelievable that a person with a "Sina" name presented himself as a Japanese. The term "Sinajin"—a person of Sina—was commonly used in Japan and Taiwan at that time as a derogatory name referring to the Chinese as a whole. It was not possible for a Taiwanese to put one's own roots of identity.

Kashima Maru[2] left Keelung on 11 August[3] as scheduled. The first stop was Hong Kong, but no Japanese passport holders were allowed to land because of the tremendous anti-Japanese feelings. The ship stopped only long enough to allow handling of cargo and to pick up one or two new passengers. There were 19 passengers on board, twelve of them Japanese, mostly businessmen or artists, all on their way to France. Shoki soon discovered that they had little in common, so he did not spend much time with them. Of course there was his good friend, Suzuki, a former classmate at Aoyama Gakuin Middle School, who was now the second officer of the ship. He and Shoki were able to find occasions to reminisce about their school days. They found out that they were the only two Christians on board. They also shared their unhappiness about Japan's undeclared war on China. Suzuki intimated that the war was undoubtedly started by the Japanese army and that sooner or later he would be drafted into the Japanese navy. In their conversations, Suzuki would add in a resigned tone of voice, "What can we Christians do? We are such a tiny minority."

On 14 August the ship continued its journey. It stopped at Singapore on 18 August, left there on 19 August for Penang, and then to Colombo[4] the capital of Ceylon (now Sri Lanka). On 25 August it set out for Aden, the capital of South Yemen. From there on 2 September it departed for Suez (the southern tip of Suez Canal) and on to Port Said. On 7 September the ship left Port Said for Naples in southern Italy; 13 September to Marseilles, 14 September to Gibraltar (a port city in the southern tip of the Iberian Peninsula). Soon the long voyage ended in London on 21 September. It took 41 days to complete the voyage from Keelung to London. It was indeed a long journey to a far-away world. The boat fares from Yokohama to London, according to the information provided by the Ministry of Railroads, published by the Japan Travel Bureau in its Automobile and Steam Ship Schedule, were £69 for special second-class and £42 for ordinary third-class. From Keelung to London would probably be £2 or £3 less. The exchange rate at the time was £1 = ¥7.5; £42 would be equivalent to ¥312. A public school teacher at that time earned about ¥50 per month. The fare amounted to about a half-year's salary of an ordinary public service person.

Adjusting to English Life and Study

On 21 September 1937, Shoki Coe's steamship arrived in London, a month after his twenty-third birthday on 20 August. The Rev. Douglas James, secretary of the Overseas Missions Committee of the Presbyterian Church of England, welcomed him at the dock. Although in Asia Shoki had received a rare university education, thus reaching a pinnacle of academic and cultural nurture, in England, the West and Europe, it seemed quite insufficient. He was unable to consult with relatives, close friends or seniors, and all things, including race, culture and customs, were new and unfamiliar to him.

Fortunately, members of the Council of Overseas Missions with some knowledge of foreign countries, were able to give special attention and care to this foreign young man. The new school term was to begin soon. Arrangements were made for him to go to Selly Oak Colleges in the western suburb of Birmingham, to get adjusted to life there, and to spend a year preparing to receive formal theological education. Formerly, Selly Oak Colleges were a group of church-run colleges involved in training Christian workers and missionaries for overseas service. However, because of changed circumstances caused by a decrease in church financial resources and reductions in overseas missionary service, the colleges had been handed over to the Department of Education, and had become part of Birmingham University.

As was expected, the young scholar Shoki Coe, just arrived from Taiwan, was unable to understand standard spoken English. His manner of expressing himself in a common Western way was not even up to par for a secondary school student. To help Shoki adjust, the Office of Overseas Missions arranged for Shoki to study at Overdale College, one of the smaller colleges in Selly Oak. Overdale was the theological training center for the Churches of Christ. At that time Dr William Robinson was the Principal. He was professor of systematic theology and philosophy of religion, a delightfully relaxed, good-hearted and caring person. He and his wife and the college tutor, Mr Gray, were all so good to Shoki that he soon got over his worries and began to feel at home.

In the April 1938 issue of *The Christian Advocate*, Shoki related his impressions and experiences at Selly Oak. In part he wrote,

> I arrived at Overdale College at about 5:00 p.m. on September 22, 1937. I felt very distant from and unfamiliar with the situation and the environment. This is a new start for my life—full of dread as well as hope. The first person to be introduced to me was a young man who was easy to get along with. With kind smiles he repeatedly pointed to the color of his own suit telling

me that "Gray" was his name. When I was yet to find out how to address him, he took my luggage and led the way to go upstairs. My tongue was frozen and no words could come out—I felt sad within. However, when I discovered that Mr Gray was my tutor, and I must attend the class he taught, I felt extremely uneasy. If I had known who he was I definitely would not have let him carry my heavy luggage—as an Oriental student I could only deeply regret that I let him do what he did. He was a very kind person. He was also a philosopher. How could he be such a delightful person?

A college where mission personnel are being trained indeed is a place filled with grateful hearts and joy overflowing with sweet spring water. Nevertheless, a foreign country with a different language and lifestyle did indeed cause Shoki to suffer from cultural shock. He wrote of his feelings at that time, saying,

> I was quiet with nothing to say every day. I thought several times, students could interact and engage each other in learning. There was an atmosphere of freshness and freedom in life here. I only wished that the weather had been better! I was not accustomed to students calling their Principal "W. R." Every time I heard it, I was shocked. And then, the Principal addressed students as "Brothers," for which I still could not feel comfortable. However, after the initial shock, I gradually felt a sense of intimacy and comradeship. It was not easy for me to follow suit, for in the Orient we have a saying, "just stay three steps behind your teacher."[5]

Shoki also moved freely among students of the other colleges and befriended them. Gradually he got to know most of the so-called "central staff" who were responsible for teaching Old Testament, New Testament, Church History, Systematic Theology, and so on. He was free to choose whatever lectures he was interested in. He took Hebrew, Greek and English. For him the teaching method at Overdale fit his style well. Because there was no pressure from examinations, he was able to choose the classes he liked, and he absorbed their contents as much as he could without worrying about the grades professors would give him. He considered this year beneficial and well spent.

A letter dated 27 October 1937 is probably the first official correspondence from Shoki after he arrived in England. The letter was posted in Overdale College and addressed to Douglas James requesting his help to deal with tuition fees, £28.10, which he owed. In the reply from Mr James on 28 October, he wrote to Shoki saying, "Your father has sent ¥1000 which has been converted to £135. Please go to a bank to open an account. I will then transfer the amount your father sent me to the account, and I will also send you one half of the scholarship the Overseas Missions will provide; the other half will be sent on April 1." It is clear that the living expenses in England in comparison with those of Taiwan and Japan in those days were extremely high. At that time in Taiwan ¥1000 was more than enough for two years' salary of a middle school teacher. That amount was barely enough for Shoki to pay for his tuition and living expenses for one year and a half.

During the Christmas season of 1937, Shoki was able for the first time to "go home" for the holidays. His "foster parents"—in Taiwanese the word literally means "guest parents"—were Dr and Mrs David Landsborough. They had retired from Chiong-hòa Christian Hospital a year earlier to return to England, where they chose to live in a suburb south of London, called Redhill. They bought a house there that included a kitchen, living room, dining room, work room, and, upstairs, four bedrooms. The Landsboroughs called the house "Formosa House." The junior David Landsborough remembered that 65 years earlier his mother asked him to go to the London Train Station to meet Shoki Coe, who was arriving by train from Birmingham, and to bring him home. From that day on, Shoki regarded the Landsborough home as his own, as freely accessible to him as his own home. He and the young David treated each other as brothers. As a matter of fact both were born in the same year, and both were born in Chiong-hòa. During the author's visit to England in 2002, while visiting the younger David, young David pointed to a photo of him and Shoki taken together at the house in Redhill, saying, "See, I have the advantage of a big body, but Shoki has a fine brain."

Study at Westminster College

After one year at Selly Oak, Shoki was able to settle down and get used to English life. He was finally able to go to the college in Cambridge that he had long anticipated. Westminster College is located in the northeast corner of the Cambridge University campus. It was the theological college that the Presbyterian Church of England used to train its ministers. On 26 April 1938, the Overseas Missions Committee decided to increase Shoki's scholarship from £40 to £60.[6]

All English Presbyterian students had to pass entrance examinations before enrolling. According to the records of 5 October 1938, of the Admissions Examination Committee of Westminster College, there were six applicants who took examinations that year and all passed. The College did not give Shoki an examination but required him to write a paper, which upon due evaluation was accepted as satisfactory to the Admissions Committee. There were six other foreign students that year: two from the United States, one each from Canada, South Africa, France and Scotland. Thus there were a total of 13 students in the entering class.

When students arrived to report to the school at its opening of a new school year, they were not required to register or to pay fees. To enroll the school only provided a book for students to sign in. In the book for 1938, Shoki signed in by using the Roman alphabet spelling of his name in Japanese, Shoki Ko, and his father's name, Simei Ko; age 24; place of birth, Formosa; and prior education, Tokyo Imperial University. In subsequent years he signed in with the same information, except of course increasing his age. However, he also dropped the word "Imperial" from his educational background. Thus "Tokyo Imperial University" became merely "Tokyo University." One may surmise that being in Europe, and seeing the formation and operation of universities, Shoki realized that there was no imperial intervention in university education. Furthermore, in comparison with the British Empire at that time, the Japanese empire in history and extent qualified only as minor league. It was also probable that, in comparing the two colonialist countries, Shoki began to experience distaste for the oppressive imperial system of Japan.

Beyond the gate of Westminster College on the right side stands a three-story section of the building used as a student residence. Until over thirty years ago, Westminster College, like Cambridge University as a whole, was a world of male students. Westminster College treated well its gentlemen graduate students who would become future church ministers. Each student was provided with twelve square meters of residence space, consisting of one bedroom for sleeping and storing clothes, and another room for studying, writing and meeting with friends. Judging by Shoki's lifestyle in later days, he must have used the study for smoking, drinking, having tea and coffee, thinking of his far-away home, contemplating his future mission, perceiving his vision, reflecting and practicing his devotional life of praying and meditation. In most cases at that time, Westminster students had already completed their university education, giving them social status and academic standing, and then came to study theology, so they were qualified teachers deserving of respect.

Displayed along both sides of the residence hallway were group photographs of teachers and students of Westminster College for every year since 1910. This display of photographs illustrates the tradition of respect and dignity in the bond between students and the school. Visitors to this part of Westminster College are able to see Shoki in three group photographs from 1939, 1940 and 1941. The 1941 photograph, includes his future neighbor and vice-principal, Boris Anderson.

Boris Anderson reminisced that in April 1940, when he arrived to begin his study at Westminster, Shoki had just begun his third year. Boris saw Shoki for the first time as he was going up the stairs of the student residence. Shoki was playing ping-pong (table tennis) in the student common room beside the stairs. The way Shoki played left a deep impression on him. Not long after that, Boris discovered that Shoki was a ping-pong champion and nobody at Westminster could beat him.

In June 1941, after due evaluation, Westminster College approved six students for graduation that year. Among them was Shoki. At that difficult time in the world, no family or friends from Taiwan could be present to celebrate the auspicious event with him. He must have wondered, "when will I be able to go home and join my family there?"

Introduction to International Ecumenism

The first World Conference of Christian Youth was held in Amsterdam, Holland, 24 July to 2 August 1939. Over 1700 people from seventy countries participated in the landmark event, which was one of the precursors to the World Council of Churches. The Conference was sponsored by several worldwide Christian organizations, including the World Alliance of YMCAs, the World YWCA and the World Student Christian Federation. The ages of participants were between eighteen and thirty-five, with an average age of twenty-five years.

One purpose of this conference was to declare to the world that Christianity is a religion of Proclamation. In the preceding hundred years, Christianity had brought its message to almost every corner of the world. The theme of the conference declared what Christianity believed—Christus Victus.

Unintentionally, though, the conference became an advocate for the "giving" side of the white European churches, encouraging European youth to be proclaimers of the Gospel. It followed previous gatherings that had, through presence and message, been dominated by European and American mission programmes and agencies. Just one year before the youth conference, the International Missionary Council met in Tambaram,[7] India, in a gathering that, through the presence of some representatives of "younger churches" touched on the shift in mission that was to come. But World War II broke out shortly afterward and the opportunity to change this pattern waited another ten years while the world map was redrawn. Professor H. H. Farmer of Westminster College was a representative at the Tambaram meeting. He was able to raise the enthusiasm of students about the theology, concepts and vision of world mission.

The Department of Youth Ministry of the Presbyterian Church of England included the following description of the global youth conference in its reports to the General Assembly:

> There were three official youth delegates (two males, one female, names listed)…and two other youth (one male, one female, names listed) participants listed on the roll. In addition, there were a minister and a woman invited by the Conference to serve as group discussion leaders. Miss Jean Frazer from our church had the honour of being elected as a member of the Presidiun of daily program proceedings. The Chairman of our Youth Ministry Committee was asked to be a participant and to hold the leadership responsibility of British delegates. Others who were related to our church included Rev. Sheffield Cheng, a Discussion Group leader, and Shoki Ko, currently a student at Westminster College, who was among the accredited Japanese delegates.

Shoki was at the right historical moment and at the right place to be invited for the conference, but who he represented reflected the realities and difficulties of mission and politics at that time.

In that era, the Presbyterian Church of Formosa did not have the financial resources, political strength and people with sufficient language skill to serve as delegates to this kind of meeting. It was also at the time when the leadership of the church had just changed hands from the English missionaries to Taiwanese (under the Japanese). Thus, although he received the authorization of the church to attend, there were no funds to enable him to go. If he had not received special attention and assistance from the office of the Overseas Missions of the Presbyterian Church of England, in particular from the Rev. Douglas James, he would have missed this significant historic opportunity.

On 24 May 1939, as Shoki Coe prepared to apply for the conference, he wrote to James saying, "If I obtain the permission from my home church in Taiwan, I would like to participate in the World Conference of Christian Youth. Please write to Principal Edward Band of the Presbyterian Middle School, Tainan. He is making arrangements for me in Taiwan. The Synod of the Presbyterian Church of Formosa at her meeting in February has given me permission to participate in this conference. Please send on my behalf the application fee of £7 to Mr. Miseshiah, the person in charge."

In a later letter to James, Shoki mentioned that he had received a letter from the Japan Christian Federation[8] that he had been accepted as a member of the Japanese delegation to the Conference, and that he would be given ¥30 per diem for incidental expenses. He observed that, "It is rather awkward to be a delegate for both the Japanese and Formosan churches. But I think I had better accept it as it happens." The reality was that since Taiwan (and Korea) were invisible as countries, the only way to list Shoki country-wise was under Japan. With the endorsements[9] and financial support he received, Shoki was invited and able to attend the conference.

It is significant that twenty-five-year-old Shoki Coe was a part of this ecumenical church gathering. He was a young and energetic theologian, coming from a non-Christian area, but competent in several languages, and a product of the mission field. After the World War, many of the "heathens" and colonial subjects gradually rebelled against European and American domination, exploitation and oppression, and demanded independence. Christian churches had to repent and be set on the path toward liberation, multicultural and multilingual realties, and indigenization. In this new era, the church required new leadership and Shoki Coe was uniquely placed to provide it. He had personally experienced colonial rule, imperialistic oppression, and the mission dominance of the Christian West, while in his studies and friendships he gained a deeper understanding of people and cultures. Shoki found that the Christian youth conference in Amsterdam helped to form his understanding of indigenous and contextual theology.

In his letter to Rev. Douglas James after the conference, he mentioned that en route to Holland he was able to give talks about the mission of the English Church. In closing he added, "I had a very pleasant journey, but worried very much about current international affairs."

The international situation certainly affected the conference. No delegates from Germany were present, and the Japanese delegation were under particular pressures before, during and after the event.

Because this first worldwide Christian youth conference met under the dark shadow of the looming World War, there was already a sense of division between enemies and allies. The whole of Europe was geared up for hostilities, and anything could trigger the war. In 1937 in Asia, Japan had started a war with China, and now showed its enmity toward Britain and United States. Japan would soon join Italy and Germany to form the Axis nations. Most people thought the Japanese government would not allow Japanese youth to participate in the conference.

Miss Shizue Hikari, one of the delegates sent by Japan YWCA, later said in her report, "It was indeed a miracle that 1,760 young people from seventy countries could come together in one place. It could be said to be evidence of 'Christus Victus' (the theme of the Conference). The organizers were worried that the Japanese delegates might not be allowed to attend, so we were cheerfully welcomed by delegates from many countries. However, at the Conference, I sensed that the physical appearance of Japanese and Chinese delegates looked to be closest in likeness but in heart seemed farthest apart."[10]

Among the Japanese delegates was a young woman theologian named Kiyoko Takeda. She met Shoki Coe for the first time at the Youth Conference.[11] However, because of the war that began the following month, there was no occasion for them to make contact with each other again until much later when both of them were involved with great success in ecumenical activities, serving as colleagues in the World Council of Churches. Kiyoko Takeda was one of the presidents of the WCC while Shoki Coe was Director of the Theological Education Fund. Back in December 1941, when the United States entered World War II, Kiyoko Takeda was a student at Union Theological Seminary in New York. As an enemy alien, her life and movement were greatly restricted, as was Shoki Coe's in England. But because their identities differed, their situations also deviated. Shoki Coe stayed in England until after the war. Kiyoko Takeda, however, was among the Japanese citizens Britain and the United States exchanged with Japan. Thus in 1942 she was able to return to Tokyo.

Another of the Japanese delegates, Kuranosuke Sasaki,[12] was a student at the School of Theology of Boston University at the time of the conference. After the United States entered World War II, he, together with other Japanese, was placed in an internment camp. Later he went to Denver, Colorado, to study and became a pastor of the Japanese Methodist Church. There were 24 Japanese delegates at the global youth counference, two of whom had non-Japanese names: Sousen Lee from YMCA, Seoul, Korea, and Shoki Ko/Coe.

The Japan YWCA journal had the following comments: "The theme 'Christus Victus' urges the youth to go beyond and overcome all difficult obstacles to be 'One Body of the Lord.'" However, the common feeling of the youth participants was: "It is likely that when we next time gather we will be meeting in fox-holes in the battle fields or on the front lines of war against each other." The World Christian Youth Conference concluded in this atmosphere of a heavy heart.[13] Germany invaded Poland the following month. In response, Great Britain and other allied nations declared war on Hitler's Germany, thus beginning World War II.

Away from Home at a Time of War

World War II began on 1 September 1939. No matter which side people were on, those in Shoki's generation could not avoid the fate of being drafted to military service. In Britain many who received higher education enlisted themselves in the army and navy in order to serve their country. His good friend David Landsborough Jr had already been sent as medical missionary in Chôan-chiu, China. The appointment by the Overseas Missions Committee of the Presbyterian Church of England happened before David completed his residency programme that he needed to receive his medical license. At the farewell parties and gatherings of friends and schoolmates and even on board the ship, David encountered many serving in the military medical corps, and he felt a bit uncomfortable. Many of his friends wore impressive military uniforms and looked handsome, sharp and enviable. When he arrived in Chôan-chiu, Japan and China were already at war. But hostilities between Britain and America and Japan did not begin until late 1941. In the interim period, Landsborough was free to move between the Japanese occupied territories and other locations. After Japan had attacked Pearl Harbor, he was no longer at liberty to move around Amoy and other coastal regions.

On 27 September 1940, Germany, Italy and Japan signed a treaty to form the Axis Alliance. Because Shoki Coe carried a Japanese passport, he not only had a hard time finding a job, but it was difficult to continue living in England. As a Taiwanese living in England, he increasingly felt the deep enmity between Britain and Japan. This increased his pain about the problem of his identity.

On 14 April 1940, the Rev. W. E. Montgomery[14] and Shoki Coe were invited to attend a meeting of the Overseas Mission Committee. Montgomery was able to introduce Shoki to the members and engaged them in discussion with him. The whirlwind atmosphere of the war caused foreign missionaries in many lands to be called home. All foreign missionaries in Formosa were ordered to be repatriated by 1940. On 17 December the secretary of the Overseas Mission Committee reported that he had received word of Shoki Coe's remarkable achievements in his studies and his projected graduation from Westminster College in June 1941. The meeting resolved to keep him in England, in as much as possible to go on speaking tours around different parts of the country to report on the work of the overseas missions. Because Shoki was neither a British subject, nor a missionary, there was no established channel for him to receive a call that would lead to ordination. Thus, the meeting also appointed him to be a mission educator of the overseas missions.

In May 1941 the Overseas Mission Committee passed two resolutions related to Shoki Coe: The first established a budget of £300 a year for their mission educator. The second located the administrative and liaison office at Westminster College. This arrangement provided Shoki with a site where he could plan for and prepare his presentations, rest between tours of duty and continue his personal studies.

On 17 June, the secretary reported to the Overseas Mission Committee that arrangements for Shoki's work were being made. The Committee instructed the Secretary to write a letter of appreciation to the principal of Westminster College for agreeing to provide office space for Shoki Coe to use. The Committee also decided that beginning 1 August 1941, it would provide £150 per annum for the programme budget of the mission educator (an amount which differed from the earlier decision). The Personnel Committee for the mission educator would be in charge of this fund.

As a theological student, though not yet ordained, he was a delightful and eloquent speaker. Kathleen Moody, who was six years younger than Shoki, remembered the occasion when Shoki came to her high school to speak about and make reports on missionary work of the overseas missions of the Presbyterian Church of England. She stated that Shoki's speech was one of the reasons she was inspired to become a foreign missionary.

Mr James, secretary of Overseas Missions, received a special letter from the Rev. Dr F. J. Smitheon stating, "I am very pleased to declare and attest that Shoki Ko has completed the required three years of theological study curriculum, successfully passed the examinations, and has been awarded a certificate of graduation." This letter amounted to a Graduation Diploma. At that time, Westminster College was an institution to train people for church ministry and did not grant a master's degree. In the same year, the Presbytery of South London, which met at Tooting, granted Shoki Ko (Coe) the status of Candidate for Ministry and declared him fully qualified to be ordained when and if he received a call.

An Enemy Alien on British Soil

In June 1941, Shoki Coe was about to graduate from Westminster College. Had the situation been "normal," he would have been preparing to go home. However, since the military regime of Japan in Formosa was exerting increasing pressure on the Presbyterian Church of Formosa, he thought it was not prudent at that time to return. Both principals of Tióng-êng Lú-tiong (the Presbyterian Girls Middle School) and Tióng-êng Tiong-hàk (the Presbyterian Boys Middle School) were now replaced by Japanese, and students and teachers were forced to participate in worship rituals at Japanese Shinto Shrines. The churches in Formosa were ordered to merge with the Japanese Church, and the activities of foreign missionaries were severely restricted and no more were welcomed by the Japanese government. By December 1940,

all the missionaries of the Presbyterian Church of England had been repatriated. Edward Band, principal of Tiōng-êng Middle School, sent a telegram to
report to Rev. Douglas James of the Overseas Mission Committee, reporting,
"We have three missionaries remaining in Formosa, but we are all leaving
Formosa on November 22, 1940."

On 30 July 1941, the acting consul general of the Japanese General Consulate in London sent a letter to the chief administrative secretary of Westminster College claiming that, "Shoki Ko's father has requested to seek the
whereabouts of Shoki Ko. According to our records, he came to England to
study at your school." The administrative secretary reported the contents of
this letter to the Rev. Douglas James of the OMC. James knew that the Rev. Ng̃
Sū-bēng, Shoki Ko's father, was in regular contact with the Overseas Missions
Office and would not have asked the Japanese Ministry of Foreign Affairs to
look for his son. Thus this claim was strange and suspicious.

On 6 August 1941, Shoki Ko notified the Japanese Consulate that he sent
a telegram to his family in Taiwan about his current address and his situation
and that he had not been able to receive their letters. The tension between
Japan and Britain was common knowledge at that time. After 8 December
1941, all communication between Japan and Britain was, of course, completely cut off. On that date, Japan attacked Pearl Harbor in the Hawaiian
Islands and declared war on Britain and the United States.

In the early hours of 8 December, Shoki Coe had just completed his assignment in the Presbytery of Newcastle and was carrying out speaking engage-
ments in Scotland. Because he held a Japanese passport, at the moment war
was declared he legally became an enemy alien and lost the freedom of movement. The news of the declaration of war spread all over Britain. The church
leaders in Edinburgh urged him to return to Dr Lansborough's residence in
Redhill, near London. At the time Shoki was a houseguest of the MacDonalds
in Scotland, and his host was first at a loss on how to handle the situation,
since Shoki was now deemed a citizen of an enemy country. After discussion
with Shoki, Mr MacDonald sent him back to Dr Landsborough's residence,
using his own name to buy Shoki a reserved berth on the night train. Thus
when the train conductor, following the usual practice, called out the name of
each passenger, he included "MacDonald"—to which a person of an oriental
appearance responded with an embarrassed, "Yes."

Legally speaking, an enemy alien is under house arrest, thereby losing freedom of movement. On 10 December, Shoki Coe wrote from the Landsboroughs' home in Redhill, "Formosa," to Douglas James to inform him that he was
now an enemy alien. On 16 December, at its first meeting after the declaration

of war, the OMC acknowledged the receipt of Shoki's letter and decided to write him to express sympathy for the difficulties he encountered as an enemy alien.

On 7 January 1942, Douglas James wrote a letter to the department in charge of enemy aliens in the British Government's Home Office requesting assistance on behalf of Shoki. On 27 January, the local security officers in Redhill agreed to grant Shoki a pass to travel further away in order to carry out his church ministries. At the same time the secretary of Overseas Missions also filed an application to the British Home Office to exempt Shoki from the other restrictions imposed on enemy aliens. On 12 February, the Under Secretary of the Home Office responded: "As directed by the Secretary of State, who is aware of the case of Shoki Ko, it has been decided to exempt him from 'the Regulations of Restriction on Enemy Aliens.' However we require that he carry a Certificate of Police Registration and report to police within one week of his arrival in any new place."

The secretary of Overseas Missions reported on 24 February that the security authorities had issued a pass to Shoki so that his ministry would not be affected and that the British Home Office had withheld restriction of movement for him. Douglas James wrote a letter to the Editor of *Christian World* in London protesting an erroneous report in the journal. He wrote, "Your report of Shoki Ko concerning his giving up of his Japanese citizenship and acquiring Chinese citizenship is not correct and not true. His ancestor migrated from China, he is a Formosan. The reason that he is a citizen of Japan is that in 1895 Formosa was ceded to Japan to become a Japanese possession. The people in Formosa did not have freedom of choice of citizenship but became Japanese colonial subjects."

The OMC realized that it was not likely that Shoki would be able to return to the Far East anytime soon. Acknowledging that he had done much beneficial work both inside and outside the English Presbyterian Church, the committee decided to ask him to continue to work for the OMC for one more year for a stipend of £220.

The Overseas Missions Secretary's report stated that the OMC would initiate a temporary cooperative programme for Shoki to work jointly for it and for the London Missionary Society. The report also stated that Shoki had requested permission to learn the Chinese official language of Mandarin. The OMC passed on these two matters to the Committee on Ministerial Candidates to make a final decision and to implement the plan.

In response to the decision of this meeting, held in July 1942, Shoki chose to study Chinese Mandarin at the School of Oriental and African Studies (SOAS). On 22 September the OMC decided to pay for his tuition and also stipulated that if he found opportunities to teach at the School, the tuition would be paid out of his teaching stipends.

At the 16 March 1943 meeting, the OMC resolved to pay Shoki Coe's stipend out of the Nielson Legacy Fund.

A Teacher of Japanese

The meeting of the OMC on 20 July 1943, noted that, because Shoki has found a full-time position at the School of Oriental and African Studies (SOAS), his second year of assignment as a mission education would terminate as of 31 July. Shoki Coe sent a letter of appreciation to the OMC for its support and assistance during the last two years.

Shoki was joined at the SOAS by two close friends. The proceedings of the OMC of 14 April 1944, noted that Boris Anderson, after completing one year of training at Selly Oak College, had enrolled at the School of Oriental and African Studies to learn Mandarin. During the summer after Shoki's graduation from Westminster College, Boris Anderson and George Hood (both close friends of Shoki) conducted youth meetings and preached at churches. Until the end of 1943, they were also mission education colleagues. They then became study colleagues at the SOAS where Shoki was a teacher while the other two were students.

During the war the relationship between the SOAS and the OMC became close. The Office of the General Assembly and Overseas Missions Office of the Presbyterian Church of England were within walking distance of the SOAS. The secretary of the OMC, Douglas James, played an important role in this relationship. His office was nearby, and all the language resources needed by him or his associates were readily available at the SOAS. Consequently, the people he sent to study at the SOAS made up the majority of their students. It may have been James who introduced Shoki to the position of Japanese language instructor at the SOAS. After accepting a position, teachers had to rely heavily on their skills and ingenuity to succeed.

The OMC itself stated in 1942 soon after Shoki began to teach that they agreed "to accede to the SOAS's offer to Shoki Ko of a teaching position. As to the terms of the adjustment of stipend that the OMC provides to Shoki, it will depend on Shoki's own initiative and voluntary decision." Over the next several years, there continued to be adjustments between the OMC and SOAS on Shoki's support. In November 1944, the OMC informed Shoki that since he had a teaching position at the SOAS and thus an independent income, he would have to pay for his health insurance with the OMC as his guarantor.

The year 1945 was one of both tragedy and joy. On 9 February 1945, the Office of the General Assembly of the Presbyterian Church of England received a direct hit by a German V-2 rocket. Douglas James, the Overseas Missions Secretary, and some other staff members were killed and all invaluable archives, records and resources were totally destroyed.

On 12 August 1944, Shoki Coe married Winifred Sounders. One month later, the dean of the Department of Oriental Studies of London University School of Oriental and African Studies, Dr E. Dorothy Edwards, presented to the Study Committee a request to issue an invitation to Shoki Coe to teach for three years. In her letter to the Study Committee, she wrote,

> Mr Douglas James swore to you not to waste the energy of Shoki Ko. He was recently married, and if he remains to teach at this school we will guarantee that he has sufficient resource to sustain his life. Therefore I recommend to the committee the following proposal: to issue Shoki Ko a three-year teaching contract beginning the tenth of this month to teach Japanese language and Hokkien language of Chinese, and his salary with proper allowances shall commence with the date when he begins teaching. If he performs well, I will not hesitate to offer him a permanent position as a lecturer in Japanese and Chinese.

At the time Japanese women married to British men were teaching Japanese at the school. However, probably no other person in London or even in the whole of England was more qualified to teach Japanese than Shoki at that time.

On 18 April 1947, when Shoki completed his three years of teaching at the SOAS, Dr E. Dorothy Edwards gave the OMC her assessment of Shoki's work:

> In October 1942 Shoki Ko came to this school to learn Mandarin Chinese. Soon after that a special military unit that needed urgently to learn Japanese required a Japanese language teacher. The school was pleased to ask Shoki to take on the task. After received consent from the OMC, we invited him to be a lecturer in Japanese. He worked diligently, and those who took up the study became his friends as well as students. He was able to inspire the interest and enthusiasm in them. In some cases the impact of his personality motivated students to develop freely their skills in translation and interrogation, allowing them to become core translators.

In her assessment, Edwards also added the following: "In October 1944, this school added a curriculum in Hokkien language, and Shoki Ko was transferred to teach that course. His achievements were outstanding. I cannot say enough for his contribution and achievements. His influence went beyond the school to the students and the curriculum, particularly in regard to his impact on students. The students acquired not only the skills in application of the language, but also an interest in China."

According to the recollections of David Landsborough Jr, Shoki's students were mostly military officers and government officials. His teaching and character were highly valued and appreciated. David's assessment was based on what he observed in 1947. Dr Landsborough, Shoki and his wife shared the same ship from London to Hong Kong. The ship made an overnight port call in Singapore. No sooner had it docked than several British navy officers and government officials came aboard to see Shoki. They were all Shoki's students at the SOAS. Next morning, two navy officers in uniforms, and four government officials in civilian clothes arrived to take the Coe family to visit the city of Singapore, and entertained them for the whole day. In the evening when they returned to the ship, they brought Shoki and Winifred some gifts (called in Hokkien/Taiwanese "tán-lō˙") that made the Landsboroughs envious indeed.

In E. D. Edwards's assessment of April 1947, the following words were also included: "His relationships with his colleagues were very cordial, and won much enthusiasm and respect from us all. When we learned that he would not be coming back the next school year to teach, we all felt very sorry."

Love and Marriage in a Foreign Land

Winifred Sounders of Seaford, Sussex, applied to the Women's Foreign Missions to be a missionary to China. In 1942 she was accepted, sent to Selly Oak for training and in 1943 began her language study at the SOAS. Winifred and other colleagues of the Presbyterian Church of England—George Hood, Boris Anderson and Shoki Coe—often got together. In fact, they had lunch together almost every day. While there may have been a wartime shortage of food, there was no shortage of conversation. Under the watchful eyes of George Hood and Boris Anderson, the love between Shoki and Winifred grew steadily.

If there was a matchmaker according to Formosan custom, it was Shoki's best friend, George Hood. Hood was three years younger than Shoki and born in England.[15] But Shoki's experience, knowledge and worldview made him mature beyond his age. George Hood always thought of Shoki as being far older than he actually was. Among his entering class at Westminster College in 1938, Shoki, with his great achievements, was the most revered and respected member.

On 3 April 1944, Winifred wrote Ms. MacDonald, the chair of the Women's Missionary Association, announcing that she was getting married to Shoki Coe. The next day, April 4, Shoki wrote Miss Galt, the secretary of the

Women's Missionary Association, and Mr Douglas James, secretary of the Overseas Missions Committee, to officially announce, "We (Winifred and I) have decided today that we will step into the covenant life of a future together. We will probably encounter many difficulties, but as we rely on God's grace and providence, we will join hands to go to the Far East to be witnesses to the Kingdom of God. Our mind is set firm, and we will not retreat."

At that time, there were clear stipulations in the rules of both the Overseas Missions and the Women's Missionary Association, that those who were accepted as candidates and received funds from the Missions for training but could not fulfill their agreement of service in foreign lands must repay all the expenses involved to that time. Winifred, having been accepted and trained to be a missionary to China, had to pay for her training and language education with her missionary service. If she were to be married to someone not a missionary, meaning that she could not serve as a missionary, she would be in breach of contract. The Coes did not have the funds to pay for Winifred's education. But in addition, as their eventual goal was to be missionaries, they thought the requirement was unreasonable. According to the recollection of Boris Anderson, Shoki was a bit sarcastic about the rules of both Overseas Missions and the Women's Missions, saying, "The Missions are like the bride's family demanding the poor son-in-law to pay a handsome amount of 'bride price.'"[16]

The letters of Shoki and Winifred, and a later letter of resignation from Winifred, gave both Overseas Missions Committee and particularly the Women's Missionary Association an enormous shock. According to the latter, all who were appointed and completed their training must serve in a foreign land for at least four years in order to be relieved of their contract. However, the Women's Missionary Association was rather humane and compassionate in handling this case, trying their best to find ways to work things out without breaking the rules. In the end, in a letter to Winifred on 1 June 1944, the Women's Missionary Association asked her to repay £115. The amount was reached according to the following formula. During her training at Selly Oak, Winifred received £80.15 from the Alexander Miller Scholarship, £70 from the Margaret Spence Scholarship, and a donation of £80 from "Bristle," for a total of £230.15. The 18 months that Winifred spent at the SOAS Language School was considered to be equivalent of two years of service at a mission field, and each year was considered a repayment of one quarter of the expenses spent for her training, meaning that she had repaid one half of the costs. Thus Winifred had to repay £115 more. As Shoki had a teaching position at the SOAS, and had some savings, Shoki and Winifred were glad to repay this amount. Winifred wrote to the Women's Missionary Association that she would pay the whole amount the following week.

On 12 August 1944, Shoki and Winifred were married. Although he was an enemy alien with no close relatives who could attend the ceremony, he was surrounded by friends and showered with their blessings. At this time of material shortage and rationed food, there was no new wedding gown, sumptuous wedding banquet or fine wine for celebration. No relatives in Formosa—even his own dearest father—knew of the event. Because the devastating Second World War was in its fifth year, communications over thousands of miles between him and his family in Formosa were completely cut off. It was not until 1946, after the war ended, that his father and his family received this news.

In the midst of these difficult conditions, the Presbyterian Church of England and the Landsboroughs at their home, named "Formosa House," provided a warm family atmosphere for the newlyweds. The "parents" of the groom were none other than Dr and Mrs David Landsborough. Ever since Shoki Coe arrived in England seven years earlier, the Landsboroughs' home had become his home. Shoki even called Dr and Mrs. Lansdsborough "Kheh-pē" and "Kheh-bó," which in Taiwanese mean literally "guest father" and "guest mother." The best man at the wedding was George Hood, and the Maid of Honor was Jean Landsborough, daughter of the Landsboroughs. Jean was born in Formosa but was sent to Shantung and Sòaⁿ-thâu to receive an English education.

George Hood, Boris Anderson and Kathleen Moody were not quite sure whether or not Winifred's parents were present at the wedding. Kathleen Moody thought that Winifred's mother had died before the occasion. According to documents left from that time, Winifred's father had given consent to the marriage and is likely to have been present. Nevertheless, Dr and Mrs David Landsborough acted as Shoki's parents, while Mrs Landsborough also assumed the responsibility of Winifred's mother. Since the junior David Landsborough had been serving since 1940 as a missionary in Chôan-chiu, China, he was not able to be present.[17]

Boris Anderson's most unforgettable impression of the wedding was the facial expression of Winifred throughout the day. There was no trace of a smile on Winifred's face during the ceremony, he recalled, not because she was not happy, but because her mind and will were firm with determination to remove any opposition and obstacles of her marriage to Shoki. For this reason she appeared to be in a state of great anxiety. Winifred was nearly thirty years old—about one year older than Shoki. She had received vocational training in infant school education and had some teaching experience. Winifred was not a scholarly type. In contrast, Shoki had graduated from the most prestigious university in Japan and had done post-graduate studies at Westminster College, Cambridge. His academic potential would likely lead him to high standing in philosophy or other fields of thought in Formosa and throughout Asia. Eventually he would be included in top leadership circles. Winifred, on the other hand, had a distinctive, maternal personality. She was caring in every detail, protective and loving.

At the time of the wedding, many friends thought that it was regrettable that among the eligible young ladies, there couldn't be somebody more suitable for Shoki—someone who might be able to assist him in his academic career and public relations. Someone willing to be like Ruth of the Bible who said, "Your people will be my people, your country my country." One friend made this comment: "If two persons of different countries are married, it is better for them to live in the country where they met and got to know each other." Some friends imagined that after the marriage, not only would Winifred not be able to assist Shoki in his academic career, she might also become somewhat of an obstacle blocking Shoki's potential of becoming a world-class theological scholar.

These friends should have anticipated that during the twelve years between the time Winifred accompanied Shoki back to his roots in Formosa until 1959 when she brought their four children back to England, that she would be an immensely capable helper in family life. Although the language she learned before her marriage was applicable in China but not at all useful in Formosa, she did her best to appreciate the heritage of the land, language, culture and history of which the Taiwanese were proud. One may well say that Shoki's great achievement in theological education was necessarily the result of a solitary battle. The unique formation of his Taiwanese identity, which shaped his worldview, could not be replicated by Winifred and their children. But nobody should discount Winifred's achievements. Winifred's maternal nature motivated her to take their four children back to England where she cared for them almost single-handedly. The oldest son earned a doctoral degree in science and the other two sons and one daughter all became physicians with outstanding careers.

While they were in Taiwan, the author took an English class which Winifred taught. He also saw Winifred come to Shoki's classroom while he was teaching to ask him to resolve some trivial family problems. After Winifred left, from Shoki's body language and facial expression, the author sensed that, due to differences of cultural background, there were differences in handling family problems. As one reads a letter written on 25 April 1944, from Shoki Coe to Mr. James of the Overseas Missions Committee, in which he speaks of racial (or cultural) discrimination, one can feel the bitterness and sweetness of Shoki's human experience. In this letter he wrote, "Our joining together as one is a gift of God, at the same time it brings with it certain responsibilities. Therefore, we two will jointly continue to fight a good fight, to let the world know that beyond and above racial divide, there is humanity, and when human sins destroy that humanity, there is still God's love that is capable of healing God's own children, and works amazing miracles."

4
Return to Taiwan (1947–1965)
National Identity and International Outlook

The Long Journey Home

World War II ended in 1945. Although Britain won the war against Germany, the price paid for victory was huge. The nation's capital, London, bore the brunt of destruction over several years from endless air raids and attacks by unmanned rockets. The city ended up a place of burned-out ruins and rubble. Winning a war meant losing an empire. The war had frozen the infrastructure of the British Empire, and even after the war, Britain was not able to reopen the mechanism that had connected it with its colonies. In fact, both during and after the war, the colonies took advantage of the situation to loosen their ties to the British Empire and accelerate their independence movements. Places such as India, Pakistan, Bangladesh, Malaysia, Singapore, Burma and Ceylon now began, one by one, to ask to be independent of the British Empire.

In those days international travel relied on ocean-going ships. During the war, most of the ships were wrecked or sunk in sea battles and their crews killed. After the war, it took more than three years to deal with the basic problems of demobilizing military personnel and reassigning colonial officials. To find berth space on a ship for a family of three to travel to the other side of the globe was quite a feat.

On 25 September 1945, forty days after Japan surrendered to the Allied forces, the Overseas Missions Committee (OMC) of the Presbyterian Church of England met. Shoki expressed his intention to the Committee to return to Taiwan in order to assist the ministry of the church there. He also requested that before he left for Taiwan he be ordained. The OMC gladly accepted this proposal but stated that the final decision would have to wait until they heard the response of the Presbyterian Church of Formosa to this proposal.

At the meeting of the Committee on 23 October 1945, Shoki Coe made observations about the situation in Taiwan and requested that the OMC return to its work there. In post-war Taiwan, because the Japanese system was abolished and the Shinto religion was abandoned, consideration was being raised about what would replace it. So there was no better opportunity than that time to proclaim the Christian faith and to rebuild the lives of Christians and the church in Taiwan. He also observed that all churches had a responsibility to maintain close relationships with the churches on the Chinese mainland.

On 20 November 1945, Shoki made a proposal at the OMC meeting to establish a scholarship in memory of the late Rev. T. W. Douglas James for students selected by churches in foreign lands to study at Westminster College. The OMC decided that the secretary and Shoki Coe should continue to work on this proposal and to report back to the OMC for further discussion at a subsequent meeting.

On 21 January 1946, Shoki again expressed his desire to the OMC to return to Taiwan to serve the church in his home country Taiwan. The Committee agreed to help him accomplish this as soon as possible and also decided to pay travel expenses for him, his wife and their son. In addition it provided him with £100 to assist with his living expenses before he found proper assignment in Taiwan.

On 27 February 1946, Shoki Coe met with Edward Band (the former headmaster of the Presbyterian Middle School in Tainan). Afterward, Band wrote a letter to the Secretary of the OMC, Mr Short, asking him to write a letter on behalf of Shoki that would introduce him to a Mr P. S. Tân at the General Consulate of the Republic of China in London and ask Mr Tân to issue Shoki a Chinese passport. Mr Short wrote the letter on 6 March as requested (although there is no copy to be found on file). One year later when Shoki took his return journey, he held a passport of the Republic of China.

By 1947 Shoki had been in England for ten years. While he was preparing to return to Taiwan, Secretary Short received a letter from the World Association of Sunday Schools, headquartered at 165 Fifth Avenue, New York City. It invited Shoki to represent the Presbyterian Church of Formosa at the Second World Conference of Christian Youth to be held in Oslo, July 22 through August 1 of that year. The OMC decided to provide financial assistance. The minutes read: "The Presbyterian Church of Formosa is very eager to send a representative to attend the meeting, and since this event will take place on his way home, to send him to attend will not only save money, but will also be appropriate."

For a second time, Shoki Coe was able to participate in a worldwide Christian youth conference. This time it was held in Oslo, the capital of Norway. The conference was similar to the one he attended in 1939. There were 1,500 participants. Both conferences left a significant and lasting impression on Shoki. At this conference Shoki met some who had been at the first event, and together they assumed important roles of leadership for the conference.

As well as assisting Shoki Coe to get a passport from the Republic of China, Mr Short also introduced Shoki's wife, Winifred, to the Chinese Embassy in London. Mrs. Coe and their young son David traveled to Taiwan with British passports. Even though by that time the Kuomintang[1] regime had already carried out its unprecedented massacre of 28 February in Taiwan,[2] Shoki Coe and the OMC did not have a sense of caution or alarm. This is most likely because the government authorities in Nanking and Taiwan had banned all news coverage of the massacre. Missionaries in Taiwan were still under a deceptive cloud, unaware of the magnitude of the situation. News spread by word of mouth, consisting only of sparse and sketchy pieces of personal information. No one knew the true story except the real directors and executioners of this tragic event, the Kuomintang regime.

In June 1947 Shoki Coe and his family left England. On board the same ship were Dr David Lansborough and his wife, Dr Jean Landsborough. David had just completed one year of sabbatical leave from the mission field to speak about his work in many home churches and was recently married. The newlyweds were on their way to their assigned mission field in Hokkien. They and the Coes travelled together as far as Hong Kong. Their ship was the S/S Empress of Scotland, filled with passengers on essential business. The ship was so full that couples had to be separated from each other into all-male and all-female cabins. For the newlywed Landsboroughs the journey was quite an inconvenience and sacrifice, and it also caused the Coes some hardship. Fortunately on this journey of over one month, the two families were able to support and help each other. On 15 August, Shoki Coe used the ship's stationery to write a report about his perceptions of, and his participation in, the Second World Conference of Christian Youth in Oslo.

When the ship docked in Hong Kong, Shoki's former classmate at the Presbyterian Middle School in Tainan, Aichi Tsai (Chhoà Ài-tì), came to see him. Aichi was on his way back from Taiwan to the United States and made this special effort to come to Hong Kong to see Shoki. Aichi Tsai was a pastor at a Japanese Church in Seattle, Washington. His wife was a "nisei"—a second generation Japanese-American. Aichi Tsai told Shoki that he had witnessed the tragic events of the 28 February massacre and its subsequent terror. One of the victims was Dr Lîm Bō˙-seng, a former teacher and chair of the Board of Trustees of the Presbyterian Middle School in Tainan. Dr Lîm was tricked into attending a presumably important meeting that needed his participation. He was not heard from after he was taken away. According to hearsay, on the following day after he was taken, the "bandit regime" secretly murdered him and concealed all material evidence, including his body. Shoki Coe believed the Rev. Aichi Tsai's information and his warning, but he was very eager to go home. In his mind he still had the impression, given by the war allies, Britain and the United States, that Chiang Kai-sek and his wife Mei-ling Song were a

Christian couple with "devoted personality and deep faith." Shoki had made up his mind to head for his homeland Taiwan after ten years of being away. Compared to far away London, Taiwan was only a short distance from Hong Kong, and the war had been over for two years. Other than Taiwan, the family had no place to go.

When the ship arrived in Keelung in September 1947, on the wharf to welcome the Coes was a tall, thin man, Chiong Khé-an.[3] Chiong Khé-an was not only his brother-in-law but the administrator of the Taipei YMCA and had great experience and ability in managing both international and local organizations. The subsequent health, growth and development of the YMCA in Taiwan owed much to his professional expertise in promoting international exchanges. During World War II young men from the Japanese colony of Taiwan were not required to serve in the Japanese military forces. Therefore, Chiong Khé-an was entrusted with the management of several YMCAs in Japan, as the secretary in charge. After the war, upon proper transfer of managerial tasks back to the Japanese, he returned to Taiwan. But he continued to be remembered and well respected by colleagues in the YMCAs in Japan.

After waiting ten long years to see Shoki, his oldest son, the Rev. Ng Sū-bēng should have been the happiest person on the wharf that day. And Shoki Coe was equally eager to see his father and to hug him. But at the dock, his father was nowhere to be seen. He had had a stroke, and although his movements were not much affected, his ability to speak was much hampered, and he had to remain at home in Tainan. For the Ng family, the return of the oldest son was a small ray of hope for relief from financial difficulties, because at that time no one had employment to support the family.

Shoki's family came to Taipei to stay for several days at the YMCA. At that time, the YMCA was using a Japanese church and adjacent Sunday School classrooms and manse. Shoki and the family stayed there until all the luggage and crates they brought back cleared customs and were claimed. Then they boarded a train and suffered a long journey to their destination, Tainan. After more than two months of travel, they completed their journey from England back to Tainan, Taiwan.

Taiwan Christian Conference 1948

After landing in Keelung, the Coes spent several days at the home of Chiong Khé-an in Taipei recuperating from the long ship journey. Both Shoki and Khé-an were qualified ministers but not yet ordained. While they were together at home, they discovered they were of common mind about developing the youth ministry in Taiwan. So they began to work together to hold a Christian youth rally in Taiwan. Eventually, in August 1948, nearly one full year after Shoki's return to Taiwan, a large Christian youth conference, with 1500 attending, was held in Tamsui.

The youth conference took place during a chaotic transition to a new colonial master. When the war ended, Japanese rules and system were replaced by an entire system brought in from China. The transfer of power resulted in a disastrous vacuum of knowledge. There were no books that could point to future directions for the youth. The books available in the stores were only barely enough to satisfy intellectual knowledge, with no stimulation or inspiration from outside, no ideas and ideals for carrying on the heritage and moving into the future. There was no source of and no resources to nurture inspiration at all. Nobody knew how the word got around, but every church seemed to know about this youth gathering. For many young people it was the first time they took a train or traveled to Taipei. What an exciting inspiration it was to see 1500 youth gathered in one place, listening to speeches, eating together, and taking a special chartered train on the Tamsui Line to ferry them to a big outdoor worship service at the Taipei New Park! What a powerful impact it left in the hearts of the participants!

These 1500 young people became the leaders of the church in the years to come. The Youth Association, YMCA, of my home church in Hong-gôan diligently promoted this event and persuaded almost all twenty members to attend. Almost all the third-year junior high and all senior high students were drawn to this gathering. Shoki Coe was teaching at the Presbyterian Boys Middle School, so he was able to encourage many students to go to the meeting. Shoki's younger sister, Siok-hūi, was a senior at the Presbyterian Girls Middle School, so she also encouraged many of her classmates to go as well. Nobody seemed to know how it happened that it was so well organized. There were older university students or theological students to lead and care for each group of younger middle school students.

Chiong Khé-an, whose work was mainly with youth and students, had outstanding organizing ability and experience and was at the same time a great supporter of church ministry. Although working within the organizational structure of the YMCA, he never forgot to coordinate his activities and programmes with the programmes of local churches. Even though Shoki Coe only met him for the first time at the dock of Keelung Port, he was immediately ready to use their three days together to begin their common dream of building the framework of a big youth rally.

That year, I had just graduated from junior middle school and passed the entrance exams of senior middle school. I felt relaxed and at ease, and could stand on the new horizon to look and to listen. To me, everything was so new and fresh, as though looking through a clear windowpane, onto a world of youth and an open future of God's kingdom, as well as a Taiwan that was full of hope.

Yet at that time, the Kuomintang government was losing its territories and its people in China gradually. It fought to hold on to every inch of territory it still controlled, while it lost the confidence of its people. The Kuomintang soldiers lost every battle they fought, and many soldiers fled even before battles began. Their runaway speed could not match the pursuing Communist troops. With the apparent speed of electronic transmission, people transmitted from heart to heart throughout all of China a deep sense of anxious disappointment, incredulity and terror.

Only in Taiwan did people still not know the true past of the Kuomintang regime, its extortion, pilferage, corruption, selfishness and incompetence. The hearts of the Taiwanese had yet to be infiltrated with the pollution created by its party officials. A deteriorating smell in economic and political realms had begun to be noticed, but young people still believed that the message of Christ would be accepted and supported by those in the position of governing authorities. Even when Taiwanese experienced the tragic massacre of 28 February, the regime had not yet lost all of China which would eventually cause the imposition of martial law. These laws would prohibit large gatherings of people and the use of the Taiwanese language—the language used at the youth conference, the official and liturgical language of the majority of people in the Presbyterian Church in Taiwan.

The Youth Conference was presided over by the Rev. Ng Bú-tong, the Vice-Moderator of the Southern Synod of the Presbyterian Church in Taiwan. In reality, he was the Acting Moderator due to the health of the Moderator, the Rev. Iûn Sū-ióng. The Southern Synod, and not the Northern Synod, assumed the leadership of the conference because the idea was first conceived by Shoki Coe and Chiong Khé-an and because it was initially considered more likely to receive the enthusiastic support of church leaders in the South whose ages were relatively young. The representative leaders of the Presbyterian Church in those days were Ng Bú-tong, 39 years of age, Shoki Coe, 34, and Chiong Khé-an, who had just reached thirty.

There were three major speakers at the conference, two of them invited from the Shanghai YMCA by Chiong Khé-an, the other one, a native son ad one who had just returned home from ten years of living in Europe, Shoki Coe. In his speech, Shoki urged the churches in Taiwan to strive for solidarity and unity. He used standard Taiwanese language to speak, and his appeal to the church was urgent and consistent with the practical realities of the situation, so the inspired speech stirred up the conference like a whirlwind. It was similar to his speech at the seventh Synod meeting of the Southern Synod of the Presbyterian Church in Taiwan which met at Táu-la̍k just a few months earlier, where he appealed for the merger and unity of the churches (or synods) in the south and in the north, the joining of the theological colleges in the north and in the south so as to pursue true unity. At the conference he repeated the words he always loved to quote, "United we stand. Divided we fall." He also gave a rather amusing and practical illustration. He said, "We must become an omelet. Do not be like fried eggs with two yolks—the status of unity of the churches (synods) in the north and in the south still unable to resolve into one. To make an omelet, you must break the egg-shells, mix both eggs and make them blend together into one."

Shoki Coe brought back home many "messages" from overseas, opening up a wider perspective for the young people. As a result, those attending the conference decided to write an open letter to urge the two synods to unite into one church. The appeals of these young people caused the church leaders and officials to give careful and honest consideration on the matter of the unity of both churches. The youth took steps for action beyond just appeals in a formal "resolution", and then put the resolution into action to work toward real unity. On 2 July 1948, the young people themselves organized a planning committee on the merger and unity of the two churches. On 3 May of the next year, 1949, a pan-Taiwan Youth Fellowship—with no division of north and south—was formed, known as, and called by the name of "T. K. C." T stands for Tâi-ôan (Taiwan), K for "Kàu-hōe" (Church), and C for "Chheng-liân thôan-khè" (Youth Fellowship).

According to Shoki's memoir, it was the kind of leader like Chiong Khé-an, who was not constrained by church politics, who was able to awake the conscience of young people to plan and implement the unity of the two churches. Also among the youth leaders who worked hard for the big youth rally, and who made great efforts to appeal for unity, was a lawyer by the name of Tân Tiâu-kéng, an elder of Tang-káng Church, to whom Shoki particularly gave credit for playing an important role in forming the TKC.[4] In his memoir, Shoki also mentioned some "brave youth warriors" in the northern church, such as Tîⁿ Liân-khun, Tiuⁿ Hông-chhiong, and an elder Táng Tāi-sêng who was a professor at the National Taiwan University Medical School.

A Young Man with Heavy Responsibilities

On 26 November 1948, the South Taiwan Mission of the Overseas Missions Committee of the Presbyterian Church of England made the following decision, as recorded in its minutes, "Whereas Shoki Coe has returned to Taiwan, whereas the South Synod has made a resolution to reopen Tainan Theological College,[5] and whereas the Principal of Tainan Theological College, the Rev. W. E. Montgomery, a Missionary of the Presbyterian Church of England, has recommended that Shoki Coe succeed him to be the Principal of the College, be it resolved that this Mission provide £300 per year to assist Shoki Coe's salary as the Principal of Tainan Theological College, £200 of which shall come out of the budget of the Tainan Mission, and £100 from the regular assistance appropriation of this Mission to Tainan Theological College."

This decision was very significant in terms of the direction of the Mission and its subsequent influence. From then on, Taiwanese citizens or "home-grown" persons would take over positions of leadership from Europeans and Americans, assuming responsibilities for "self-governing," "self-nurturing" and "self-propagating."[6] The existence of a person such as Shoki Coe in Taiwan was something worthy of being celebrated. Nevertheless, at that time in history, the Presbyterian Church in Taiwan still had a long way to go to achieve financial self-sufficiency.

On 22 August 1949, Shoki Coe was ordained and installed as principal of Tainan Theological College. From the family point of view, Shoki Coe became the third generation to be ordained as a minister. His father, although old and weak after suffering a stroke, was very happy to learn that his son was now a full-fledged ordained minister and had become the principal of the Theological College.

Shoki Coe felt a heavy responsibility as principal of the College. He was only the third principal since its founding. Being only 35 years of age, he asked himself if he was adequate for the job. In those days, it was considered necessary for the principal of a theological college to be involved in all aspects of church ministry. Responding to this great expectation, Shoki became absorbed in church activities and programmes on all levels of church life, assuming roles of advisor or leader. From the perspective of education in Taiwan at that time, his academic background ranked him as one of the most educated people in the academic world. As a teacher, he had experience from the School of Oriental and African Studies in England and as a teacher of English at the Presbyterian Boys Middle School after he returned to Taiwan. However, as a pastor, although he had been saturated with the stories and pastoral experiences of his father and grandfather, he had not been able to put his knowledge and skills into practice. The Rev. Boris Anderson, who was two years younger than Shoki and had just been transferred from Hokkien, became his vice-principal. Both of them, without much experience, were suddenly entrusted with taking important roles of leadership in churches all over the island.

Fortunately, there were two experienced and qualified teachers at the Theo-logical College, Rev. Iûn Sū-ióng and Rev. N̂g Chú-gī. The Rev. Iûn Sū-ióng had much pastoral experience. He had been moderator of the South Synod during the most difficult times of the war. In his position, he took on the impor-tant role of negotiating the issues related to the affiliation of the Presbyterian Church in Taiwan with the Nippon Kirisuto Kyodan.[7] The Ninth Synod of the Presbyterian Church met on 9 January 1948, at the church in Táu-lak where the Rev. N̂g Chú-gī was pastor. This was the first Synod meeting that Shoki Coe attended after returning to Taiwan. At this meeting the Synod voted to re-open Tainan Theological College. Shoki had known the Rev. N̂g Chú-gī since student days in Tokyo, when Shoki was at the Tokyo Imperial University, and the Rev. N̂g at Tokyo Theological College.[8] The Rev. N̂g Chú-gī was the strongest advocate for the reopening of Tainan Theological College. He taught at the college for over one year, but soon after Shoki became principal, left to pursue further studies at Union Theological Seminary in New York. Fortu-nately, Ms N̂g Lí Siù-hiân (Mrs. N̂g Chú-gī) remained at the college to assist Shoki in general business affairs and the financial accounts of the college.

Challenges of Financial Management

Shoki inherited a theological college with a long history. Having been closed due to the war, it suffered from lack of proper care and financial resources. The school buildings showed the effects of the hard times they had been through, with broken doors and windows that had undergone repair after repair, and furniture that was old and dilapidated. Several buildings inside the compound once known as Sin-lâu[9] were in such disrepair that they could hardly be used to house returning missionaries or teachers. They had been so brutally damaged by wind, rain and the hot, subtropical sun that from the outside these buildings looked like old, bent-over persons. Inside, the walls were stained with mould of a dirty greyish-green colour.

When Shoki Coe became principal, the economic and social conditions in Taiwan were in a period of extreme disarray. After the 28 February incident, massive numbers of military personnel were deployed to Taiwan to carry out the subsequent repression by the Chiang regime. At the same time, Chiang's military corps were being defeated all over China by Chinese Communist guerrilla forces. Between 1947 and 1949, the Chiang regime lost every inch of its territory on the Chinese mainland. Chiang brought the remnants of his military and government bureaucracy, a total of nearly one million people, to occupy Taiwan. Sometimes primary schools even had to suspend their classes in order to allow troops to be housed in their classrooms.

Taiwan's economy was under tremendous stress. In a short span of a few years, the resources that had supported a population of six million now had to support a population of seven and a half million. Now every four persons had to support one new resident in Taiwan. In addition, the new arrivals enjoyed special privileges, arranged by the ruling authorities. The privileges of the ordinary arrivals might not have been as desirable as those of their bureau chiefs, highly placed managers or even immediate superiors, but they were still better than the conditions of the established residents of Taiwan, who suffered daily from the miseries of hunger.

Toward the end of 1945, the exchange rate between Japanese Yen to US currency was ¥1= $1. The Japanese ¥ was the currency used in Taiwan until Japan surrendered, at which point the government converted to Taiwan dollars. However, in 1950, Taiwan dollars were converted to "New Taiwan dollars" with a rate of forty thousand Taiwan dollars to one New Taiwan dollar. This meant the rate of inflation was soaring.[10] A rice merchant recommended to Shoki that he pay him in advance for eight weeks of rice, and he would deliver rice to Shoki's home every week for the next eight weeks. But after five weeks, the merchant stopped delivering. He had gone bankrupt and closed his shop. Still, given soaring prices, Shoki really didn't lose money. At a time of flyaway inflation, the prepay method was to the advantage of the prepayer.

In 1950, the tenth stated meeting of the South Synod of the Presbyterian Church in Taiwan met at Sin-heng Church in Ko-hiông (Kaohsiung). The Synod meeting included an annual report from Tainan Theological College. For the first time, Shoki Coe as principal had to make this report to the Synod. When he came to the financial section of the report, he displayed his unfamiliarity with accounting practices. In particular when he had to report an unfavourable transaction for the College, he felt extremely embarrassed. One elder-commissioner attending the Synod by the name of Gô˙ Thian-sek asked him whether there was an auditor to oversee the accounts of the College. Shoki Coe was even more embarrassed and red faced when he had to admit that all the account records were in a small notebook in the pocket of his jacket. So, he requested the Synod to assist him in setting up a healthy and proper accounting system for the college. On the matter of academic affairs, he reported that there were only three full-time professors and three or four part-time or volunteer lecturers. This unfavourable condition continued until 1952 when he wrote to Mr. Fenn, the Secretary of the Overseas Missions Committee of the Presbyterian Church of England, reporting that he and Boris Anderson had to teach more than twenty hours a week. On top of that he had to do administrative work and raise funds from churches. He requested assistance to increase the teaching staff so that the college might expand its student enrollment to meet increased demand.

Because of the soaring rate of inflation, Shoki Coe had to use donated funds to buy and store rice to pay for his teaching and administrative staff (whose salaries were partly paid in rice and partly in cash) and sustain the needs of the student body. In those days all students received free room and board. Thus large sums were required to run the college. The terrible economic and social conditions were not only an enormous challenge to Tainan Theological College, but also to Shoki personally.

On 7 March 1951, the First General Assembly of the Presbyterian Church in Taiwan met at Siang-liân Church in Taipei. It was a joint meeting of the North Synod and the South Synod. The Assembly consisted of twenty minister-commissioners, twenty elder-commissioners, three missionaries, one stated clerk from each Synod, and the principal of each Synod's theological college. The Assembly voted that the united Presbyterian Church in Taiwan would apply for membership to the World Presbyterian Alliance and also the World Council of Churches. No opposition was expressed to the former organization, but the latter did not receive unanimous support.

Several factors caused some complications in regard to joining the World Council of Churches. As the Communists took over China and the Kuomintang regime retreated to Taiwan, nearly a hundred Protestant denominations of all shapes and forms, Roman Catholics, and no less than a thousand European and American missionaries came with it. The Christian landscape was totally changed. The new situation was far more complicated than the previous simple condition in which the Presbyterian Church had almost a monopoly on Protestants in Taiwan.

Consequently, at the suggestion of Shoki Coe, the Assembly decided to apply to join the WCC in principle, with the final decision to be made by a special committee of 23 persons appointed by the General Assembly after consultation with both mother foreign missions.[11]

In 1951 several special church-related visitors arrived from overseas, particularly from the United States, to visit Tainan Theological College. One was Dr Stanley Smith, representing the Nanking Theological Seminary Board of Founders.[12] By that time, the bamboo curtain had closed off mainland China. All foreign missionaries were driven out and no new mission personnel were allowed in. The Christian community, while not eliminated, was functioning under severely limited conditions; indeed, its contact with the outside world was severed. Because Dr Stanley had done advanced studies at Westminster College, he was a fellow alumnus with Shoki Coe and Boris Anderson.

Having taught at Nanking Theological Seminary and interned by the Japanese as a prisoner of war during the Sino-Japanese War, he was well-qualified to represent the seminary's Board of Founders. After hearing a report from Shoki about Tainan Theological College, he toured the campus, carefully looking into the condition of the buildings and reviewing the college's condition. He was both enthusiastic and concerned about the status of theological education among Chinese Christians.

After touring the campus, he said to Shoki, "I have not seen your library yet." Shoki, looking embarrassed, replied, "The College doesn't have a library." In fact there was a sort of library. Entering from the college's main gate, on the left side of the building there was a room of about three by five meters in size, which had been designated as a reading room as it hardly qualified to be called a library. Shoki explained that the reason the library collection was so inadequate was that during the seven years the college was forced to close, nobody took care of it. Thus most of the original books, documents and resource materials were scattered and lost. Dr Smith replied that because a library was essential for study, the need must be resolved as soon as possible.

Before Dr Smith departed, he spoke to Shoki of his hopes, and asked Shoki to write a proposal based on their discussions and send it to him to be used in raising funds. The funds indeed came in 1952 and enabled Shoki to start a series of pastors' refresher courses.

Another important visitor was Dr Henry "Pit" Van Dusen, president of Union Theological Seminary in New York City and chair of the Nanking Board of Founders. At that time, I was a first year student at the college. For daily worship, first year students were seated in the chapel's front pew. At the time of his visit, I was seated at the center of the front pew. Shoki asked the students and faculty members present to choose a song to welcome Dr Van Dusen. I volunteered hymn 333 as one that was familiar to all and that we could sing well. Shoki announced it, and all joined in singing the well-known words, "Come, Let Us Sing Praise, Sing Praise to the Lord." Everyone sang with gusto in four-part harmony. As the sound filled the whole chapel, all felt that the Holy Spirit had also filled the building. Students and faculty still believe that the singing of this particular hymn touched the heart of Dr Van Dusen in a way that aroused hope in him for spreading the gospel, not only in Taiwan and Asia, but throughout the whole world. This was the gift of a group of zealous young theological students.

It is not clear if Dr Van Dusen drew inspiration from this group of enthusiastic young theological students or from prior planning when he announced that he was going to set up a special study programme for leaders of young and emerging churches,[13] and that Shoki Coe would be asked to head this program. It did not begin until 1959–1960, when Shoki finally found time for it. In addition to Shoki himself, the Rev. Lâu Hôa-gī from Taiwan was also invited to participate.

I remember an incident that occurred around the time of Dr Van Dusen's visit to the college. Shoki was riding his bicycle through a small alley between the Presbyterian Boys Middle School and the Girls Middle School, when a lush bamboo plant overhanging one side injured one of his eyes. For about two weeks he felt so uncomfortable that he, who had never taken a day off due to illness, had to suspend his classes. The incident left an unforgettable impression on me.

In 1951 Dr Frank Cartwright, the executive director of the Nanking Board of Founders, paid a visit to Tainan Theological College. After his visit, his name became a catchword for a huge source of financial assistance. In Taiwanese everyone referred to him as "Khà-tō-lâi," which means [when you have need], "Give him a call, and assistance will be forthcoming."[14]

Due to the close relationship between the Tainan Theological College and the Nanking Seminary Board of Founders, Shoki Coe was able to connect with the US Methodist Church in 1953. This started with a visit of Bishop Ralph Ward from New York, who was accompanied by two Methodist missionaries in Taiwan, to Tainan Theological College. Bishop Ward was a missionary in China and was well respected. However, Shoki Coe did not have a very good impression of the Methodist church then, because Bishop Ward and Dr Frank Cartwright were quite different types of people. Bishop Ward gave the impression of being rather elitist and formal, while Cartwright was a popular, open and easygoing person. The impression Bishop Ward gave Shoki Coe was of an "oppressive ruler" similar to people such as Chiang Kai-sek and Mei-ling Song. Fortunately, when Tracy Jones (then secretary in charge of Asian affairs for the Methodist Church, also former missionary in China) and Dr Eugene Smith (general secretary of the General Board of Missions of Methodist Church) came to visit Tainan Theological College, they made Shoki Coe's impression of the Methodist Church change for the better. In reality, the Methodist Church had a great share of and influence on the policy of the Nanking Seminary Board of Founders.

In 1953 Shoki Coe completed four years of service as the Principal of Tainan Theological College. The first twelve students who had entered the college when he began his service now graduated. Among the twelve graduates were four women, the first-ever women graduates. One of the graduates was Ko Chùn-bêng, who later became the Principal of Yushan Theological

College, a college that has specialized in training pastors for the churches of the aboriginals of Taiwan, and then became the general secretary of the Presbyterian Church in Taiwan. While he was general secretary, he led the church, on behalf of the people of Taiwan, to make three statements about the current situation and the future destiny of Taiwan. His faith in, and loyalty to, Christ led him to be charged with "harbouring seditious persons" by the Kuomintang regime, and he was convicted and imprisoned in April 1980. He was imprisoned for four years, three months and twenty-one days. Shoki Coe considered Ko Chùn-bêng as the "most outstanding and distinguished minister and church leader" of all his students.

The Wretched Problem of the Domicile Registration System

In 1900 the Japanese government in Taiwan set up the domicile registration system. For the colonial rulers of Taiwan, this system became one of the most effective and powerful tools of control. However, until the massacre of 28 February 1947, and the total withdrawal of the Kuomintang from China in 1949 to take control of the sole territory—Taiwan—the Kuomintang regime had carried out the domicile registration system only half-heartedly at best. But after fleeing to Taiwan, the Central Government realized how effectively the Japanese government had utilized the system. Without much effort they were able to tidy up the system for their own use as a weapon for controlling the populace. The new regime began its strict implementation of the domicile registration system.

After Shoki Coe returned home to Taiwan, he faithfully abided by the law as a loyal citizen and went to register his domicile.[15] However, he immediately encountered problems created by his international marriage. He returned to Taiwan in September 1947, not long after the massacre of 28 February had taken place. People were still gripped by terror. Civil service personnel were getting by with ambiguous practices, and people felt insecure, especially the educated people. Those who had received Japanese higher education sought ways to become anonymous, going underground to escape with their lives. Shoki's friends who were British citizens advised, as Shoki's wife, Winifred, also hoped, that she and their son David keep their British citizenship. Shoki Coe brought his family home and lived together in their quarters in the Sin-lâu compound. Very few people knew that in the eyes of the Kuomintang, Shoki Coe was unmarried.

During the years when I was a student at Tainan Theological College, I was required to move my registration to the college address, where the head of the household was Principal Shoki Coe. I was able to obtain a copy of the registration from Shoki's brother, Dr N̄g Bêng-hui, as they were both in the same household. Strange statements were recorded under the entry of Shoki Coe, such as:

> Removed to the redesignated No. 34th Household of Neighborhood Group No.5, of Chôaⁿ-pak Section of the East Ward of the Municipality of Tainan, at No. 228 East Gate Road, in the 40th Year of the Republic, 13th Day of the 10th Month (i.e., October 13, 1951). In the 42nd year of the Republic, 23rd Day of the 11th Month (i.e. November 23, 1953), the migrant address was removed to the 41st Household of the 5th Neighborhood, Chôaⁿ-pak Section, East Ward of Tainan Municipality, at No.228 East Gate Road, Tainan. The Head of Household, Shoki Coe, included in the Household are migrant registrants.

From the day Shoki Coe became principal, he also became head of the registered household of the Theological College. All resident students joined the big family, the household headed by Principal Shoki Coe, at 228 East Gate Road. All students were honored and felt their intimate relationship as members of a family.

Yet the domicile registration records contained double entries. On one hand Shoki Coe was registered as head of the household of the Theological College. On the other hand, he was also registered in the household of his stepmother n̄g Gô˙ Eng-thô, residing at No. 22, Lane 1, Phok-ài Road, Tainan, as a family member, and that he was the first son of n̄g Sū-bēng (father) and Lîm Kim (mother).[16] But Shoki's entry after the word "spouse" was left empty. This empty line amounted to saying that Shoki was still a single person, not yet married. There was also no mention of his children. I discussed this matter concerning Shoki's domicile registration records with a registration staff member. The person said that omitting the spouse's name was not in accordance with the rules of domicile registration. Thus I suspected that the Central Government must have given a special directive to the municipal registration office about this matter either to demean or brush aside Shoki Coe, or to provide a reason to denigrate Shoki's credibility and character—as it was later used.

When in 1951 Shoki Coe applied for a passport to travel overseas the first time, the entry column clearly indicated that he was not married. In his memoir Shoki said that when he protested to the authorities about the mistake, the official replied, "Your spouse is a foreign citizen.... If, and after she is naturalized, she can apply for a domicile registration, then she will be registered and legitimized as your spouse." This was the way the officials of the Central Government tried to deal with and intimidate any persons connected with foreign citizens or had some form of foreign protection. It would seem that while they did not dare to directly harm such people, they would do everything within their power to create difficulties for them and to disparage them.

It made Shoki Coe extremely angry that rumours were spread around the educational institutions and church circles saying, "What kind of a person is Shoki Coe! How can he be qualified as a Christian minister and principal of a theological college? He lives with a foreign woman not his wife and has four children by her!"[17] Shoki intimated to me that he was put in this position by Chinese officials who wanted to disgrace Taiwanese leaders for the purpose of causing them to lose moral authority, leadership power and spiritual integrity. They wanted to demonstrate that they were a bad lot—a bunch of second-rate, lowly, menial and inferior people of shady character. This government practice seemed to reflect the same corrupt spirit that had led to the 28 February massacre that was intended to wipe out Taiwanese leadership and Taiwanese consciousness.[18]

First Travel Abroad after Returning Home

Shoki Coe's first journey abroad after returning to Taiwan took place in July 1951. The trip was made in response to Bishop Stephen Neil and Dr Raja Manikam's invitation to visit Geneva, Switzerland. The purpose of the visit was to discuss mission strategy in Asia and the membership of the Presbyterian Church in Taiwan in the World Council of Churches. Although the trip was short, it was important and probably the first step in Shoki's involvement in the world arena.

During the visit, Shoki not only met Bishop Neil and Dr Manikam but also Dr Marcel Pradervand, general secretary of the World Presbyterian Alliance. Together they talked about the state of affairs of the Presbyterian Church in Taiwan and its relationship with other churches. In 1949 Bishop Neil, on a visit to the Presbyterian Church in Taiwan, had encouraged the Church to join the WCC. By the time of Shoki's visit, the Rev. Hugh Macmillan, English language secretary of the General Assembly of the Presbyterian Church in Taiwan, had informed the WCC that the two synods of the Presbyterian Church in Taiwan had formed one General Assembly and that the General Assembly had decided to join the WCC. Hence the Council's officials were able to discuss this matter with Shoki. From Shoki, they learned that the General Assembly had not firmly agreed to join the WCC but had entrusted the final decision to a special committee who would consult with the overseas missions boards of the two mother churches, Bishop Neil wondered whether it was the appropriate time for the organizing committee for the Second Assembly of the WCC to accept the Taiwan Church's application. Would it be better to wait for the next meeting to settle this matter? Shoki carefully explained the process and the deliberation at the Assembly. Upon hearing this explanation, Bishop Neil was much relieved.

It was during his visit to Geneva that Shoki Coe first met Dr Henry "Pit" Van Dusen, president of Union Theological Seminary in New York. This meeting was an important turning point for Tainan Theological College. The development of the college owed much to the great help given by Van Dusen. The Presbyterian Church in Taiwan, after being nurtured to maturity by the mother Presbyterian Church of England, gained its freedom to extend its external relations. The assistance given by President Van Dusen on behalf of the Presbyterian Church USA, a leading Protestant denomination in America, represented an entrance into a new ecumenical, international path.[19]

Boris Anderson Joins the College

In 1947, when Shoki Coe returned to Taiwan, he moved into half of a duplex house. In February 1948, Boris came to Taiwan to address a missionary group on the subject, "Trends of New Testament Theology Today." He said that this was a test run for him to see whether he was qualified to teach New Testament at a theological college. In September 1948, Boris Anderson was moved from Chôan-chiu, China, to Taiwan, where he moved into the other half of the duplex. Between the Coes' and the Andersons' residences there was a connecting doorway. If there was business to discuss or information to share, they could use this entrance. The door seemed to have been built there on purpose to aid communication between the two sections of the house. Several times, the Andersons woke up at night seeing little David, Shoki's eldest son, standing in the doorway, peering into their side.

Between 1948 and 1963, when the Andersons left to go back to England, these two households were very close in many aspects. In both college business affairs and in family life, they supported each other very much. Until 1959, when Winifred and the four children returned to England, the two families were very close, like one family.

In July 1951, when I took the entrance examination for Tainan Theological College, the Rev. Boris Anderson was in charge of conducting my oral exam. Soon after that the Andersons left for a sabbatical year in England. On board the same ship back to England was the Rev. Ñg Bú-tong, preparing to study in England for a year, and Dr Gô˙ Ki-hok who planned to be in England for three months of further studies. The Rev. Boris Anderson spoke several times of the experience of that particular trip. He said that the Rev. Ṅg Bú-tong was a zealous, honest and serious preacher, preaching what he believed must be said. In 1952, at the beginning of the next school year, he was back teaching at the college leading the second year class in which I was enrolled.

The College Becomes a Security Target

In the early 1950s, as the Kuomintang lost all their territories except for Taiwan, their rule over their Taiwanese hardened. Tainan Theological College felt directly the surveillance and oppressive tactics of the regime. Here are but two typical examples: One evening, past midnight, a group of Mandarin-speaking secret police/plain clothes security personnel knocked at the entrance door of Shoki Coe's residence, calling loudly, "Principal Coe!" to ask him to open the door. Shoki went through the connecting door to the Anderson family's quarters. After a short discussion, it was decided that Boris Anderson would answer the door. He stood on the second floor porch and spoke to the police, five or six of them, down on the ground floor at the entrance, and asked, "What do you want?" They answered, "Somebody would like to invite Principal Coe to entertain him." Boris Anderson answered in Chinese Mandarin, "If you want to invite him, why come after midnight? He is not in. This is a time for sleeping. Your loud voices will disturb people's sleep!" They continued to call, raising their voices even louder. Boris then in a rather rude tone said to them, "This is a residence for foreign nationals. We will have to report this to the British Consulate, and ask them to file an official complaint to your government to stop this kind of disturbance." They continued to shout for about thirty minutes before finally leaving. The next evening, Mr. L. Singleton locked the outside iron gate of the missionary compound. Shortly after midnight, there were loud rattling sounds at the gate, but nobody responded. This kind of disturbance continued for several days. During daytime hours, whenever Shoki went out of the house, Boris would accompany him.

At that time, two distinguished lay Christians stood out—Dr Hâu Chôan-sêng and Tân Tiâu-kéng. Shoki Coe and Boris Anderson asked them for their advice. Dr Hâu Chôan-sêng was a member of the ruling Kuomintang Party, so he was able to bring some effective result. He requested that if the special security authorities intended to arrest a church member, Kuomintang members who were also church members should be notified in advance. After that there were no more disturbances.

Another incident occurred during October 1952. Early one Sunday morning, special security personnel appeared on the Theological College campus.

After I reported it to Shoki Coe and Boris Anderson, Shoki asked me to call the Rev. Iûⁿ Sū-ióng and the Rev. Niû Tek-hūi to come. The security police wanted the college to hand over to them a fourth year student by the name of Toh Êng-siông. The courtyard of the campus instantly looked like a faculty meeting. The faculty members' discussion with the security police was interesting to observe. Because the security police could speak only in Chinese Mandarin, the Rev. Niû, a native of China, would then translate what was said into English. The college faculty members would reply in English, then the Rev. Niû would translate English into Chinese Mandarin, back and forth. This was indeed a strange scene. In a theological college in Taiwan, its faculty spoke only English and Taiwanese!

It happened that Toh Êng-siông was on his fieldwork preaching assignment in Pak-káng Church that day. The security police waited for him and arrested him after his fieldwork preaching, informed the Theological College and Principal Coe of the place where he was being detained, and promised not to inflict physical punishment. In December, close to the time of his release, when a big dinner was held at the college, a special portion was prepared and sent to him in prison.

In this manner, during the early 1950s, the Kuomintang regime continued to exercise terror tactics, directed especially toward educated and elite Taiwanese in an attempt to intimidate and eliminate them. By the fall of 1952, the Kuomintang authorities had suppressed all obvious opposition powers throughout Taiwan, and were now better able to distinguish the real "communist bandits" from persons with foreign connections and global relationships. This led to less harassment of this latter group of people.

In September 1954, I was drafted for six months and trained to serve in the military's communications corps. I served in the same regiment with the Rev. Tīⁿ Liân-bêng and the Rev. Tân Chhong-hoat, and the same company with the Rev. Sun Hông-kî. In the camp sleeping quarters there were long rows of wooden beds. The one who was assigned the bed immediately next to me one day showed me a certified card indicating that he was a special security person. He spoke about his assignments. At that time, people with those cards had the following privileges: (1) to take all public transportation free; (2) to report on any person in secret, and the person would be arrested immediately; and (3) to receive the regular salary of an ordinary position plus the special allowance of a security officer.

Shoki probably became a security target because someone wrongly accused him in order to receive special award money. The person could have lived inside the Theological College campus or nearby. All he would need was a scrap of paper or a note as evidence for his secret reports. Toh Êng-siông recalled that while he was a student at Ka-gī Agricultural Vocational School, a teacher was especially fond of him. Later this teacher was found to be associated with communists. By association, Toh was wrongly accused of the same connections. At the time of his arrest, if he had not been a student at Tainan Theological College, and receiving advice and protection from Dr Hâu Chôan-sêng, lawyers Tân Bêng-chheng and Tân Tiâu-kéng, he, regardless of who he might be, would have been eliminated and there would not have been a Rev. Toh Êng-siông to serve the church.

At the time of the 28 February 1947 event, a lawyer, Elder Tân Tiâu-kéng of Tang-káng exerted special efforts to save the life of a person who had come from China to Taiwan after the war, from unreasonably angry Taiwanese. However, after the Kuomintang government and troops "pacified" Taiwan by suppressing all rebel elements, Elder Tân Tiâu-kéng disappeared, without a single trace or information of his whereabouts. Fortunately the person whose life he had saved earlier made great efforts to search for him. Two months later, he found and saved Elder Tân from a secret prison.

Recollections of Daniel Beeby

In 1950 the Rev. Daniel Beeby arrived in Taiwan. His original assignment was to teach at the Presbyterian Boys Middle School. While living at Tainan Theological College and adjusting to life in Taiwan, he was also thinking about his mission in Taiwan. He had heard that the United Board of Christian Colleges in China,[20] located in the United States, had been entrusted with a fund valued at $1,300,000 to support higher educational institutions in China, which was now to be used for Christian institutions of higher education in Asia. He discovered that in Taiwan there were no church-affiliated institutions of higher education. With this knowledge, he wrote a letter to the Board in New York.

Daniel Beeby's information came as a surprise to the Board. In reply, the Board invited Beeby to investigate and explore the means of education that might best reflect educational ideals responding to the new demands of the time. So he wrote to the Overseas Missions Committee in England, request-ing a three-month leave for travel in the United States to investigate the pro-grams and facilities of Christian universities and colleges. Having completed the tour, he wrote a report suggesting a form of education that valued a com-bination of both brains and hands, an institution that would emphasize work and study as equally important. That was the original ideal on which Tunghai University was founded.

Daniel Beeby thoroughly respected the judgment, authority and leadership of Shoki Coe. When he returned from his exploratory tour in the United States early in 1952, he found that Shoki Coe had already requested the Board of Directors of the Theological College and the General Assembly of the Church to appoint him as a professor of Old Testament. Although at the time Beeby thought Shoki to be one-sided and a bit high-handed, he eventually accepted the appointment to meet the needs of Tainan Theological College. This later influenced him to do two years of doctoral studies at Union Theological Seminary in New York. As he reflected on this unilateral decision and the twist of events, he felt that the grace of God was at work. In 1972, when he became *persona non grata* and was kicked out of Taiwan by the Kuomintang regime, he was in a quandary. Where would he find a job? In this critical situation, Selly Oak College offered him a teaching position in Old Testament Studies. He could continue to use Selly Oak College as a base for educating and nurturing Taiwanese and people from the Presbyterian Church in Taiwan as warriors and scholars of democracy.

When Daniel Beeby was originally sent as a missionary to Amoy (in South Hokkien, China), his starting salary was £200 per annum. He felt miserably poor. But when he came to Taiwan, he discovered that the local minister's salary at that time was only one tenth as much as his. The impact of life and culture in Taiwan was for him a great awakening.

Daniel Beeby experienced two occasions of huge currency devaluation. The first one was when he was still in Hokkien, China. Before he left Amoy, he experienced the devaluation of the Chinyuan currency of China from one million to one. The second occasion was when forty thousand Taiwan Dollars was exchanged/devalued to one New Taiwan Dollar. Although Taiwan's society, families and church were enduring the nadir of economic depression, the fundamental reason that the island was still able to maintain steady growth owed much to the fact that its economy was grounded on a modernized system and that it had established universal education. Shoki Coe, together with leaders of the church, was able to lead Tainan Theological College out of the wasteland into a new, bright age of spiritual advance for the citizens of Taiwan. This alone would qualify Shoki for a place of preeminence in the spiritual history of Taiwan.

Preparing for the WCC Assembly

In the spring of 1953, Dr Hans H. Harms, Associate Director of the Division of Studies of the WCC in Geneva wrote to Shoki Coe to come to Geneva in August, to take part in planning the section on world evangelism, including its contents, methods, and scheduling, for the forthcoming Assembly of WCC. Shoki Coe first came to Geneva to report his arrival and then went on to Bossey, a village near Geneva, to the planning meeting. For Shoki Coe, WCC had to put up US$800 toward his travel expenses of US$1,200. Dr Harms had to write to Dr R. E. Fenn, the Secretary of Overseas Missions of the Presbyterian Church of England, for help to make up the deficit of US$400.

This meeting marked the first official and practical involvement of Shoki Coe with WCC affairs and his work with Dr Henry "Pit" Van Dusen. Dr Van Dusen introduced Shoki Coe to the leaders and dignitaries of churches around the world. He said to the leaders that Shoki was the principal of Tainan Theological College, "a leading, if not the leading theological seminary in Asia." Then he said to Shoki Coe, "Through Dr Stanley Smith and Dr Frank Cartwright, and through your letters and reports to them, I feel that I have known you for a long time." While they were in Geneva, Dr Van Dusen was quite determined that Shoki Coe establish a relationship with the United Board for Christian Higher Education. They also discussed establishing a Christian university in Taiwan.[21] Van Dusen proposed that the theological college should be a part of the new Christian university. Shoki thought differently. He knew that during the colonial rule of Japan, the Japanese did not permit Taiwanese to have their own school; likewise, the Kuomintang colonial rulers' policy would not let Taiwanese have their own school to provide education to enlighten and to manage their own destiny, or permit Taiwanese to be educated with the ideas of self-determination.

In Geneva Shoki Coe also met many other important people, including the head of the Bossey Institute Canon Wendel; Canon Wickham (later to be a bishop); Reverend Maury, father of Philippe Maury, who later became a colleague. He also had the opportunity to become reacquainted with people he had met at the Amsterdam Youth Conference of 1939, including Robert Bilheimer, Daisuke Kitagawa, Paul Abrecht and Victor Hayward. There was also Dr D.T. Niles, a theologian from Ceylon who was one of the speakers at the Amsterdam meeting of 1939, and also took an important role at the Oslo conference. He was a church leader from Asia whom Shoki Coe continued to be in contact and work with.

Dr Pradervand, whom Shoki met on his first visit to Geneva, also informed him that prior to the WCC assembly in 1954, the Seventeenth General Council of the World Presbyterian Alliance would meet in Princeton, and of course, the Presbyterian Church in Taiwan should have representatives at both of these worldwide meetings. Shoki Coe considered the year 1954 as an important year for the Presbyterian Church in Taiwan, as this was the first WCC assembly since the Presbyterian Church in Taiwan had indeed joined the WCC. In addition, prior to this there had never been an officially appointed representative of the Presbyterian Church in Taiwan present at the General Council of the World Presbyterian Alliance.

This trip also provided Shoki Coe with a good opportunity to use summer vacation time to visit England. Since he left England in 1947, he had not experienced such freedom. Prior to 1937 the educational system was Japanese imperialist education, which left no room for freedom at all for the educated Taiwanese. After 1947, under the martial law of the Chiang Kai-sek regime, there was no freedom of movement, speech and assembly. So as soon as he stepped into England, Shoki Coe felt that his spirit was liberated and set free. When he visited the office site of the Overseas Missions Committee of the Presbyterian Church of England, which had been totally destroyed by the German V2 rockets, he found it still lay in rubble. The people in England were still living in difficult conditions after the war, but the atmosphere of freedom and the warmth of human relations remained.

Although the British Empire was in a state of ruin, the government was determined to rebuild the society, and looked forward to launching a society that would care and benefit all. The British social system was not communist, nor was it capitalist. There was also a change of government, which happened at around the time when Shoki Coe left England. The former Prime Minister Winston Churchill, a great leader of the British Empire during wartime, lost power in the 1945 post-war election. Yet the British spirit did not change.

Dr Fenn, the secretary of the Overseas Missions, arranged to hold a meeting for sharing information and discussion among concerned people at Marylebone Church in London. The first part of the meeting shared information of recent developments and the situation of the church in Taiwan, and what former missionaries to Taiwan should do. There was also information about the status of the Presbyterian Boys Middle School and the Girls School. Present at the meeting were Mr F. G. Healey, a former secretary of Overseas Missions; the general secretary of the Presbyterian Church of England, the Rev. Edward Band, former headmaster of the Presbyterian Boys Middle School in Tainan; and Dr David Landsborough. The second part of the meeting involved discussions with Ken Slack and Alan Price, two schoolmates of Shoki Coe at Westminster College, on the subject of school education in general, especially about theological education, and how to strengthen the college, such as through college instruction and teaching staff.

After the meeting, Shoki Coe went on to Cambridge to visit Westminster College. He met Mr Elmslie, the principal then, and Professor Whitehorn, a former principal. This was the first visit to his alma mater after he graduated from there in 1942. The discussion with them was focused on a 1953 graduate of Tainan Theological College, Tiu^{n}Tek-hiong, whom Shoki Coe wanted to send to study at Westminster College for two years.

Immediately following that visit, Shoki Coe went to Scotland to visit New College in Edinburgh, hoping to see Principal Bailie. He was not in, so Shoki Coe met Professor Porteous (professor of Old Testament Studies), and spoke of an outstanding alumnus of New College, Dr Campbell Moody, who was a missionary in Taiwan. Campbell Moody was a legendary evangelist in the coastal villages of Chiong-hòa. He travelled through villages, playing a trumpet and calling, "God is looking for his lost children," to attract an audience to come to listen to his evangelistic message and to believe in Christ. He later contacted tuberculosis and died in Taiwan. Shoki's visit had important and successful results, as he was able to make arrangements for Mr C. S. Song, who was to graduate from National Taiwan University Philosophy Department in 1954, to study at New College. Shoki Coe then visited the MacDonalds, who were his hosts when World War II had broken out and Shoki instantly became an "enemy alien."[22]

He also visited Trinity College in Glasgow where he met a church history professor, John Foster. Shoki Coe particularly remembered him, because they both were at Selly Oak the same year. Shoki Coe was then a student, and John Foster was a teacher who had authored a book, *Past and Present*. The founder and the first principal of Tainan Theological College, missionary, Thomas Barclay, was an alumnus of Trinity in Glasgow. At that time Shoki Coe did not have a student to send from Tainan Theological College to Trinity College, but still wanted to build a bridge between the two colleges.[23]

From Glasgow, Shoki Coe headed back to Marylebone Church in London, where the Presbyterian Church of England had made arrangements for him to give a special lecture, and Principal Elmslie had come specially from Cambridge to preside over the meeting. However, Shoki had contacted flu after arriving in England, and instead of resting, relied on aspirin to continue his travels and meetings. He was so tired when it came to the lecture in London that he fainted, and was not able to give the speech as planned. When he woke up all the audience had left. He felt that this was one of the most regrettable experiences of his life.

Immediately upon his return from his trip to Europe, Shoki Coe went to see the Rev. Ng Bú-tong, the general secretary of the Presbyterian Church in Taiwan (who was then still the general secretary of the South Synod, and had just returned from overseas studies). They discussed the two important worldwide meetings of the church to be held in the United States the next year, and that it was important for the Presbyterian Church in Taiwan to present reports to both meetings. At the time their residences were all in the Sin-lâu and Theological College compound, and it was easy to get together. Based on their discussions, the Rev. Ñg Bú-tong wrote a plan for evangelism that was over ninety pages and set dates to call a "Pre-Evanston" conference of the Presbyterian Church in Taiwan,[24] to be held at Tainan Theological College, 22–24 February 1954. The result of this Pre-Evanston conference was the genesis of the so-called PKU ("Pōe-ka Ūn-tōng" which in Taiwanese means doubling the church evangelism movement) of the Presbyterian Church in Taiwan. The target as well as momentum for this evangelistic campaign was looking forward to the one hundredth anniversary of Protestant witness in Taiwan (1865–1965), with the hope to double the number of churches and members between then and the one hundredth year celebration, along with the hope to have at least one church in every township and village in Taiwan.

Experiencing a Continent

In spite of his busy work and tight schedule at Tainan Theological College, Shoki Coe took off for the United States with many "missions" to accomplish: business related to the WCC, theological education, mission and evangelism in Asia and Taiwan. No personal business or benefit was on his task list.

Shoki Coe probably flew from an airport in England to New York for this first trip to the United States. In 1954 all passenger flights were propeller air-crafts and most likely required two fuel stops across the Atlantic. The whole trip must have provided him with much food for thought.

He experienced the meaning of a "continent." For the forty years of his life while he lived under the rules of Japanese and British empires, all his education and living experiences were on islands. When he took a ship to go to England, or to return to Taiwan, all the ports he stopped by were only on the edges of the continents of Asia and Europe. While he was on the North American continent, he could experience a whole day or even days of an automobile journey before seeing a city, and the trains had to provide sleeping and dining facilities. He better understood what Revelation 21 meant about "the sea was no more."

Shoki was also struck by the size differences between people. He realized that American people were generally tall and big. The Europeans he had come to know were generally taller than Asian. When he met Dr Henry "Pit" Van Dusen for the first time, he thought he was an exception, but after he arrived in America, he realized that the people there were not only tall but also large.

Shoki speculated the cause was that "Americans consumed large amounts of beef and steak." The American barbecue must have impressed Shoki. As he was in America during the summer, he witnessed the many barbecue grills set up in the backyards of homes and apartment buildings, parks and campuses. The outdoor feasts were fantastic, and obviously different from the English style, which was indoors, with very carefully and meticulously arranged table setting with special silver and plates, full of "atmosphere." The American style, Shoki discovered, was half a pound beefsteak, a quarter of a chicken, a whole potato wrapped in tinfoil and roasted, and more. All were far more than what one person could—or should—eat.

Shoki found that American culture adored "bigness." In 1954, and even up to thirty years later, the United States had the largest building and the tallest skyscraper, the longest bridge and the longest suspension bridge. The country had large farms, super large automobile factories, steel mills, aircraft factories. Even in the area of higher education and the development of specialists, the United States was able to gather intellectuals and highly educated people from around the world to its research institutions. Shoki also saw large-scale theological seminaries that ranked among the top theological institutions of the world. Coming from Tainan Theological College which was not only small but had very rudimentary facilities, Shoki felt crushed under the pressure of size and stature.

Yet, after experiencing the "big" North American continent, Shoki wanted to emphasize that "small is beautiful." While the concept of "ecology" did not really exist at that time, Shoki felt that conspicuous consumption, with its greed, desires and practices, would bring negative repercussions on human beings. Christian love must bring the world self-control, humility, caring and sharing.

Visiting American Churches and Theological Seminaries

For a young and clear-minded head of a theological institution, this visit to the United States was the best field education he could have received. In a short span of time, he was able to see many seminary facilities and dialogue with and learn from a large number of top theological professors, leaders of different denominations, theological educators, staff members and heads of mission agencies and foundations.

The most important thing he learned was how to refine and extract his own goals in life. Through his struggles over the last five years, he had clearly found that the life of the church of Jesus Christ is in her proclamation of the message of Christ. And at the heart of ministry and proclamation was one's commitment to what one proclaimed. There was a wrestling in Shoki's heart.

It was in this wrestling that he discovered himself, the church in Taiwan, the whole society in Taiwan, and found the place of Taiwan and its people in the world arena. Shoki Coe's focus became enlightening people who were in ministry to live out effective interaction within the real human situation in Taiwan.

Shoki Coe repeatedly emphasized to me, "I am not a theologian, although I lean toward theological position and theory, to make my call and my appeal. I clearly find and know that my mission is to be a theological educator. A theological educator tends to be an activist; that is why I engage in dialogue incessantly and constantly with people of other lands and the world, and people within Taiwan, to inform and to appeal. I give attention to those who are still in training, and those who are already in the ministry. I call and appeal to these people to know the reality and the genuine situation. Taiwanese who strive to commit themselves and are loyal to the genuine situation in Taiwan, equals their commitment to the world and to the ministry of Christ in this world."

Under the leadership of Henry "Pit" Van Dusen during the 1950s, Union Theological Seminary in New York became the largest centre of theological inquiry in the US, and even the largest theological seminary in the world. The seminary was located in the neighbourhood of some of the most glamorous and prestigious academic institutions, such as Columbia University, Jewish Theological Seminary, Barnard College, Julliard School of Music. The famous Riverside Church stands there as its next door neighbour. On top of this, the future "Interchurch Center" at 475 Riverside Drive was under construction. There was truly no better place for an educational, ecumenical institution to carry out its activities and interaction with the world.

The setting and environment of Union Theological Seminary indeed left a deep impression on Shoki. However, his deepest and most unforgettable memories were the arrangements for him to meet and discuss with world famous theologians, such as Reinhold Niebuhr, John Bennett, D. D. Williams, James Muilenburgh.[25]

Shoki's meeting with Reinhold Niebuhr here, although not his first, was pleasant and memorable. When speaking with Niebuhr, Shoki mentioned that he had read most of his books, which had greatly influenced Shoki's ethical thinking and political theology. Niebuhr was very concerned about the situation in the Far East, and he understood the situation well. It was a good opportunity to talk with him about the situation in Taiwan. Shoki told him of the so-called "white terrorism" that Taiwan was facing, and how the "Chinese (or rather Kuomintang)" government in Taiwan had arrested, tortured and executed people who held different opinions, and then branded them as "communist bandits."

Neibuhr told him of a similar situation that was going on in the United States at that time that was known as "McCarthyism." In America then, anyone who was suspected to hold communist ideas or have association with people of that ideology would be persecuted and arrested by the government authorities. Niebuhr's ethical and political ideas were that there was no perfect and reasonable democracy, but Christians and the church must take up the role of bearing the responsibility of being a conscience of the state and society within the framework of a democratic ideal.

There were three "young and energetic" faculty members at Union Theological Seminary then—Bennett, Williams and Muilenburg—who maintained contact and friendship with Shoki after his 1954 visit. In sharing his thoughts with them, Shoki gradually led to the issues of how to achieve excellency in theological education, especially for the ministers of the churches of "younger" and "developing" nations, their training and the necessity of continued education. Shoki Coe asked them for assistance in strengthening the teaching faculty of theological colleges in these areas, and especially at Tainan Theological College. Shoki found in them a very sympathetic ear, especially from D. D. Williams. At that time Williams was involved with Richard Niebuhr and one other who had been commissioned by the North American Association of Theological Schools to review the existing curriculum of schools. They were able to examine these issues with Shoki Coe with considerable expertise and knowledge. Ever since Shoki's meeting with them in 1954, similar issues arose at different times in North America, even in Singapore and other places in Asia, and Europe, and subject matters even extended to ethics, politics and the international situation.[26]

During Shoki's visit at Union Theological Seminary, Dr Van Dusen made special arrangements for Shoki to see Dr Beach, the librarian at the seminary. Dr Beach spent a considerable amount of time showing Shoki the library facilities, and explained its own catalogue system. Shoki was impressed with the size and efficiency of the library. Of course, there was no way that Tainan could catch up with Union in a short time, or even in Shoki's lifetime. Dr Beach promised to donate spare and duplicate copies of its library books to Tainan. He did indeed do so in the following years.

Dr Van Dusen also arranged for Shoki Coe to meet Dr Morris, the librarian at Yale Divinity School. Dr Morris was a "teaching librarian" and had a wide range of knowledge and expertise, holding the rank of professor. This fact greatly influenced the direction and policy of the library at Tainan when it was rebuilt. Later when the Association of Theological Schools in South East Asia was planning its first workshop for librarians, the preparatory committee unanimously chose Dr Morris to conduct the workshop. When Shoki Coe was working for the Theological Education Fund of WCC, Dr Morris was engaged to give advice to libraries and the training of librarians of theological schools in Latin America and Africa.

In addition to visiting the library and librarian of Yale Divinity School, Shoki was able to visit the dean, Dr Liston Pope, and professor of Christian Education, Dr Paul Vieth, and another professor, Dr Charles Forman. Shoki requested that the Divinity School accept students from Taiwan for further studies. Yale Divinity School is part of Yale University, so its dean is responsible for the operation of the school. Therefore, Dean Pope was the policy maker of the school. Like Dr Van Dusen, Dr Pope had vision, and they were all involved in the strategy and planning of the church, and rendered great support to WCC programs. Two years later, in 1956, Dean Pope on his way to Bangkok for a WCC-related conference, made a special stop in Taiwan to visit Tainan Theological College.

It was in Princeton, before the General Council of the World Presbyterian Alliance, that Shoki Coe met Dr John Mackay, the President of Princeton Theological Seminary, for the first time. Dr Mackay was president of the Alliance and the host of the meeting. He was a giant in ecumenical circles and a great theologian. The Alliance constituted one quarter of the members of the WCC family; Dr Mackay also occupied an important leadership position in the WCC. These were such precious moments for Shoki, that at this busy time, Dr Mackay was willing to take time out to meet him. The time in Princeton was short. But he was able to see Dr Homrighausen, and through his introduction to meet Principal Dr John Bailie and Dr T. F. Torrance (of New College, Edinburgh, both of whom Shoki missed when he visited there), and Professor J. Hromadka of Czechoslovakia. And it was there that Shoki met the dean of Princeton Seminary for the first time, Dr James McCord of Austin, Texas, who was to contribute greatly to the training of ministers from Taiwan. Dr McCord succeeded John Mackay to become president of Princeton Seminary. During his years as president, many ministers from Taiwan were accepted there for further studies.

The 1954 WCC Assembly and Taiwanese Identity

The World Council of Churches (WCC) was founded in Amsterdam in 1948. This is a worldwide Christian organization, like a United Nations of Christianity, which aims to include all Christian denominations in efforts for Christian unity through renewal, dialogue and prayer, and to seek mutual tolerance and acceptance and cooperation. Prior to the First World War, some major denominations already had some consensus. Soon after the war, movements such as Faith and Order and Life and Work (of the church) combined to form this council-type of organization. Although it is an ecumenical and worldwide organization, the Roman Catholic Church, the US Southern Baptist Convention, non-denominational churches, and many charismatic and Pentecostal churches are still not willing to join.

The Presbyterian Church in Taiwan became a member of the WCC in 1951, so the WCC's second assembly in Evanston was its first. The Presbyterian Church was the only denomination in Taiwan with enough members and churches to qualify for membership. In 1954 at the stated meeting of the General Assembly of the Presbyterian Church in Taiwan, Shoki Coe was appointed as the official representative, and the Rev. Tân Khoe-chùn, the Rev. Gô' Éng-hôa, and the Rev. Iûn Sū-ióng as observers to the WCC assembly. These same four persons also served as official delegates to the Seventeenth General Council of the World Presbyterian Alliance just prior to the WCC assembly, also the first for the church in Taiwan to participate.

For Shoki, the WCC assembly, where church leaders transcended national and denominational boundaries to gather for fellowship and worship was a very inspiring, impressive and challenging experience. But Shoki also felt that it was too big. It was very hard to get to know people or have meaningful participation except in discussions in small groups or committees. Real ecumenicity, he felt, only takes place and finds meaning in a locality—a home, a college, a church, a nation or a region. As the delegate from Taiwan to Evanston, Shoki brought gifts from Taiwan and the Taiwan church to the assembled worldwide church. The fellowship and the sense of solidarity from the worldwide meeting were the gifts the delegates could take back to each church, nation and region, to continue to carry out the mission of Christ entrusted to the church, in its various and glorious ways and shapes.

The subject of China's becoming communist was a major focus for deliberation in the section meeting on Mission and Evangelism of the WCC assembly. After the founding of the People's Republic of China in 1949, all foreign mission personnel were expelled, all evangelistic activities were forbidden throughout the country, and China disappeared from the missionary strategy. The discussions and opinions offered by the participants appeared to be pessimistic, and the atmosphere was grave and gloomy. The chair of the discussion, Dr D. T. Niles, a church leader from Ceylon (Sri Lanka), asked Shoki Coe to express his ideas as a "Chinese" from the perspective of mission.

The following is a summary of Shoki Coe's speech:

More than six years ago, in October 1947, one of the reasons that I returned to Taiwan was that I regarded myself as a Chinese. But upon my return and living under the martial law of the Chiang Kai-sek regime, I began to ask myself, "Am I a Chinese or only a Taiwanese?" Because there was little difference between living under Japanese rule or Chinese rule, Taiwanese were still treated as second-class citizens. "Chinese" is a very vague term; to call a person "Chinese" is like calling a person European or Anglo-Saxon. I have never visited China, and I am not qualified to represent "Chinese" in expressing any opinion as Dr D. T. Niles has asked me to do. Of course we have Chinese in Taiwan; we call those who came to Taiwan from China after the Second World War "A-soaⁿ-á"[27] and ourselves "Han-chû-á." (Taiwan's map looks like a sweet potato shape island.)

I fully understand "mission impact," because during the war, when I was still in England, I used to call myself "Chinese" in my speeches, describing with enthusiasm and liveliness the Chinese troops, under the leadership of a brilliant Christian general, who bravely fought against Japanese troops, and the inspiration of the world famous Christian "Madame Chiang." Like many people, I drew beautiful and colourful pictures! However in the last six years or so, when I observed with my own eyes, Chinese troops are basically undisciplined, the officers of any rank are corrupted and rotten to the core, and it is not hard for me to understand why the Kuomintang was so totally defeated by the hands of the Communists. And I say, I cannot understand why mission agencies of Christian churches encounter such great obstacles.[28] However, I believe this is also God's providence in missions. I agree with many who repeatedly say at this debate, that God's judgment should begin with the people of God within the household of God. As a Taiwanese Christian, I am reminded of a sermon the minister preached at the church in Redhill (a suburb of London), calling the people in the world to heed these words from the Scriptures: "On the left hand God doth work with, but I cannot behold" (Job 23:9).

When Shoki Coe saw so many church leaders groaning as though it were the end of the road because missionary activities came to an end in China, he felt that it was time to call attention to the special situation in Taiwan. Here was an opportunity and a new hope. Suddenly, as if by special inspiration, he said, "there is a China in the world, but there is also a Taiwan. Although mission work in China has made many Christian churches feel frustrated and disappointed, God will stretch out his left hand to open a new opportunity of mission in Taiwan." After this speech, even Shoki himself was surprised by this sudden inspiration. He thought of this as a new breakthrough with fresh meaning, as it was an occasion for him to make a statement that Taiwan had an independent status. Afterward, when D. T. Niles wrote his report, he mentioned "one China, one Taiwan," and used the commentary of the Book of Job written by the Pastor of Redhill to give additional comments on the subject.

Ecumenical Difficulties in Taiwan

During the seven years between the WCC assemblies held in Evanston in 1954 and New Delhi in 1961, there was interest in ecumenism in Taiwan. Other than the Presbyterian Church in Taiwan, there were churches that were involved with the ecumenical movement, such as the Episcopal, Lutheran, Methodist and American Baptist. After much consultation and negotiation, they cooperated on two important efforts for the church. One was the celebration of the one hundredth anniversary of Protestant witness in Taiwan. The other was the formation of the Taiwan Ecumenical Consultative Committee. Although these two achievements did not receive much international acclamation, those who worked to bring them about did struggle to witness the cooperation and unity of the church.

For the Presbyterian Church in Taiwan, WCC membership was a very lonely struggle on a rough and bumpy path. No other denomination in Taiwan was a member of this worldwide Christian organization. The reasons ranged from straightforward to complex:

1. A WCC member church must have a minimum membership in the tens of thousands.

2. The Kuomintang tried to monopolize international relations and its diplomatic function, and found the PCT's relationship with the World Council of Churches—which enabled news to enter and leave Taiwan without censorship—threatening.

3. There were member churches of WCC in communist countries, so if the ruling authorities allowed the representatives of Taiwan to participate in such an organization, there was fear that the defence line of "anti-communism" might break down.

4. Those Christians who were adamantly anti-communist with the aim to defend the church purposely slandered the WCC as a pro-communist organization in front of the ruling Kuomintang.

5. Language was a key factor in the inability to make government officials understand the relationship between the WCC and the Presbyterian Church

in Taiwan. There were powerful Mandarin-speaking members among the Episcopal, Methodist and Presbyterian churches, who held important positions in the government of the ruling Kuomintang. In Taiwan they were not in reality church members of these denominations, but rather the policy-making position holders for international and internal relations of the ruling authorities. There was no way for these "Mandarin-speaking only Christian" officials of the Ministries of the Interior and Foreign Affairs in Taiwan to understand and experience the kind of firm foundation and strong international ties that the churches in England, Canada or Japan were enjoying through mutual dialogue and interaction of churches. Although the Presbyterian Church in Taiwan did not have much expertise in using Chinese Mandarin, it was able to use several languages, especially in this era, when the witness of God and confessional statements must be made in plain language that the worldwide church and international community could understand.

In this difficult situation, there were some Mandarin-speaking ministers who maintained their integrity in Christian faith and character. One of them was Rev. Chou Lien Hwa, who maintained good relationships with Shoki Coe and the Rev. N̂g Bú-tong. While Shoki was not able to use Chinese Mandarin to communicate well, and there were no other leaders capable of interacting with high officials of the Central Government of the Kuomintang, the Rev. Chou Lien Hwa seemed to be able to take the role of an intermediate, a good friend at a difficult and dead end situation. The Rev. Chou Lien Hwa left for the United States to study theology for six years, before the Chinese communists had taken over the whole China Mainland in 1949. He came to Taiwan in 1954. Whenever Shoki Coe and Chou Lien Hwa carried on a conversation they used English. Chou had zeal and expertise, and he and Shoki Coe were theological educators, and shared the passion for the "indigenization" of Christian faith and theological ideas.

Chou Lien Hwa wrote in his memoir how he came to know and to work cooperatively with the people of the Presbyterian Church in Taiwan toward the end of the 1950s. He wrote:

It was the time before the one hundredth year anniversary of the Presbyterian Church in Taiwan. We were preparing for a big celebration. It has been said that Chinese never celebrate one's own birthday alone; the celebration must be in a setting of gathered people. So, the churches other than the Presbyterian Church in Taiwan got together and organized a party preparation committee, and I was elected to be the chair. During that period of time

the Presbyterian Church in Taiwan was very actively carrying out its "Doubling the Church" campaign. In many churches in the south the membership
increased more than twofold. They were not "political," just honestly carrying out the work of expanding the church.[29]

Chou Lien Hwa continued to write about how he worked with Shoki Coe
and Ng Bú-tong to establish ways whereby they evaluated and steered forward
theology and church.

> There were two colleagues, the Principal of Tainan Theological College Shoki
> Coe, and the General Secretary of the General Assembly of the Presbyterian
> Church in Taiwan Ng Bú-tong, with whom I often talked through the night,
> discussing the strategy of the mission of the church, from after suppertime
> until about two to three o'clock early next morning. Shoki was an idealist full
> of energy and passion, he had a lot of ideals and strategies; he was a good
> speaker, not actor; on the other hand, Bú-tong did not utter a word, as he
> quietly and carefully listened. Some might ask me, then what did you do?
> I was a person to raise questions. I often asked why do you have to do it in
> that way? Do you think it is workable? After the discussions I tried to cheer
> up others, or at times to throw a wet blanket. The next morning Bú-tong
> and I rose up early, but did not bother to go say goodbye to Shoki, then went
> straight to take an ordinary express train to return to Taipei. Bú-tong was a
> man of little words, but a man of action. He would carry out what was said
> the previous evening one by one. They two were the perfect match, and they
> brought the Presbyterian Church to its apex era.[30]

On 22 November 1963[31] Bishop Charles Gilson of the Episcopal Church
and Chou Lien Hwa extended an invitation to the Presbyterian, Lutheran, and
Methodist church leaders to gather at Tunghai University to form a Taiwan
Ecumenical Consultative Committee. This Committee aimed to develop cooperation among churches and their missions, until it culminated in attempting
to draft a common statement on "national affairs" in 1971. There was prog-
ress but unfortunately, there was too much difference in political backgrounds
among the denominations. Thus the Presbyterian Church in Taiwan was left
alone to brush up the final wording, and issued the its historic first statement.

After the General Assembly of the WCC in Evanston, Illinois, in the summer of 1954, the following General Assembly was held in New Delhi, India in
the winter of 1961. Shoki Coe was invited to participate. Unfortunately, however, Shoki had been singled out by the Kuomintang government, and was not

initially able to get his Exit and Re-Entry Permit. The authorities employed a delay tactic. The meeting was to start soon, but the permit just was not forthcoming, and Shoki was anxious.

Fortunately there was a "President's Chaplain," Chou Lien Hwa, who offered a helping hand. Chou Lien Hwa first went to see the Minister of the Interior, Lien Chen-Tung. Since it might have been an inconvenient environment at his office, Chou went to see him at his residence. Minister Lien told the Rev. Chou that there was a whole stack of secret reports on Shoki Coe, so he did not dare to issue the permit. Chou then asked Lien, were these reports coming from the same source? Would it be possible to send someone to Tainan to see whether the one who filed the reports had violated the normal rules and done something beyond the call of duty? Was the reports' filer credible and were the reports accurate? It looked like Lien did not have enough power to remove this "mountain". So, Chou went to call on Chang Chun, the secretary general of the Presidential Office for help. Chang Chun happened to belong to the highest policy-making body of the Kuomintang which included Tseng Hsu-pai, Tao Hsi-sheng, and Hsieh Ran-zhi. It was necessary to call for Ng Bú-tong and Shoki Coe, and together all seven met at Chou's church, Grace Baptist Church. Ng Bú-tong and Shoki Coe prepared a report concerning the Presbyterian Church in Taiwan to the committee. Early the next morning, the Deputy General Secretary of Kuomintang Hsieh Ran-zhi made a telephone call to the Office of Exit and Reentry Control, and Shoki Coe was asked to pick up his permit by 10 a.m.[32] Thus, Shoki was able to represent the Presbyterian Church in Taiwan to go on to New Delhi to attend the WCC assembly.

The Growing Family in Taiwan

In 1947, when three members of the Coe family set foot in Taiwan, they were not completely ready to face the challenges ahead. Although it had little impact for baby David, his 34-year-old mother Winifred experienced great culture shock. Everything was strange—culture, language, food, weather, land, water, and the entire environment, even the wind that blew. Her lack of material goods plus her busy life did not give her time to stop and learn to readjust. In addition, there was enormous pressure of runaway inflation. The savings that the Coes had from England, which they changed into local currency, in a few short months became a useless pile of waste paper. The missionaries on the Sin-lâu missionary compound, such as Mr L. Singleton and the Rev. R. Montgomery and his wife, after being repatriated during the war, had returned. But among them there were no younger people of Winifred's age who could support her. This exaggerated her loneliness.

Nearly two years after they returned to Taiwan, on 3 May 1949, their second son, Michael, was born. On 30 November 1951, the Coes had another happy event—the birth of their daughter Eileen. Although the Coes' residence was in the Sin-lâu compound and the Theological College was within the extended walls of Sin-lâu, Shoki was too busy in his duties of administration, teaching, preparing of lectures, meetings, and so on, to spend much time with his family. Winifred not only had to care for the family and raise the children, to meet the needs of the Theological College, she also helped teach English. On the recommendations of Dr Chioh Oán-seng, the Coes hired a woman named Tiuⁿ Chìn-lú (also known as A-tan) to assist in caring for the family. A-tan was a very bright woman, quick to learn and with a generous personality. She respected her employer and family, followed their instructions, and was loved by the whole Coe household. With Shoki as match-maker, she married Tiuⁿ Chì-tiōng (also known as Teng-a), a caretaker at the Theological College, and raised her own family.

Using her farm family background, A-tan supplemented the Coes's nutritional needs by raising goats for milk and growing vegetables uncontaminated by parasites, for their salads. While supplying nutrition for their table, she also helped to reduce their food bills. In the summer of 1947, Shoki Coe had applied to the Embassy of the Republic of China in London for a Chinese passport to travel back home to Taiwan, while Winifred applied for a British passport with David's name included. 1947 was the year of the massacre in Taiwan. With terror gripping the island, the people there felt very insecure. For this reason, Shoki's British friends persuaded the Coes to maintain British citizenship for Winifred and David.

When Shoki went to the East Ward Office of Tainan Municipal Government to carry out his registration, he thought that it would be a routine procedure. But instead the consequences were complex beyond comprehension. About one month later, the registrar's office made an extraordinary condition. It notified Shoki that unless Winifred was naturalized as a citizen of the country, Michael could not be registered. This was a totally unexpected blow. The municipal office explained that this ruling was made by direct order of the highest authority, the Ministry of the Interior. The British Consulate in Tamsui advised that, because of the instability of the political situation in China, it would be better for Winifred and David to retain their British citizenship. Thus for the time being, Shoki let Winifred keep her British citizenship, and asked Dr Landsborough and Miss Gretta Gauld, the Chief of Nursing staff, to issue a birth certificate for Michael, to give the British Consulate proof of Michael's British citizenship. The result was that his name was inserted in Winifred's passport.[33]

Later when Eileen was born in 1951, and the youngest son Andrew in 1955, the same procedure was followed as in Michael's case to establish their British citizenship as members of Winifred's family. However, the repercussions of this attempt to register Michael's birth at the Municipal Ward Office were far-reaching. It served as a starting point of harassment by the Central Government.

From 1952 onward, every year when Shoki Coe renewed his passport of the Republic of China, in the entry for "marital status," the Central Government intentionally wrote "single, not yet married." Shoki's repeated protests and requests of amendment were to no avail.

Starting from the incident of Michael's domicile at the Registrar's Office, Shoki received a monthly notice to ask why the Coes refused to register their children as citizens of the Republic of China. Shoki knew many officials at the East Ward Office as well as the Municipal Government Office. He told them it was not he that refused to register them, it was the government that refused to register them as Chinese nationals.[34] This kind of harassment continued for ten years until 1959 when Winifred took the children out of Taiwan. At that point the monthly notice ceased to arrive.

Unfortunately, in the Presbyterian Church in Taiwan there were pastors and elders who became the voices for the Kuomintang and spies and informants on church family affairs. The Government, through a front organization, the Christian Council, also called the League for Anti-communism and for Defending the Church (sponsored by an organization associated with American clergyman, Carl McIntire), and a legitimate agency of the General Assembly of the Presbyterian Church, began to spread rumours that disgraceful things had happened in the Coe family. The slanderers cited this disgrace as the reason that Shoki resigned his position as the moderator of the General Assembly in 1965, soon after the Church's Centennial Celebration. The following year, 1966, at the General Assembly of the Presbyterian Church, an elder-commissioner suddenly rose up to make a motion to reprimand Shoki Coe for having lived with a woman to whom he was not married and having four children by her. Although few commissioners paid any attention to this motion, this incident called for the church to re-examine itself and to recognize how much the Coes had suffered by this type of slander.

Precious Sabbatical Leave

By 1958 Shoki Coe had been principal of the Theological College for ten years, and he needed to take a year of sabbatical leave. This leave had several levels of meaning to him. First, he could be totally relieved of his duties in administration, personnel issues, teaching and building headaches. Second, he could replenish and renew his spirit. Third, he would be able to review, discern, analyze, and put in order and perspective, what he had read, taught and experienced. And fourth, he could get in touch with new theologians, new theological educators and church leaders of the world, to receive some stimuli, challenges, and enlightenment in learning from them.

At this point in time, his wife Winifred had reached utter physical and spiritual exhaustion and was not healthy. She needed rest to restore her health. Their children, particularly David, had reached the age that required formal British education, which was a particular wish Winifred had.

As Shoki was making plans for the next step in his future, four invitations emerged on the horizon. Overdale College in Selly Oak, Birmingham, England invited him to take on the one year William Paton Lectureship. This position would provide suitable living quarters that would allow the whole family to be together to enjoy the warmth of family life, yet on the other hand, since he would continue to teach, there would be little chance for Shoki to "replenish" himself.

The University of Chicago School of Theology invited him to be a visiting professor for one year, teaching Christian mission, research and mission education. This invitation could provide some income, but not enough for travel costs for the whole family, and as it was only one year it could only provide a fragmented piece of long-term education for his children, so it was not adequate. On top of that, it was not a good position for his own replenishment.

The Executive Director of the Nanking Seminary Board of Founders, Cartwright offered him a teaching position at Drew University Theological Seminary to teach a course on mission in Southeast Asia. The benefit was a little better, but the shortcomings were similar to that of the previous offer. Finally, an invitation came from Dr Van Dusen, President of Union Seminary in New York. This invitation was similar to what was offered before, except that it was now in greater detail. He was asked to teach "Theology of Mission to the [whole] World", and he was promised that he could freely choose whatever courses he would like to take at the Union to replenish himself.

Shoki chose the fourth invitation. However, this did not satisfy Winifred's expectation that their children receive what she considered to be "proper education" in an adequate environment, which of course, Winifred thought that only England could provide.

Therefore, Shoki Coe made some inquires to the Overseas Missions Committee of the Presbyterian Church of England to see whether it would be willing to pay for the education and living expenses of the Coes. On 10 November

1958, he wrote to Mr. Fenn, the secretary of the Overseas Missions, saying, "Although I have a strong desire to stay with my family in England for a year, I think that I can only be with them for a month in England. My itinerary is as follows: in July 1960, I will participate in the theological workshop, and a conference of the heads of Christian universities and theological schools in South East Asia, and then proceed to England, and from there to the United States. I hope that the travel expenses for me to go through South East Asia and Europe to New York and back will be paid by Nanking Seminary Board of Founders."

The records of the Overseas Missions Committee of the Presbyterian Church of England provided sufficient reason for Winifred's return. Winifred, not having been appointed a missionary, stayed outside the missionary circle. The OMC encouraged her to receive a thorough physical examination from Dr Landsborough. Although Shoki Coe asked the OMC to provide her with airfare, the committee only agreed to pay for her ship passenger fare.

In the years 1959 to 1960, through such arrangements, Shoki Coe and his whole family were able to return to England, from where he continued to New York for one year. While at Union Seminary, he was able to teach and at the same time did some study and research. After his year at Union, he travelled by way of England and spent time with his family before returning to Taiwan.

There is no way of knowing whether, before she left, Winifred had any intention of returning to Taiwan. In fact, she remained in England, while Shoki went to New York and then returned to Taiwan. Shoki was very busy with his church work and was not able to share in the nurture of his children. He did not have time to relate his Taiwan family history to them, although in his memoir Shoki reported that he had tried to share this tradition with David, who spoke fluent Taiwanese and had attended the local Taiwanese primary school, Sèng-lī Kok-hāu. Yet David was always proud of being British. Living in England during the formative years deprived the children of the experience of growing up in Taiwanese society. Consequently, whatever impressions of Taiwan they gained from their father were only external facts about Tainan Theological College and the tidbits from the OMC. They did not the surroundings and history of Taiwan. This was the sad case for many Taiwanese people. They were like the Jews about whom the Apostle Paul wrote, "I have received (the gospel), but my own people have not experienced it." Although Shoki had his own family, he was like Paul, always on the road, travelling the world—a truly global person.

In the spring of 1961, Knox College in Toronto, Canada, granted Shoki Coe an honorary doctor's degree, Doctor of Divinity, to honour and acknowledge his outstanding contribution as a theological educator, a church leader in Taiwan, as well as his invaluable contribution in the field of theology in South East Asia, and his leadership in the worldwide church such as WCC.

The Kuomintang Government and Tainan Theological College

The Republic of China under the Kuomintang was not a country ruled by laws. Whenever it encountered any difficult issues or realities, it would pull away all the foundation of laws, apply a "suspension" policy and use authoritarian methods, namely applying the "Temporary Regulations during the Time of Suppressing Rebellion to Maintain Stability," on top of martial law. The government tried to eliminate the best and elite of Taiwan, but it could not effectively touch the ones that drew significant international attention, Shoki Coe and Tainan Theological College. Through Shoki's work in England and connections in the World Council of Churches, he was well known by many across the globe, as was the school he headed. There were constant visits of church leaders from Europe, Americas and Africa to Tainan, and the college had already established friendly international relations. They did not have any relations whatsoever with the Central Government of Kuomintang.

But at the time, Taiwan Theological College in Taipei was different. Its principal, the Rev. James Dickson, had personal, friendly relations with the administrative chief of Taiwan, Governor Wu Kuo-tzeng, because they were formerly schoolmates at Princeton, and the governor gave personal consent that the students at the Theological College in Taipei, while at school, would not be subject to the draft into military service. For that special privilege, many students chose to go to Taiwan Theological College, instead of Tainan, to do theological studies.

Under the rule of the Kuomintang in Taiwan, the government basically did not care about a "school for religious studies." It reasoned that if no attention were given, this kind of school would naturally disappear. The government thought that theological colleges were places like monasteries for people who denounced worldly life, and that once these people entered there, they would not return to society to care about life in society, communities, churches and their members. They would be similar to Taoist priests learning their practices from their masters individually like apprentices. But theological seminaries and colleges are different. They have a long history and tradition and are also interconnected with international communities as well as with local churches and community.

The standing of a professor of a theological school was never accredited and recognized by the Ministry of Education, and thus, was not subject to government evaluation, and the church did not seek recognition of the degrees of graduates of its seminaries by the government authorities. During wartime, and even after the war, the government did not even delegate to the Ministry of Education to give consideration or supervision and evaluation of the academic standing of these schools, but instead just lumped them together with other religious establishments to go under the jurisdiction of the Ministry of the Interior. The officials of the Ministry of the Interior were not competent to do the necessary review tasks, and had no desire to do these duties as well. And thus the theological schools were left in limbo, not taken seriously for their curriculum and academic content.

When both Shoki Coe and the Rev. Ng̃ Bú-tong were involved in establishing Tunghai University, church leaders in the United States, particularly Stanley Smith, proposed that Tainan Theological College should merge with this forthcoming interdenominational university. The church leaders in the United States had little experience and knowledge of the situation of different denominations and their inter-relations or status of cooperation. At the time, the whole of Taiwan was saturated with missionaries of all shades and forms; other than Presbyterian, the number of missionaries was almost the same as the number of members of each denomination. Since these missionaries were evacuated from the China mainland to Taiwan within a short period of time, they still did not have opportunity to resume their denominational apparatus in Taiwan. Their national leaders were few in number, and not in touch with the situation, nor did the missionaries know their immediate environment and neighbours. In contrast, the Presbyterian Church in Taiwan had about six hundred to seven hundred churches spreading all over Taiwan.

The church leaders of different denominations other than the Presbyterian Church were primarily members of the Kuomintang, and held important government posts. These other denominations were only connected in organizational structure. Therefore, the existing reality of founding an interdenominational university could be said to be the result of negotiation and consultation between two parties, namely "the Presbyterian Church in Taiwan" and "Christians of Kuomintang officials." Of course there was a de facto third party, an organization that was related to the National Council of Churches of Christ in the USA, the United Board for Christian Higher Education in Asia.[35] This third party only set up the initial "founding committee", and when an appropriate succeeding body was established, control was immediately transferred to this body, and the United Board ceased its direct control. Thus, the United Board sent the new body, the Board of Trustees of Tunghai University, an enormous amount of funds to carry out its task. As was well known, except for the first few years of its founding, Tunghai University was virtually controlled by Christians of the Kuomintang, with little participation by regional or local churches, either denominational or ecumenical groups.

In retrospect, Shoki Coe's hesitance to consent to the merger of Tainan Theological College with Tunghai University was justified. He thought that if Tainan Theological College had merged with Tunghai, he would have done a great disservice to the church by surrendering the operation and control of theological education to the hands of the government, and the Theological College would have disappeared from the map of the Presbyterian Church in Taiwan.[36]

Shoki Coe did make inquiries about the conditions by which the Ministry of Education would give accreditation to a theological college. These conditions included: (1) Instruction must be in Mandarin Chinese; (2) Allowing government interference and intervention, such as employing "military officer-instructors", setting up courses in "military education", placing a political "weekly assembly" on the curriculum schedule, conducting a flag raising and lowering ceremony daily; (3) Establishing a "security" office (to spy on the political opinions of staff and students); (4) Probably changing the admissions policy with more input from outside the church, recommendation of applicants from the session (consistory) would have to be abolished, and the admissions policy would incorporate the requirements of the policy of the Kuomintang's "Unified Admissions" system.

The Kuomintang's policies did not stop at letting "theological colleges walk their own lonely paths" and at one time issued an order to prohibit theological colleges from calling themselves "college," (hak-īn, hsue-yuan in Mandarin). Instead, they must change their names to be called "institute" (su-īn, shu-yuan in Mandarin),[37] thus becoming a "theological institute" with no academic standing whatsoever. As far as I remember, Shoki Coe just totally ignored this order, and never abandoned the historical designation of the name of the college. Neither did the Presbyterian Church in Taiwan allow its theological institutions to be called "Sîn-hak Su-īn" (theological institute). The courageous stand that both Shoki Coe and the Presbyterian Church took deserved commendation.

All male students at Tainan Theological College nervously awaited the day when their studies would be abruptly interrupted and they would be drafted into the Kuomintang's military force. When the draft order arrived, the draftees had to leave everything to get ready for the first round of basic training and service (essentially brainwashing on behalf of "China" and learning military skills), or "continuing military education", if one had already had the first round of training and service. The draftees had only a few weeks to report to duty. The basic training times varied from four to six months, the length of service varied between one to three years. The content of "training" included the "immoral and evil nature of communism, stressing that communists were an undisciplined, unscrupulous bunch of rebels, and destroyers of noble Chinese culture, and only the government of Kuomintang was a good and law-abiding one, etc."[38] This was but empty talk; there was no noticeable evidence of good deeds worthy of mentioning. What one saw was but exercises of power and brainwashing as the defence line to ward off any sudden attack from China.

The difficult situation and troubles that the students of Tainan Theological College encountered were large. However, each of the graduates of theological colleges who served in the churches of the Presbyterian Church in Taiwan still had to overcome obstacles and dangerous paths to reach the front line of the mission field.

Centennial Celebration of Christian Mission in Taiwan

British missionary Dr James Maxwell began his medical work and missionary activities in Taiwan on 16 June 1865. By 1965 Christian mission had completed one hundred years. Ten years prior to that, the church in Taiwan had a mission initiative of "Doubling the Church and Members Movement" as a way to celebrate the centennial year. The celebration by the Presbyterian Church in Taiwan was presided over by the Rev. Shoki Coe, moderator of the General Assembly of the church that very year. The position of moderator of the General Assembly normally was elected for a term of one year, and no one was to succeed himself for a consecutive year for a second term. However, Shoki Coe was the only one who was elected and served as moderator two times, the Fourth and the Twelfth General Assembly (1957 and 1965). There was no limit for the position of general secretary. So the Rev. Ńg Bú-tong was elected and had held the position since 1957 when the position was created. The reason that Shoki Coe was elected for a second time to be the moderator, was to announce to the world the Taiwan church's acknowledgement and appreciation of Shoki Coe's forward-looking vision and leadership. It also acknowledged how he had worked along so effectively with the General Secretary Ńg Bú-tong, who in 1955 had initiated the overall strategy of the "Doubling the Church Movement" which now had born tangible fruits as part of the Centenary Celebration.

The two Synods (North and South) of the Presbyterian Church in Taiwan had come together as one General Assembly on 1 May 1951. However this union was mostly symbolic; it did not bring the whole church together or enable the dynamism of the solidarity of the church. Nevertheless this first unified meeting dealt effectively with the issue of joining the WCC and once the relationship between the church in Taiwan and WCC began, Shoki Coe began to bring the church in Taiwan into the international arena. One after another, international exchanges, care and concern, studies, support and relations with foundations and funds started to appear on the doorstep of the church in Taiwan. With this support and input, the Presbyterian Church in Taiwan was able to consolidate and avoid disaster by walking one step ahead of the divisive plots and challenges of the troublemakers who displayed the banners of "Anti-Communism, Defend the Church." The "Anti-Communism, Defend the Church" clique were pro-Kuomintang, befriending the power that was, as well as the "anti-Taiwan" group of people, headed by none other than the "pure gospel" leader Carl McIntire. Beginning from the day that the Presbyterian Church in Taiwan became a member of the WCC until 1965, this group of "anti-communist" Christians used every opportunity to find fault in the church of Taiwan, to scream aloud in criticism, and to make accusations to the government in Taiwan that the WCC was a "pro-communist" organization, and to other churches in Taiwan that WCC was a "liberal" group (which at the time meant not believing in the absolute authority of the Scriptures or in miracles). They even called it "Anti-Christ."

In order to make the Fourth General Assembly of the Presbyterian Church in 1957 a genuinely unified church, both synods voted to discontinue the functions of "synod" and to allow each presbytery to directly relate to the General Assembly and participate in the work of the Assembly. From that time forward, the General Assembly would meet yearly. So it could be said that the first real General Assembly elected Shoki Coe as moderator and Ng Bú-tong as general secretary. The "Doubling the Church" Movement was in its third year. There was great enthusiasm and confidence in the church to move forward to the future.

The year 1965 was the Centenary Celebration of the formation of the Presbyterian Church in Taiwan (and Christian Mission in Taiwan). The Tenth General Assembly of the Presbyterian Church in 1963 voted to hold a solemn special celebration and to invite related churches and agencies to join the celebration, in all twenty churches and agencies. On 16 March 1964, invitations went out to those who were willing to join. On 15 April they gathered to meet at Taipei YMCA for an exchange of ideas. A Preparatory Committee was organized, and the Rev. Chou Lien Hwa (Baptist) was elected Chair, the Rev. Fang Ta-lin (Methodist) the Recording Secretary, the Rev. Ng Bú-tong Executive Secretary.[39] The week of 16–22 June was set for Celebration Week: 16–17 June was designated for celebrative activities in Tainan; 19–20 June in East Coast Taiwan; and 21–22 June in Taipei. There were six celebration events in Tainan: Celebration of One Hundred Years of Mission, Thanksgiving Service, Parade, Thanksgiving Service for the Achievements of the Doubling the Church Movement, Music and Entertainment, and Exhibition of Historical Documents and Material Objects. The most colourful and significant event was the Thanksgiving Service for the Achievements of Doubling the Church Movement, held in the afternoon of 17 June at the Athletic Field of Tióng-êng Middle School (the Presbyterian Boys Middle School), and presided over by the Moderator of the General Assembly, the Rev. Shoki Coe.

The Rev. Chou Lien Hwa, the Chair of the Celebration Preparatory/ Organizing Committee wrote the following report of his involvement and related issues. From the early stages of preparation, the founder and leader of the ICCC (International Christian Council of Churches),[40] Carl McIntire appeared on the horizon. Chou Lien Hwa wrote what happened when the celebration events began:

> Carl McIntire appeared, he wore a badge of a news reporter and exercised personal supervision. The first rumour appeared: two representatives from USSR were going to crush the gate. On this matter I was quite certain and confident that it was not going to happen, because I had made a telephone call to the Entry and Exit Control Office, to report to them that there was a list of approved foreign guests from the Ministry of Foreign Affairs, and that the list had already been given to them, so I was not responsible to "keep the gate," it was up to the immigration officials to do their job. Later, we learned that these two were from the World Presbyterian Alliance,[41] its general secretary, and moderator of the Swiss Reformed Church, their spoken English carried German and Swiss accents so as to be mistaken as representatives from the Soviet Union. They had their passports with them, why the immigration officers did not bother to examine them carefully? They eventually entered the country. But this was only just the beginning of troubles to come.[42]

On the day just before the celebration in Tainan, Chou Lien Hwa was summoned to the office by the Chief of Staff of the Garrison Command's Headquarter in Taipei. The Chief of Staff wanted Chou Lien Hwa to give consent to the following four items:

> A parade would be permitted, but there shall be no sound;
> During the parade, no handout of documents (bills) will be permitted;
> There are quite a few ruffians in Tainan, there must be no contacts or fights with them;
> All activities must end by 11 P.M.[43]

When Chou Lien Hwa returned to the Tainan Hotel, he encountered another sinister thing. The receptionist on duty was told to say that the hotel was full, and that the hotel would not welcome any guest from the Soviet Union. But Chou Lien Hwa insisted that the two best suites be given to the two distinguished guests, and that an American guest would be transferred to another hotel. Chou prevailed.

Next morning, Chou Lien Hwa had to face such questions as "WCC is a pro-communist organization," "presence of Soviet Union representatives," and so on at a press conference. He was too pressed with time to change his clothes to make it to the ten o'clock worship service at Thài-pêng-kéng Church. As the chair of Preparatory Committee, he had to preach. He just put on a choir robe to preach.[44]

That evening, before the parade began, all printed materials, which were originally intended to be distributed at the parade, were destroyed, as was the printing plate at the printer's shop. The parade was organized into two hundred church members per group, and each group was managed and led by a church leader, silently marching—even hymn singing was not allowed. However, the whole parade was very well organized and disciplined; it also was a very dignified parade, and the organizers and leaders felt at ease and pleased. Before eleven o'clock that evening, the last person in the parade had reached the final destination, and the parade was then dismissed. Thus, in this manner, a significant parade of religious nature at a time of martial law was carried out successfully. However, for the parade that was planned to take place in Hoa-liân, although a permit had been obtained from the Police Department, the Centenary Celebration Organizing Committee, upon consultation with local Christian leaders, decided to cancel.[45]

For this Centenary Celebration, there were about two hundreds guests invited from overseas. The delegation from the Presbyterian Church of Canada was thirty persons strong, as was the delegation from the Presbyterian churches in the US. There were also delegates from the Executive Committee of the World Alliance of Presbyterian Churches and representatives of different mission boards and moderators of churches, numbering about forty, and about one hundred representatives of sister churches and overseas Chinese churches in Southeast Asia. They were all enthusiastic participants of this historic event.

The delegation of Presbyterians from the United States was led by the moderator of the United Presbyterian Church, USA, William P. Thompson. William Thompson was elected to be the stated clerk of that church about ten years later. In one of his speeches at a conference on "Church and Human

Rights," he spoke of his impression of the Centenary Celebration of the Presbyterian Church in Taiwan in this way:

> In the summer of 1965, my wife and I visited Taiwan in a party which included twenty-seven persons from the United States. We went to participate in the celebration of one hundred years of Christian witness on that island. We were inspired by the zeal and faithfulness of the Taiwanese Christians whom we met and we rejoiced at the success of the "Doubling the Church Movement" with which the Presbyterian Church in Taiwan observed the centennial. We visited Taipei, Tainan, Kaohsiung, Taichung, Hualien and many other places—everywhere impressed by the energy and the accomplishments of the people.
>
> For me, the climax of the entire experience occurred in Tainan. Following a great rally of Christians in the athletic park, thousands of those in attendance formed a column and marched through the streets of the city carrying lanterns lighted by candles following a band playing "Onward Christian Soldiers." Hundreds of thousands of their fellow citizens lined the streets watching in silence. My friend, Shoki Coe, who was then the moderator of the Presbyterian Church in Taiwan, invited me, because I occupied the same office in the United Presbyterian Church in the USA, to accompany him at the head of the parade. As I joined the marchers, I sensed the tension which pervaded the situation.
>
> I learned that the authorities had granted permission for the parade very reluctantly. It was the first parade permitted under auspices of any other than the government itself. Apparently fearful that the route of the parade might spark a political incident, the officials modified the route of the parade several times, the last only hours before the parade itself. The marchers were forbidden to sing; hence, the single hymn which the band played over and over. At one point, as we turned a corner, a sound like gunfire rang out. Apprehension drained away when it was identified as firecrackers set off by a spectator.[46]

After the June celebration, there was an All-Taiwan Sunday School Rally in Taichung on 5 August and an island-wide Christian Youth Rally in Tainan on 18 August. There was a special celebration sports event held in the athletic field of the Tióng-êng Girls Middle School, 17–22 August. Also scheduled as a concluding part of the celebration series of activities, was the Second Conference on Mission and Evangelism Strategy at Tainan Theological College, 25–30 October. Representatives of partner mission agencies from overseas and local church agencies were invited to participate.

At the time, the secretary of Overseas Missions of the Presbyterian Church of England, the Rev. Boris Anderson, who was the immediate neighbour of Shoki Coe in Tainan from 1948 to 1959 and had been vice-principal of Tainan Theological College, was present at the Centenary Celebration. He had in-depth knowledge of Shoki Coe and his family and was very familiar with the history of the Presbyterian Church in Taiwan in the last one hundred years. He came bringing some historical materials from England for the display at the Centenary event, and also brought with him a short history of the relations between the church in England and the church in Taiwan that he had written, as a resource for the church in Taiwan and partner churches to be used for the forthcoming mission strategy conference in October.

Boris Anderson also did a very significant and meaningful thing for Shoki Coe and his wife, Winifred, as a gift to them for the celebration of the church's one hundred years anniversary. He made arrangements and raised funds from the Overseas Missions' connection for the moderator's spouse to join her husband at the Centenary Celebration. He also especially made it possible for their youngest child Andrew to accompany Winifred. When Andrew left Taiwan with Winifred he was only four years old; returning now, he was a more mature nine-year-old boy. It was summer months, school was not in session, so his class work would not be affected and there were other relatives who could take care of the other three siblings who were left behind in England. In this way, half of the Coes were able to be together as family, and to celebrate this rare event of the one hundredth anniversary of the Church in Taiwan.

60黃能傑牧師於1903年12月28日就任

Fig. 1. The ordination of Nĝ Lêng-kiat on December 28, 1903, at Lâm-á-khe^n Church. Photo courtesy of the Archive of the Presbyterian Church in Taiwan.

Fig. 2. The Rev. Nĝ Lêng-kiat and his second wife Tân Oat-ti and daughter Ka-biaū. Nĝ Lêng-kiat married Tân Oat-tī a widow, after Giâm-hân died. She had been a nurse at the Chiong-hòa Christian Hospital when she was young, 1909. Photo courtesy of Nĝ Ki-chhiong.

Fig. 3. Shoki Coe (front row, first on left) is about four years old in this family photo, c. 1918.

Fig. 4. The Rev. Nĝ Sū-bēng, Shoki Coe's father, c. 1940.

Fig. 5. The Rev. Nĝ Sū-bēng, his wife Lîm Kim, and the family (front row from left), Shoki Coe, Bêng-hui, An-hui, Siok-eng, and Éng-hui, c. 1925.

Fig. 6. Shoki Coe (middle) and his cousins during summer vacation when he was a high school student. On left, Âng Su-êng (son of Shoki's father's sister), and right, Lîm Sūi-hûn (Shoki's maternal uncle's son), c. 1932.

Fig. 7. Shoki Coe (second row, second from left) and friends at Tokyo University YMCA Hostel, c. 1935. Source: Toshikazu Miwa.

Fig. 8. Shoki Coe (back row, center) and students at the Tokyo University YMCA Hostel before a meal, c. 1934. Source: Toshikazu Miwa.

Fig. 9. Shoki Coe (third from left standing) and friends at a Christmas skit at the YMCA Hostel, Saturday, December 24, 1934. Shoki was a main character and director of the skit. Source: Toshikazu Miwa.

Fig. 10. At the YMCA Hostel every Sunday, there were about one hundred children who came to the Sunday School operated by the Y residents. Here Shoki stands with some of the children he taught, c. 1935. Source: Toshikazu Miwa.

Fig. 11. Shoki Coe and David
Landsborough Jr. in front of
the Landsborough home, 1937.
Source: David Landsborough.

Fig. 12. The Landsboroughs during World War II, (from left) David Landsborough
Sr, Jean, a student from London named Marjorie Messenger, Shoki Coe, Mrs. Landsborough, c. 1938.

FIg. 13. Westminster College faculty and students, 1940. Shoki Coe is second from left in the middle row. Source: Westminster College.

Fig. 14. Wedding photo of Shoki Coe and Winifred Sounder, with George Hood (left) and Jean Landsborough (right), 12 August 1944.

Fig. 15. Shoki and David Coe, c. 1945–1946.

Fig. 16. First graduating class of Tainan Theological College since Shoki became principal, March 1950. The moderator of the South Synod and the principal are sitting in the front row. Source: Tiuⁿ Tek-hiong.

Fig. 17. The Coe family before they left Taiwan for England (circa 1957). Source: Ko Chùn-bêng/ C. M. Kao.

Fig. 18. Shoki Coe and colleague Desmond Tutu and his wife, in front of the Episcopal Center, New York City, c. 1981. Source: Gūi Sūi-bêng.

Fig. 19. Shoki and Winifred Coe at home after retirement.
Photo taken by Tiuⁿ Chhian-hūi,, and provided by Sun Hông-tìn.

Fig. 20. Shoki Coe's visit with Lee Teng-hui, vice-president of
Taiwan, in 1987. Clare Anderson is sitting in the background.

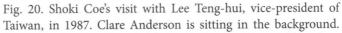

5

Contextualization in Action (1965–1980)
Organizing Ecumenical and Political Movements

During the busy time of celebrating the one hundred years of the gospel reaching Taiwan, Shoki Coe was also personally busy in making preparations and necessary arrangements for his pending resignation as principal of Tainan Theological College. In his letter of 27 July 1965 to his friends, he mentioned that he had already accepted a position as Associate Director of the WCC's Theological Education Fund, which would use London as its base of operation. As this was to work with theological education, he hoped he would be able to come back to Asia for a visit every now and then. If he and his friends in Taiwan thought that this future visit would include Taiwan and Tainan Theological College, they were wrong, because after he left Taiwan in November 1965, his name was blacklisted. Not until 1987, with great effort of the then vice-president of the country, Lee Teng-hui, was Shoki finally given special dispensation to return and walk on the soil of his native land, a full 22 years after he left. He had been free to travel around the world and to all other Asian countries, but his native land Taiwan was not able to welcome him home for such a long time. This was one tragedy of his life.

Fulfilling the Mandates for the Theological Education Fund

The theological college Shoki Coe loved was handed over to Dr Choan Seng Song, who had just completed his doctoral degree requirements at Union Theological Seminary in New York. Just like Shoki, who was only 35 years old when he took over the college, his successor, Dr C. S. Song, was 36 years old at the time. As the moderator of the Presbyterian Church in Taiwan, he felt he must give the church a proper transition into the second century of the history of the church in Taiwan. So Shoki decided to stay on until November, when the conference on mission strategy, "Marching Forward Together into the Second Century," was over before he took leave.

Shoki Coe resigned as principal of Tainan Theological College in 1965 to return to England as the associate director of the Theological Education Fund of WCC. The director of the Fund, whose office was based in New York, had the main task for raising and managing funds. As associate director Shoki Coe was responsible for the operation and work assignments and established the assistance and supporting programs for theological education around the world that continued for 14 years. He could also choose the location for his office. The headquarters were set up in a church located at 13 London Road, Bromley, Kent, a suburb of London. A main factor for choosing this location in Kent was that Winifred and children had already settled for a few years in a house they purchased further south in Seaford, Sussex.

The Theological Education Fund was established in 1958 as part of the integration process of the International Missionary Council with the WCC. When the IMC decided to merge with the WCC, it set out to establish an agency that would assist "the third world, mission field, and younger churches" to take up the task of developing ways of "self-support and self-propagation," that is, for the churches that were "on the way to catch up" to train their theological students and ministry corps. The main instigators of the Fund were mostly from "older" or "senior" churches and agencies of Europe and North America. Those from North America included United Board for Christian Higher Education in Asia and the chair of this agency, Dr Henry Van Dusen. Van Dusen respected Shoki's ability very much and took him under his wing, so Shoki was invited to attend the International Missionary Council in Ghana in 1958. Shoki was then elected a member of the Research Commission on Theological Education of the Council. With this background, Shoki Coe was able to participate in this rare opportunity of launching a new program. Nineteen years after this, in 1977, he was able to see the conclusion of the Theological Education Fund which he directed and let its continuing organization, the Programme on Theological Education, carry on the next phase of development.

During its early founding period, the director of the Fund was Dr Charles Ranson. Dr Ranson was with Shoki Coe at the First Institute of Theology held in Bangkok in 1956. At that time there was no seminary in Asia that had courses of study leading to an MDiv degree. However, at that meeting the theological schools in South East Asia began to join hands to work together. By the following year in 1957, the Association of Theological Schools in South East Asia (ATESEA) was formed. In 1966, fifteen schools of ATESEA came together to form South East Asia Graduate School of Theology and initiated a joint Master in Theology degree program.

During the International Missionary Council in Accra, Ghana, in 1958, three mandates were given to work for theological education in the third world. After the fund was established, these three mandates were set out in three different stages in order to be effectively implemented.[1] The first mandate was implemented from 1958 to 1965. The main goal of the fund's first mandate was to raise the academic standard of students in theological education institutions as much as the situation would allow; improve and strengthen indigenous theological education; promote regional responsibilities; and encourage creative theological thinking that would lead to a higher academic level to meet the need of continuing education in the field and the diverse needs of ministry.

The second mandate was implemented from 1965 to 1971. It was felt that in theological education there was a tendency to focus only on raising the academic level. Therefore, the second mandate set another directional goal to deepen the identity with indigenous communities and situations. The excellence of theological education would lie in leading students, when encountering the gospel, to be competent in taking into full consideration their own culture, ways of thinking, and the realities of the human situation, thus leading the church in dialogue and interaction with its living situation and environment. This mandate required both teachers and learners to have a deeper understanding of the realities of the cultural and religious situation they were in so as to be able to understand better their own missionary communities as well as the world and situation they had been sent into. Then they would be able to carry out their entrusted tasks in life effectively.

The third mandate, implemented from 1971 to 1977, was to continue pursuing the path of contextualization, of what came out of the indigenous effort, with the aim of renewing and changing the direction of theological education. During this mandate, the fund concentrated its energy on discerning and discovering what theological education in the third world could give to the worldwide church in terms of fresh and creative visions and hope.

The immediate superior and the director during the first six years of Shoki Coe's work at the Theological Education Fund (1965–1971) was Dr James F. Hopewell, and the head office was still located in New York, while the secondary office was set up in Bromley, Kent, England, where Shoki Coe was the supervising staff. In addition to Hopewell and Shoki, there were three other associate directors, each responsible for a continent or area of the world—Africa, South America, Europe and North America. Shoki Coe's main responsibility was Asia, Australia and the Pacific region. In order to carry out his duties, he had to visit theological educational institutes in the region he covered, so he was constantly on the road, spending about half of his time travelling.

Holding a Republic of China passport to travel was indeed a troublesome affair, because that country kept on breaking diplomatic relations with more countries in the world. And all these countries that cut relations with Taiwan particularly took note of China's opinion, that Taiwan was not a country at all. So it was very difficult for Shoki to obtain visas to these countries. After suffering all sorts of inconveniences and even insults, Shoki decided in June 1966 to begin the process of application to the Home Office of the British government to be naturalized as a British citizen. After one year, on 20 June 1967, he finally received his certificate of naturalization as a British citizen. In the application paper he requested that his legal family name be changed to Coe. During the years between 1937 and 1947, he had been known as Shoki Ko, using Japanese pronunciation, so a change from Ko to Coe did not change the pronunciation, only the spelling.

In September 1969, the president of Princeton Theological Seminary, James I. McCord, as the chair of the World Alliance of Reformed Churches, and on behalf of the Executive Committee, extended an invitation to Shoki Coe to apply for the position of general secretary of the World Alliance. Shoki Coe felt that he wanted to put all his energy into theological institutions and theological education, that he was not keen about being involved in church politics and that furthermore he did not want to be separated from his family again. In 1965 he and Winifred had purchased a house in Seaford, named "the Bye." So he responded with "thanks, but no thanks" and continued his work in an associate position.

Shoki Coe was elected the director of the Theological Education Fund in June 1971, to have overall responsibility in raising the standards of theological education and the training of ministerial staff on all continents. Although he oversaw all the work, he still maintained a particular responsibility for work in Northeast Asia, namely Korea and Japan.

In 1971 and 1972, Shoki without reservation invited a theological educator from Africa, Desmond Tutu, and a woman theologian, Ivy Chou, to be his associates to work with the two who were retained from the former administration. Thus Shoki now had a total of four associates to work with him. Aharon Sapsezian was responsible for Latin America and the Middle East region; James Berquist South Asia, South Pacific and Caribbean; Ivy Chou Southeast Asia in conjunction with the Foundation of Theological Education in South East Asia; while the entire African continent and Madagascar were entrusted to the hands of Desmond Tutu. This period of time could well be called the golden era of TEF. There was a director and four associate directors, with a total of 14 staff in the TEF office.

In July 1975, Desmond Tutu was asked by the first Bishop of Johannesburg to serve as the dean of the cathedral. Both Shoki Coe and Desmond Tutu considered this to be a great challenge, and difficult tasks would be ahead of him. They finally agreed that Desmond had to resign from the work at the Theological Education Fund to engage in the movement to struggle for human rights by abolishing racism and achieving racial equality. So Desmond Tutu resigned and together with his family moved back to Johannesburg. Archbishop Tutu was a recipient of the Nobel Peace Prize in 1984.

During the 1970s, when Shoki Coe was responsible for theological education in Asia, which included Korea, the Korean church was severely suppressed and persecuted by the Park Chung Hi regime. In July 1974, the general secretary of the National Council of Churches in Korea and Professor Moon of Hanguk Theological Seminary were arrested, and the former dean of Yongsei University College of Theology was imprisoned for eight months before he was released. In addition five other theological professors (three from Yongsei University and two from Hanguk Seminary) were suspended.

In the director's report of 1975, Shoki mentioned, though not directly related to theological education, that all Asian countries except Japan were under dictatorial governments; even India was in the hands of powerful authoritarians. In the annual report of 1976, Shoki included the ordination of the former Associate Director Desmond Tutu as Bishop of Lesotho in Southern Africa. On 9–10 February 1976, Shoki Coe and his associate who was responsible for theological education in Latin America, Dr Aharon Sapsezian, attended a Consultation on Attempts of New Methodology in Theological Education held in Sao Paolo, Brazil, and then visited other places in South America. Shoki used the breaks in his travel itinerary to attend a preparatory meeting for the formation of the Brazil Chapter of Formosans for Self-Determination.

On 21 July 1977, Shoki Coe's work as the director of the Theological Education Fund ended, thus marking the completion of the fund. On that day, the office at Bromley, Kent, England, closed to give way to a new organization, the Programme for Theological Education (PTE), which began on 1 August under the directorship of the Rev. Dr Aharon Sapsezian. The office was moved from England to Geneva, Switzerland. And from that day on, Shoki Coe's position was consultant to the Programme for Theological Education with an office in Geneva. Other than travel to Asia and other places in relation to his job, or short periods of office work in Geneva, Shoki was able to spend time working at home in Seaford, England, continuing to be in constant communication with the office in Geneva. This continued for two years until he finally cast off this burden.

According to his annual report of 1977 (July), from the beginning of the third mandate of TEF that began in 1971, he received US$760,000 undesignated, and US$1,700,000 designated funds. Now the TEF was able to leave undesignated funds of US$700,000 and designated funds of US$750,00 for PTE. For twenty years, from the start to completion of TEF, the fund received about US$13,000,000. For the first mandate (1958–1964) it disbursed about US$5,600,000, and for the second mandate (1965–1970) $4,000,000, and the third mandate (November 1971–1977) about US$13,000,000. The director mentioned especially that during his tenure, he had given financial assistance to about seven hundred theological education institutions in developing areas of the world.

In the summer of 1979, just before Shoki Coe's retirement, with the financial support of PTE and the cooperation of the Christian Conference of Asia, a consultation was held in Hong Kong on Chinese theological education. The hosts were Tao Fong Shan Christian Study Institute and the Christian Conference of Asia. The participants included people from Taiwan Theological College, Tainan Theological College, Theology Department of Fujen Catholic University (Taiwan), Jesuit theologians from Taiwan, Trinity Theological College in Singapore, the Religion Department of Chung Chi College of Hong Kong Chinese University, and others. Also in attendance were Tiuⁿ Sūi-hiông and Tiō Chhong-jîn from Taiwanese churches in North America. This was one of Shoki Coe's last major undertakings before he retired.

Organizing a Movement for Taiwanese Self-Determination

The "Formosan People for Self-Determination" movement was initiated by the Rev. Dr Shoki Coe, the Rev. Dr Nĝ Bú-tong, Dr Lîm Chong-gī (medical doctor) and the Rev. Dr Chôan Sēng Sòng on 20 March 1973. On that day there were representatives, such as Tiân Hông-bō˙, Lîm Tiat-hu (Albert Lin), Nĝ Khun-giâm, Chiu Gô˙ Siù-hūi, numbering about twenty from different places getting together to establish this movement.

From its beginning, Dr C. S. Song had served as its secretary, publishing an occasional journal named *Chhut-thâu-thiⁿ* (English edition) to make known the desire and hope of Taiwanese and the statements issued by the Presbyterian Church in Taiwan. The journal strived to introduce and interpret them to Taiwanese living overseas and church leaders around the world and to solicit their support. Fortunately, the Rev. C. S. Song kept a file and bound copy of the journal as records and documents, for any researchers who wished to know about the persons involved and the issues discussed during the period between March 1973 and January 1980. In the preface, the Rev. Song reflected on their motive for forming the movement. He said,

> We came together to discuss, to debate, to agonize over the issue, to search for strategy and to brainstorm each other's thoughts. Our motive was not for selfish reasons; we did this for the sake of political thoughts of Taiwan. Our zealous love for Taiwan made us have no other choice than to do this. What we do is but a return of the grace and gift we have received. We do not care about our

busy professional schedules, we commit ourselves to this movement, because we believe, as Christians, our love of Taiwan must be turned into practical love of this land and people. We, four persons, Dr Shoki Coe (minister), Dr Lîm Chong-gī (professor), Dr Nĝ Bú-tong (minister), and Dr Chôan Sēng Sòng (minister), do not desire anything but democracy and freedom of Taiwanese people.[2]

In response to the "Public Statement on Our National Fate" of the Presbyterian Church in Taiwan on 29 December 1971, the founders of the Self-Determination Movement, on 25 December 1972, based on "Christian Understanding," made a statement, "Declaration of Taiwanese (Formosans) for Self-Determination Movement." It states, "[Self-determination] is closely linked with our own future and destiny. Regardless of who we are, we cannot deny that we have sacred rights of freedom to determine our own destiny. Therefore, we appeal to all Taiwanese at home and abroad to come together to strive and solemnly announce to the world our firm desire to fight for our own reasonable choice of freedom.[3]"

The main goals of the "Taiwanese for Self-Determination Movement" are[4]: (1) to attain a stronger manifestation of Christian conviction of human rights for Taiwan; (2) to promote the cause of self-determination for the political future of Taiwan; and (3) to diligently work to build a democratic and free society in Taiwan.

The plan of action is: (1) to mobilize Taiwanese Christians at home and abroad to exercise Christian responsibility toward Taiwan; (2) to sensitize the political consciousness of the people of Taiwan at home and abroad; (3) to gain wider public support—individually and corporately; (4) to relate to other Formosan organizations striving to fulfill the same goals; and (5) to create a political front that would demand recognition by the governments presently involved in determining the future of Taiwan.

In the middle of April 1973, four initiators and founders of the Self-Determination Movement jointly wrote an open letter to fellow Taiwanese. The whole text follows:[5]

Our Dear Fellow Taiwanese in Taiwan:

Through this open letter and the attached documents, we wish to send you our greetings and to inform you of what we have been doing for the future of Taiwan. As you no doubt realize, this is a very critical time for Taiwan. Our future is at stake. If we do not act now, the chance of our surviving the international power politics is slight. To be fully aware of the critical situation is the first step toward guaranteeing our freedom and human rights.

During these past few months, those of us who are very much concerned about the destiny of Taiwan became extremely alarmed by the possibility that the future of Taiwan would be decided without our participation. We, that is, you and me, those of us who regard Taiwan as our homeland, are to be bypassed, ignored and exploited for the political interest of the ruling powers, both domestic and foreign. Can we continue to keep quiet in the face of such imminent danger? Should we once again submit ourselves to ruthless manipulation by those who have power over us? Are we to raise no question as to who we are, why we have no right to determine our own political future? And should we pretend to give support to the illusion of "Recovering China" only to bring downfall upon ourselves? Or can we allow ourselves to be deceived by economic prosperity into believing that nothing disastrous may happen to Taiwan?

The answer is a thousand times and three thousand times No! That is why we started the movement called Formosan Christians for Self-Determination. If you read the attached documents with care, you will have no difficulty in knowing our basic intention and purpose. The right of self-determination is the sacred right for all human beings. But the sad reality of the world is that no one is going to recognize our sacred human right unless we claim it, fight for it and appeal to the conscience of the people. That is why we have to speak out, make our cause known and keep bringing it before the nations of the world.

The movement for the self-determination of Taiwan has been receiving strong and enthusiastic support from the Taiwanese in the United States of America, Canada, Japan and Europe. And on March twentieth of this year, a news conference was held at the National Press Club in Washington, D.C., for this important cause. There and then we pledged to stand behind the Movement and work toward the goal of self-determination.

We also ask you to stand behind our common effort. You should keep yourself informed of what is happening internationally. You should also seek occasion to discuss your concern with your friends. Let us remember those of us both from and in Taiwan are determined to take the matter into our own hands, unless we decide to fight for our own rights, we cannot hope for a bright future. When the moment of decision arrives, let us be ready and united in making the right decision to ensure our freedom and rights.

We remember you constantly in our thoughts and prayers.

Yours sincerely, (Signed)
Shoki Coe, Wu-tong Huang (Nĝ Bú-tong), Tsung-Yi Lin (Lîm Chong-gī), Choan Seng Song

Four initiators and founders of the Self-Determination Movement also called a consultation, "Salvation Today for Taiwan," from 28 February to 3 March 1974 in Wuppertal-Barmen, Germany. There were 132 representatives from all over Europe participating in this meeting. The consultation adopted a statement that was read at the Germarkerkirche Evangelical Reformed Church during the worship service. This was the church in which forty years ago, at the time of the Nazi regime in Germany, the German Confessional Church expressed its resistance to the dictatorial regime that had caused tens of millions of people to suffer cruel treatment.[6]

Shoki Coe gave a special address at this "Salvation Today for Taiwan" consultation in Germany. Following is the transcript of the address:[7]

Honored guests: fellow Taiwanese, and fellow Taiwanese Christians.

As the Chairman of the organizing committee of this conference, it is my great pleasure and honor to extend to you all a warm welcome.

I would like especially to welcome cordially our honored guests who are also our hosts, because here in Germany—our host country—the Churches have supported us both spiritually and materially. For the support I wish on behalf of all people of Taiwan to express deep appreciation. We share a common faith in Christ which transcends national and racial divisions.

I wish also to extend a special welcome to those of our fellow countrymen who are not Christians, but who share with the rest of us the deep concern about the future destiny of our homeland and people. We look forward, as we proceed with this important conference, to have dialogue and consultation among all of us as we deliberate our own future, namely, the future of the 15 million people of Taiwan, at this critical time.

Today is the twenty-eight of February. I do not need to explain what this date means in Taiwan's calendar. But for some of our honored guests I must explain its significance.

Twenty-seven years ago today a tragic event was taking place in Taiwan. The people rose against the oppression of the occupying forces under the command of the Nationalist General Ch'en Yi. He and his soldiers had proved to be not the hoped for liberators from Japanese oppression; instead they had themselves become oppressors. The price paid by the people of Taiwan for that rebellion was the bloody massacre of more than twenty thousand Taiwanese, including many of our national leaders. This dreadful event marked the beginning of the search for our Taiwanese identity, and for true liberation.

Furthermore, the place where we now meet (Wuppertal-Barmen) is also very significant in the history of the Church in Germany. It is not necessary for me to explain this to our hosts, but most of my fellow countrymen may not know that in this place forty years ago, the confessing Church of Germany took its stand against the Nazi regime.

Keeping in mind the time and place of this meeting, we can see more clearly the two-fold purpose of this consultation. On the one hand, our Consultation is a response to the message of the Bangkok Conference on "Salvation Today"—that salvation be re-discovered and re-affirmed as liberation, in which the authentic self-identity of all peoples as human beings will be assured; on the other hand, it is a response to the confession made by our Church in Taiwan two years ago, affirming that the right of people to determine their own destiny is the right given by God.

Therefore, our aim and purpose is to understand more clearly and more deeply what this means, and what we should do about it.

In conclusion, may I give a reminder that 1974 is to be celebrated as the Year of Human Rights, and many consultations are taking place in different parts of the world. Thus, what we endeavor to do in this consultation will constitute part of the world-wide effort of those who seek visible and concrete manifestations of Human Rights in particular situations. So, with these, I hope and pray that our coming together will be meaningful and fruitful in all we say and do.

By March 1974, there were about thirty branches of the movement established in different parts of North America to carry on the responsibilities of planning and activities. And after the consultation, the "European Branch of Self-Determination" was established with the leadership of the Rev. Roger Chao (Tiō Iú-gôan) to continue the task.[8]

One very significant event occurred on 6 September 1974. One hundred sixty-five Taiwanese came together in Vienna, Austria, from Brazil, the United States of America, Canada, Japan and Europe. At this gathering, they organized the "Worldwide United Association of Taiwanese." The purpose of the association was to promote fellowship and mutual help among the people of Taiwan and to unite the people of Taiwan both at home and abroad into one great family to protect and defend to the best of their ability the human rights and welfare of Taiwanese compatriots. Mr. Koeh Êng-kiat was elected as the president of the association at this meeting.[9]

In April 1975, in the event of, or as a result of, Taiwan's Chinese Kuomintang regime's order to ban the publication and confiscate existing copies of the romanized version of the Taiwanese language Bible, the Self-Determination Movement members were able to rally twenty denominations and church agencies to issue a joint statement.

In response to the confiscation of Bibles, on 18 November 1975, the Presbyterian Church in Taiwan issued a statement "Our Appeal." The statement points out that the government's reason for banning and confiscating romanized Taiwanese Bibles is that it contravenes the policy of promoting the "national language." This policy is itself unconstitutional. As the nation's constitution guarantees the freedom of religion, the government must not act against the nation's constitution. Based on the principle of freedom of religion guaranteed in the constitution, the statement, among other things, appeals to the government to return the confiscated Bibles and to permit publication and distribution of Bibles in any language. The statement reiterates that the purpose and meaning of the church's earlier statement "On our National Fate" in 1971 was based on Christian faith and conviction to fulfil its mission to pursue justice, freedom and peace, and thus to continue the appeal for solidarity to work toward that end.

The Fifth WCC assembly met at the Kenyatta Conference Center in Nairobi, Kenya, 21 November–10 December 1975. There were nearly 2,500 participants from more than 150 nations around the world in attendance, but it also was noted:

> What a profound sadness it is to realize Christians in Taiwan were conspicuously absent. Where is Taiwan in this world community? Where are Taiwanese Christians in this worldwide Christian fellowship? From East Asia most of the countries were there—Japan, Korea, the Philippines, Malaysia, Indonesia, and so forth. But Taiwan was a missing link. People asked why? They were saddened by the absence of representatives of the Presbyterian Church in Taiwan, a church which had two hundred thousand members and over one thousand congregations. The reason for their absence was simple: the Nationalist government refused exit permits to their delegates.[10]

Due to the absence of delegates of the Presbyterian Church in Taiwan, right after the assembly the general secretary of the WCC, Dr Philip Potter, wrote a letter to the Rev. Ko Chùn-bêng, the general secretary of the Presbyterian Church in Taiwan, to show his solidarity and sympathy, as well as support for the statement, "Our Appeal."[11] Similarly, on 11 December, the president of the World Alliance of Reformed Churches, Dr William Thompson, and its general secretary, Dr Edmond Perret, also jointly sent a cablegram to Rev. Ko Chùn-bêng, commending the courage of the church in Taiwan and promised through the publication of the alliance and governmental channels to disseminate the statement "Our Appeal" to all parts of the world.[12]

On 16 August 1977, as President Carter of the United States of America was on the verge of implementing normal relations with China, the Presbyterian Church in Taiwan issued another statement, "Declaration of Human Rights." In terms of the history of Taiwan, this declaration signified an in-depth expression of Christian faith, which is full of love for the land and people and an honest proposal in response to a people who were oppressed and suppressed by authoritarian powers. Everybody who participated in the draft of this declaration had their will written in anticipation of possible dangerous consequences. The words that drew most attention to the people and government authorities were these: "In order to achieve the desired goal of independence and freedom for the people of Taiwan in this critical international situation, we urge our government to face reality and take effective measures, whereby Taiwan may become a new and independent country."

At the stated meeting of the Twenty-Fifth General Assembly of the Presbyterian Church in Taiwan, meeting on the campus of Tainan Theological College, 27–31 March 1978, two significant resolutions were made. The first one was the election of the general secretary of the General Assembly, and second, the approval of the report of the Standing Council of the General Assembly which included the item of what it had earlier approved, the "Declaration of Human Rights." With an extremely careful and thorough process in paper balloting, the voting of both items took place. On the reelection of the Rev. Ko Chùn-bêng (C. M. Kao) as the general secretary, 225 votes of yes, 49 votes of no, eight votes blank (that is, abstention) were tallied. Thus the Rev. Kao was elected successfully. As for the issue of approval of the report (that is, retroactive approval of) "Declaration of Human Rights," the tally was 235 approved, 49 against, ten abstentions. So, the declaration became the official statement of the Presbyterian Church in Taiwan.

This action of solidarity of the Presbyterian Church in Taiwan had far-reaching repercussions. The Chinese Kuomintang authorities arrested, prosecuted, convicted, and imprisoned the Rev. C. M. Kao for "harboring a seditious element (person)," Mr. Shih Ming-teh (Si Bêng-tek), whom the authorities considered to be the main culprit of the "Formosa Incident"[13] in December 1979. The arrest happened on 18 April 1980. From that day on Shoki Coe put even greater efforts into rallying the Self-Determination people to work toward the release of C. M. Kao and the ultimate goal of saving Taiwan from further imprisonment and oppression. In reality, after the arrest and imprisonment of the Rev. C. M. Kao, the Self-Determination Movement had concluded one stage. The initiators of the movement ceased to use "self-determination" as the core of their activities. The reasons were:

1. In the "Formosa Incident" itself, and the subsequent imprisonment of the Rev. C. M. Kao, the entire Presbyterian Church in Taiwan was sucked into the whirlpool of Taiwan's democratization movement. Due to the involvement of persons like C. M. Kao and other clergy, the Chinese Kuomintang from then on was no longer hesitant to regard the Presbyterian Church in Taiwan as a political entity.

2. The "Formosa Incident" was a careful plan of the Chinese Kuomintang authorities to wipe out the leaders of the democracy movement as "rebels" or "seditious elements." There were numbers of church members and ministers of the Presbyterian Church in Taiwan among those convicted. The church believed it should suffer alongside the oppressed, whether they were Christians or not, as part of its mission.

3. The movement of democratization of Taiwan was the social and political expression of the Self-Determination Movement. In this manner, the Self-Determination Movement which had started as a Christian body, now broke its boundaries, and joined the greater movement for the "Chhut-thâu-thin"[14] (liberation) of Taiwanese, and attracted wider public response and support.

On 15 December 1979, the "United Front for Establishing Taiwan Nation" was organized. Its important constituents included United for Independence of Taiwan, Formosan Association for Public Affairs, and the Taiwanese Self-Determination Movement. The Self-Determination Movement emphasized the human rights and freedom of the people and did not regard itself as a political organization. However, the Chinese Kuomintang had determined that the Presbyterian Church in Taiwan was an organization which was more political than religious, because it had earlier made a public statement of "Declaration of Human Rights" (1978) to appeal to Kuomintang authorities to make Taiwan a new and independent country, applying its Christian faith to social concern to work closely with people of the same mind. So the authorities used the Formosa Incident of 10 December 1979 as an excuse to arrest many church people. The leaders of the Self-Determination Movement, particularly people like Shoki Coe, then set out to raise funds to be used to defend political prisoners and to seek their release. By connecting and interacting with the people in Taiwan, through all means of communication, the overseas Taiwanese self-determination people tried to raise the conscientious awareness of Taiwan identity and engage in education to promote the idea of establishing a nation. Therefore, after 1980, the year Shoki Coe retired from TEF/PTE, he began to work closely together with Professor Peng Ming-min (Phêⁿ Bêng-bín) and Professor Chhòa Tông-êng to tour all over North America to promote the idea, to raise funds and to call for solidarity of Taiwanese of the same mind to work together for a common goal until his death in 1988.

6

Active Retirement (1980–1988)
Final Reflections

While continuing his active concern for theological education, maintaining connections with the ecumenical church and fellowship, responding to occasional requests for his personal appearance, and being actively involved with the Taiwanese Self-Determination Movement, Shoki Coe tried to stay home in England after his retirement in 1979.

His former colleagues, students and friends scattered around the globe still maintained their high respect and love of him, and desired to see him. He was also a very hospitable person, so many came to his home, "the Bye," in Seaford, Sussex, England, to visit him. His wife was also very kind and sincere in receiving visitors from the younger generation. Many of the moderators, or pastors from Taiwan, when visiting Europe or coming for further studies, made a special effort to come see him at "the Bye," which was almost turned into a hostel. Shoki and his wife set aside one room as a guest room.

Hospitality at Home

They might not provide big meals like Taiwanese and Americans who were accustomed to entertaining guests, but they did provide proper English family meals for visitors with sincere hospitality. The visitors might have found that the Coes did not live a life of plenty. Food in England was not as plentiful as in America or even in Taiwan. They lived on very limited pensions, and life was simple.

I visited the Rev. Shoki Coe two times at the couple's home in Seaford. Both times Mrs. Coe was away receiving treatment for an eye ailment. Because Shoki knew little about cooking, he had to follow carefully the instructions given by his wife to put the meat pie that had been prepared and seasoned into the oven, set the prescribed temperature, and bake for thirty minutes. For soup, Shoki heated up the precooked soup, and for salad he took fresh vegetable salad out of a container. From Shoki's friends in Japan, I learned that he was particularly fond of Japanese and Chinese cuisine and often said, "At home there are only English dishes to eat, so I always think of the cuisine of my homeland."

Some former students or friends from Taiwan would invariably bring something with a Taiwan native flavour as gifts on their subsequent visits. One characteristic of Taiwanese is that they do not care very much about big and elaborately decorated houses or beautiful and expensive clothes, but they do care very much about what they eat, to the extent that whenever they see a relative or a friend, they would always ask, "Have you had enough to eat?" All Shoki's former students who visited him had the impression that their master, to whom they owed much gratitude, did not have the good fortune of enjoying good food. They were living in a rather remote corner of a foreign land, where it was hard to obtain Taiwanese food, and they lacked the skills to cook native Taiwan dishes. Visitors, after taking leave of them, would ask friends in England to try to find something with a homeland flavour which might be obtainable in England to send to the Coes to express their honour and appreciation.

Seaford is a small town in southern England with a residential population of 1,600. It is on the shore, and at one time in the past a tourist town. The Coes' residence was not far from the shore and was built on top of a cliff on higher ground, so there was no beach connected with it or any access to the beach. However, to the Coes it was a place to explore the beauty of nature. Shoki rented a small hut in the nature park, where he stored some tools to gather natural plants on the slope, clothing for exercise, drinking water and so on. On good days, he could roam around and be an explorer in the natural environment.

Whenever a former student came to visit, if he had time and the weather was favourable, Shoki would act as a guide to take the visitor for outdoor sightseeing. Once when Tiuⁿ Chhian-hūi came to see him and Winifred in Seaford and they did a little bit sightseeing of historic sites in the outskirts of the city, Tiuⁿ Chhian-hūi realized that Shoki was wearing his decades old "most favorite suit jacket." He carefully took good care of that jacket. Tiuⁿ Chhian-hūi was much moved by this incident. It also showed Shoki's simple lifestyle, hardworking and thrifty, in order to save precious resources for his children's education and to help the needs of churches around the world. Shoki tried to save expenses on food and clothing, but he had to spend for the maintenance of the house. He said that one time when a big wind swept over his house, three tiles were blown off the roof and the cost of repairs caused him quite a headache. To fix each tile properly in place, the labour cost him over £100 each.

The Coes' residence had a big lawn in the backyard. Shoki told me that he was an expert in getting rid of weeds. He would demonstrate, taking an iron bar with a flattened tip, sticking it into the ground, giving it a little twist to one side, and then the weed came out with its roots and could be easily disposed of. The lawn was green, clean and lovely. He must have spent a lot time giving it proper care, with fertilizer and water, to keep it that way. There was a strip of land reserved to plant flowers and some green vegetables. The flowers were blooming beautifully at the time of my visit.

On one occasion Shoki invited me to take a little walk with him to the town. On the edge of town, there was a church and Shoki pointed out that it was a United Reformed Church where he had been actively participating. Due to his vast knowledge and experience as well as active participation, he was elected an elder of that church. I was quite taken aback. Why an elder? Once a minister, is not that person a minister for life? Shoki said, "I am retired from a minister's position and rest from it, but I am an 'elder' now. I must be actively involved in the tasks of an elder now. I need to continue to be active." I was quite moved by Shoki's attitude toward life and his untiring spirit of service to the Lord. It has been more than twenty years since that meeting with him, yet my heart is still burning hot with that inspiring experience.

The most frequently used airports and air travel routes for Shoki Coe after his retirement were between London and New York. He would be present at occasions when he was asked to give speeches, to conduct a wedding for a friend's family, or to raise funds for Taiwanese causes particularly in relation to the church and future of Taiwan. He was a frequent speaker at gatherings of the Taiwanese Christian Church Council in North America.

Mrs. Gô˙ Lâi-hó was in charge of student life, and a counselor to students, when Shoki Coe was principal at Tainan Theological College. Her residence in New York became a regular hostel and temporary residence for Shoki Coe in New York City. On some occasions, those who cared about the church and their homeland Taiwan would volunteer to raise funds to defray his travel costs. Whenever Shoki was in New York, and had enough time, he would visit Taiwanese churches on the East Coast of the United States. In addition, the Rev. Ông Chài-heng, an alumnus of Tainan Theological College who was a pastor in Chicago, also did his part in helping out with the cost of Shoki's travel and programme in the United States.

During Shoki's visits in the New York area, Mr. Gūi Sūi-bêng (also known as Ben Wei) was his personal driver, taking him to visit and conduct his business. In every visit, Shoki would be going back and forth between New York City and Washington, D.C. In New York City, there was 475 Riverside Drive, the Interchurch Center, which housed many national offices of different denominations and many ecumenical agencies. And in Washington, D.C., of course there were the White House, both houses of the US Congress, the embassy of the Kuomintang Chinese government, and Taiwanese political activists such as Phêⁿ Bêng-bín, Chhòa Tông-êng, and Tân Tông-san, who had contacts with members of the Congress or Senate whom they could ask

for support for Taiwan when any proposal came up on the floor which would
be beneficial to the people of Taiwan.

On every returning trip to London, after Shoki accomplished his mission
in North America, supporters and friends such Gô˙ Lâi-hó, Gūi Sūi-bêng and
Ông Ài-lân would load his luggage with special food to take home. Between
1975 and 1980, Shoki made at least two trips to San Francisco, one in 1976
and the other in 1978. I was his guide and driver, taking him to visit some
tourist sites and taking quite a few photographs.

The Last Visit Home

From the time he resigned as principal of Tainan Theological College in 1965
to assume a position with the WCC until July 1987, Shoki Coe wandered outside of Taiwan. Due to his great influence and inspiration to so many students
and his high visibility in the international arena, the Kuomintang regime did
not attempt to arrest him but tried to prevent him from further influence
in Taiwan through his advocacy for the self-determination for Taiwanese.
The Kuomintang regime placed him on the black list of names permanently
banned from returning home.

In 1987 President Chiang Ching-kuo announced that the martial law that
had been in effect for fifty years would be repealed. The repeal of the law was
due to the fact that the opposition political forces grew stronger every day
and that Taiwan had acquired the bad reputation of being a country with the
longest martial law in the world. It could no longer stop the tide of genuine
"democracy," nomenclature they had been using without warrant for years.
Within that year, the application of the Presbyterian Church in Taiwan for the
return of Shoki Coe was granted with much help from Professor Lee Teng-
hui, who was vice president of the country.[1]

After 22 years away from home, it was to Shoki like a dream to be able
to return. When he had first left Taiwan to study in England and had to stay
there during the Second World War, he ended up away from his homeland
for 11 years. This time, because of being placed on the black list, his exile was
twice as long. Many friends and former students, upon hearing the news that
Shoki Coe was to return home to Taiwan, even came back from abroad just
wanting to hear what he had to say about the mission and ministry of Taiwan,
as well as wishing to give thanks to God for his contribution to the ecumenical church and his struggle for Taiwan. All were happy to see him but at the
same time were laden with a heavy heart, as they would also have to say goodbye. Shoki Coe had had lung cancer for about a year, and he had been given a
prognosis of about four months to two years to live.

From 29 to 31 July, Shoki was at the Presbyterian Bible College in Sin-tek to attend a mission consultation on the theme of "Opportune Time for Mission in Taiwan." He was asked to speak in the afternoon of the second day on "Reviewing Mission Theology at This Time in This Place" to lead off the discussion. Due to his health, he was only asked to speak for twenty minutes and then was followed by two other speakers, each for forty minutes, Nĝ Phek-hô on "Its [Mission Theology's] Relation with Indigenous Culture" and Táng Hong-óan on "Its Relation with Indigenous Religions." Unfortunately there was no recording or transcript of Shoki's lecture. However, there was another lecture on the subject of "What Is theological education?" in which he briefly spoke of theological education and its implications for Taiwan and world mission.

On 2 August, because of the rare occasion of Shoki's return to his alma mater, Tióng-êng Tiong-ha̍k (Presbyterian Middle/High School) was joined by Nĝ Bú-tong, Boris Anderson, Lîm Chong-gī and a whole host of alumni that filled up the auditorium of the school to hold a thanksgiving worship service.

On 3 August, Tainan Theological College conducted a special convocation to honor Shoki Coe, outstanding alumnus Nĝ Bú-tong, and distinguished former professor and Vice-Principal Boris Anderson with honorary Doctor of Divinity degrees. The following is the transcript of Shoki Coe's speech at this occasion, titled "What Is Theological Education?":

> This is probably my last opportunity to give a public lecture on what I consider to be theological education. I am pleased that the college I loved so much has bestowed on me an honorary Doctor of Divinity degree and asked me to speak on this subject.
>
> I spent my lifetime as a theological educator, and so to answer this question, a verse from Paul's letter to the Galatians came into my mind, "My little children for whom I am again in the pain of childbirth, until Christ is formed in you" (Gal 4:19).
>
> Any genuine theological education must include three layers of the "form of Christ." Theological education is a serious matter, like a mother's birthing of a child, just as Paul said, "…[like a mother] is in pain of childbirth, until…" Today I am speaking of this matter in front of my colleagues in theological education.
>
> Let us begin with what is obvious (and perhaps what is easy to see), theological education is involved with theological formation. It is not only in the accumulative knowledge of theology—mind that I do not look down on this kind of knowledge—I consider we must not become a theologian who can only quote and refer to somebody else's knowledge in theology. Other than

learning the knowledge, we must endure the pain of childbirth, until the heart and mind of Christ is formed in every person. We do not only aim at having Christ's mind in us, but also in others' mind, that all may have Christ's mind among each one of us all (Phil 2:5). So that every one will be able to say, "It is not I who is thinking, it is Christ in me who is thinking."

Secondly, the purpose of theological education is involved with ministerial formation. This is also obvious and easy to see. In reality, whenever the higher the academic level of theological education is achieved, the less ministerial formation seems to happen. There is one thing I need to give further explanation. During the mission consultation, someone suggested that if a clergy person is to be assigned to engage in theological education, there must be a prerequisite of five years of ministerial experience. This suggestion was put aside without much discussion. The reason was that Dr Thomas Barclay and I were cited as examples. It seemed that it was under a very extraordinary circumstance, extraordinary examples were cited, and this was not something to call for. When I worked for the Theological Education Fund, there were a number of theological educational institutions, which I visited, whose theological teachers did not have enough ministerial formation, thus causing considerable trouble in these institutions. What we mean by "ministerial formation" is not confined to acquisition of certain skills or techniques. In like manner, I do not look down on these skills and techniques; other than these skills and techniques, we must endure the pain of childbirth, until the ministry of Christ is formed in every one. This ministry is what our Lord has said of himself, "I came to minister, but not to be ministered unto," "I came among you like a person who ministers." We must wholeheartedly minister until we can say, "It is not I who minister, but it is Christ in me who ministers."

The last but not the least, and it is the most difficult task for a theological educator to do—this area has been often forgotten or totally ignored by many theological schools or universities, and regarded as nothing to do with their education. This is what I call "life formation." Theological education must be involved in "life formation." We must endure the pain of childbirth until the life of Christ is formed in each and every one of us, "until we all attain to the unity…to the maturity, to the measure of the full stature of Christ" (Eph 4:13). This painful and joyful expectation of Christ's life formed in each and every one of us, is indeed the most important part of theological education. The most glorious and joyful moment of a theological educator is when his or her students cannot only say, "Christ who in me thinks," "Christ who is in me ministering," but also can join Paul to say, "It is not I who is living, it is Christ in me who is living."

If a theological educator gives attention to these three formations, he or she will give attention to the nurture of a whole person of the people of God. The mission and life of the church must rely on this kind of whole person of the people of God to carry out. If theological educators truthfully and faithfully take seriously this word "until," and "until" these three layers of the forms of Christ are formed in us, they will indeed care about every Christian's wholesome life. Even theological educators like me who have reached this age can only honestly and humbly join Paul and say, "Not that I have already obtained this or reached the goal; but I press on to make it my own, because [or just as] Christ Jesus made me his own" (Phil 3:12)—Christ is formed in me. [2]

Shoki Coe, in response to the honour and welcome of his invitation to visit Tainan Theological College, prepared a "last will and testament." He arrived in Taiwan on 28 July 1987, but the will was signed on 21 July in Seaford. In this will he especially entrusts his eldest son, David, and second son, Michael (as executors), to take £20,000 out of his estate to be given to the Overseas Missions of the United Reformed Church whose office is located at Tavistock Place, London, to establish a lectureship at Tainan Theological College. In order to truly achieve this memorable gift to Tainan Theological College, Shoki brought a copy of his "last will and testament" to Taiwan and gave it to Principal Tiuⁿ Tek-hiong.

After a busy schedule at Tióng-êng Middle School and at Tainan Theological College, Shoki Coe was able to visit relatives and old friends in Tainan and other places in the southern part of Taiwan. During this time, he stayed at the principal's residence. The principal at the time was Tiuⁿ Tek-hiong, who began his theological study at Tainan Theological College the year Shoki Coe became principal of the college. He graduated in 1953 but remained at the college to do research and teaching assignments. On 7 August, Shoki Coe said goodbye to the city, where he grew up and which he considered his hometown, Tainan, and flew to Taipei.

While Shoki Coe was in Taipei, he stayed with another of his former students, Ko Chùn-bêng (a.k.a. C. M. Kao). Ko was in the same class as Tiuⁿ Tek-hiong and graduated the same year. Upon graduation he spent most of his time working in theological education equipping people to minister to aboriginals of Taiwan. In 1970 Ko was elected to be the general secretary of the General Assembly of the Presbyterian Church in Taiwan, and during his tenure in 1980, he was arrested and convicted of harbouring an alleged "rebel and seditious person." He was imprisoned for four years, three months and twenty-one days, until he was released in early fall of 1984. [3]

When he was in Taipei, Shoki Coe saw for the first time "The Mission Building" —head offices—of the Presbyterian Church in Taiwan, located at Lane No. 269, Section 3 of Roosevelt Road, Taipei, where the office of the general secretary is housed.

Hearing that Shoki Coe was a houseguest at Ko Chùn-bêng's home, the leaders of the newly organized People's Progressive Party, Iû Chheng, Iâu Ka-bûn, Chiu Chheng-giòk, made a special trip to see this forerunner of the Tai-wan democratic movement.

Special arrangements were made for Shoki Coe to meet three political VIPs when he was in Taipei. They were Li Hoan, the Secretary General of the Kuomintang, David Dean, Director of the American Institute in Taipei (AIT)[4] and the most important and the key person, Vice-President Lee Teng-hui.

After 22 years, these two colleagues in higher education were able to meet again. Shoki Coe and Lee Teng-hui both reminisced about their past and felt as close as before. They talked for about three hours. Shoki Coe complained that though martial law was repealed, it was replaced by the national security law. Through and through it changed only the form but not the substance—"oā[n] thng bô oā[n] liàp."[5] The new law which says "advocacy of communism and divi-sion of the national territory are not permitted" is basically self-contradictory. Not only did Lee Teng-hui not deny this but also said that indeed there were many self-contradictions. Lee said that in order to repeal martial law quickly, there were not sufficient deliberations regarding the new replacement law. If the law had not been passed before Chiang Ching-kuo died, it might have had to wait a minimum of eight years before the repeal of martial law. Lee Teng-hui said that if the partial law had not been repealed, the government would be merely the servant of the Garrison Command. Only when the partial law was repealed was there a chance to change the essence of the nation.[6]

After the visit with Vice-President Lee, Shoki also had a formal visit and conversation with the secretary general of Chinese Kuomintang, Lee Hoan. In their formal conversation, Shoki Coe honestly and straightforwardly told Lee Hoan that the treatment of Taiwanese as "compatriots" by Kuomintang was even worse than that of the "foreign" Japanese colonialists. In Shoki's memoir, he related how he told Lee Hoan about the entry of his marital status as "not married" on his domicile registration and his passport, which was subsequently used to accuse him falsely of "living with a foreign woman without marriage" in order to shame and discredit him. He also mentioned that his activities and those of other Taiwanese were twisted and coloured with red in the media in Taiwan, their names blacklisted and news falsified. While the Kuomintang let in the Taiwanese people who were well known in the world, Shoki felt this was part of its "public relations show." Up until 1987 the Kuomintang was not willing to let those activists who were outspoken in the international arena to participate in the transformation of policy on national affairs.

Shoki Coe also had an opportunity to see David Dean, the Director of the American Institute in Taipei (AIT), accompanied by Nĝ Bú-tong, Lîm Chong-gī and Ko Chùn-bêng. Before he became the Director of AIT, David Dean was an official in the US State Department in Washington, D.C. In the aftermath of the Formosa Incident and Ko Chùn-bêng's arrest, Shoki visited him to seek the means for Ko's release. At that visit in Washington, D.C., David Dean consoled Shoki and said "Time is on your side." And at this meeting in Taipei, they were able to speak of the developments in the intervening years and some interesting happenings. Dean said that when Cyrus Vance was Secretary of State, he accompanied him on a visit to China. When Vance met with Deng Xiao-ping, he asked Deng, quite unexpectedly, if the United States could set up a consular office in Taiwan. Deng refused, but the United States, Canada, United Kingdom, Japan and other European countries eventually opened offices in Taiwan that in effect did the work of an embassy. However, looking back on history, Shoki Coe considered that since the severance of diplomatic ties with the United States, that time turned out to be very unfavourable to Taiwan. In 1971 when the United Nations decided to give the seat of "the Republic of China" in the United Nations to the People's Republic of China, the United States had the intention of supporting a seat for Taiwan as a separate nation and supported the idea of a China and a Taiwan. But instead, through the choices of the Kuomintang, the Taiwanese were still kept outside the political process, suffering from the consequence of its severed ties with nations. This reality caused Shoki's deep sense of "m̄-kam-goān" before he died. In 1988 Chiang Ching-kuo died and opened up the opportunity for a Taiwanese, Lee Teng-hui, to succeed him.

Reminiscence and Exhortation of Final Business

A few years ago I wrote to David Coe, the eldest son of Shoki Coe, requesting his help in providing family photographs or anecdotes that I might share with Shoki's former students, colleagues or friends. His reply on 29 April 1998 reminded me of the sacrifices Shoki and his family had no doubt had to make for Shoki to fulfil his career and passion for Taiwan. This is part of what David said in the letter:

> This is an issue concerning opinions. There are three important lines of development of my father's biography: 1. There is the story of his birth, growing up, education, etc. 2. There is his work, his idea of the mixing religion and politics,

which he continued to hold unceasingly, even after he began working with ecumenical agencies; it grew even stronger and not less. 3. In his *Memoir*, there is no meaningful mention of his relationship with his family either partially or totally. Of course during the short period of time before his death, when he was racing with time, he wrote his *Memoir*, and he was even unable to complete it before his death. On the other hand, he was always in crises and dangerous situations, and he tried consciously and intentionally not to let his family get tangled in his political life. On the matter of his family life, my opinion is, if he was silent on this matter, it must be his intent to do so. If you (i.e. the author) merely asked for some family photographs, that you may begin your story with them, then this kind of family photograph collection is still in the process of being made. If and when it is made, the family story must be told by the family.

At the end of his letter David added, "I hope this is not too negative of a response to you."

In 1988 both Shoki and Winifred died. At the time they had five grandchildren from their sons and daughter. David holds a PhD in science and the three other children are medical doctors and have carried on their profession. David had moved to England in 1955, when he was only 11 or 12, for education. His mother moved back to England with David's three other siblings only in 1959. And it wasn't until 1965, when David was an adult, that his father returned to England.

In about 1978, when Shoki Coe was visiting the San Francisco area, I took him for sightseeing. When walking up a small slope, he clearly had problems breathing. I said to him jokingly, "I thought you were a football (soccer) player, were you not?" He replied, "O Sūi-hiông, I am getting old." "What kind of problem?" I asked. He said, "My daughter Eileen took me to the Naval Hospital for examination, and she pointed to my chest, and said, that is where it is wrong." He continued to say, "When I went to the hospital, the hospital gate guard had to straighten the gun to salute her, then I realized that she was a ranking officer of the armed forces." Then I remembered that I had not seen him smoking the last several times I met with him; he used to be a chainsmoker when he was in Tainan or working in England. He used to say that smoking made him calm, and let him have time to think. It was about 1979, when he retired, that he stopped smoking entirely. According to my classmate the Rev. Tè Tiong-tek, on the occasion when he visited Shoki in England, he asked Shoki why he stopped smoking. He said, "It is too expensive to smoke cigarettes in England. When you buy cigarettes here, you do not buy by the pack, you can only afford to buy a single cigarette or a few at a time." Tè Tiong-tek could not but exclaim about the economic conditions of England in the 1970s, which were worse than Taiwan by comparison.

When Shoki Coe returned to England after his last visit to Taiwan, the bad news circulated that he had lung cancer and had reached an incurable condition, to which the medical experts predicted that he had at most two years time for treatment. As a clergyman and as an educator of pastors, he was psychologically prepared.

However, there were three things that made his heart heavy. The first was his wife's health condition. Winifred could not see well and was in need of somebody at her side constantly to care for her. The second was that friends and relatives who all thought that Shoki had invaluable life experience, plus thoughts and theology, had requested him to put them in writing. It was quite an unexpected turn of events, that the body of an athlete all of a sudden became so vulnerable and weak. With the diagnosis that he had only two years' allowance, it was too short to carry out so much. The third concern for Shoki was the liberation of Taiwanese that had always been his conviction— people of Taiwan would bind together to work out their own destiny. The goal was still far away. Every time when he thought of this, a deep sense of his "m̄-kam-goān"[7] returned.

Since 1986 there were signals that the martial law would be repealed in Taiwan, for in that year, Chiang Ching-kuo announced, "I am a Taiwanese." It had been two years since C. M. Kao was released from prison. In Taiwan the "anti-Kuomintang" people and those who held the attitude of "half-believe and half-doubt" scattered around the world dared to try to break through the anathema of a "monopoly political party" to organize the Democratic Progressive Party. The Christian church's version of the Democratic Progressive Party could be said to be the concrete manifestation of the interpretation and public dissemination of the three statements of the Presbyterian Church in Taiwan. Therefore, the Presbyterian Church in Taiwan also took the opportunity to solicit a response to the three statements from those Self-Determination Movement participants abroad, and jointly they might explain their true meaning and their messages of Christian witness. The process of the return of the two Ng giants[8], Ng Chiong-hui (Shoki Coe) and Ng Bú-tong of the Presbyterian Church in Taiwan was a necessary step and important agenda for the church. So after carefully considering the names on the black list, they processed the application for Ng Bú-tong. His successful return had immediately prompted the application for Shoki Coe's return.

Before the news of the repeal of martial law was out in the open, Shoki Coe and I had a rather lengthy and sincere discussion. I assumed that the Chinese

Kuomintang, in order to continue its rule over Taiwan, must loosen its grip a little bit so that it could provide a show of its "intention of democratization." The Chinese Kuomintang also clearly knew that the elite Taiwanese were not "revolutionaries" with military training but civilians. They were weak and powerless and could appeal only to the world through diplomatic means. I felt, therefore, that the Kuomintang must be totally eliminated. However, Shoki Coe's opinion was that the Kuomintang would certainly fall but that the important issue was the way it would fall and when the time should come for Taiwanese to exercise self-determination. Taiwanese must not be pushed and pulled down and fall down with it all together. I also observed that Shoki Coe seemed to have confidence in the Taiwanese members of the Kuomintang.

In this lengthy discussion, Shoki Coe also mentioned several incidents that still made him feel "m̄-kam-goān"—unacceptable:

1. Since his youth, Shoki never identified himself as Japanese. For example, there was the incident when he was a primary school child, called insulting names by Japanese children, and he got into a fight with them. Another incident happened on the way home from Japan on board a passenger ship, when speaking Taiwanese with his younger brother Bêng-hui caused his brother to be unreasonably punished by his Japanese instructor. There were other times when he protested the unjust treatment of his compatriots as third class citizens.

2. During his years as a student in England, he was often asked to speak Chinese or wear Chinese clothing to identify himself as Chinese.

3. During the war, although he did not want to identify as Japanese, due to strategic necessity he was asked to teach the Japanese language; by demand he was required to learn Chinese Mandarin. He respected the war of resistance to the Japanese led by the government based in Chungching and even had to accept and believe the allied countries' position that the "war of resistance against Japanese" (in China) was a "just war."

4. He had to deal with the embassy of the Republic of China in London to obtain his passport and be treated with the same status as an "overseas Chinese."

5. The Chinese Kuomintang regime used the domicile registration system to insult him purposely, under the pretence that his wife was not a naturalized citizen, refused to classify him as a married person, and falsely called their children illegitimate.

6. He took a normal Christian channel endeavouring to establish Tunghai University, to connect the Presbyterian Church in Taiwan with WCC, yet he

was regarded as a "seditious element" (the same as other people who worked for democratization). His name was on the black list, purposely given unreasonable delay in obtaining his exit and reentry permit, and later on, when working for WCC, was denied an entry permit to Taiwan.

Now that the "golden" age of Chinese Kuomintang is over, and even the dusk is approaching, it still does not want to repent, does not want to admit that its end is near and still continues to raise betrayers of people, uses deception, arbitrarily and wrongly changes historical facts, and is likened to a vampire sucking away the results of people's sweat and blood. Not only does it not give people a chance to make their own choice, it does not give true information. It strangles the freedom of the press and monopolizes the media, even to use the Chinese version—a "great unified China"—as its basis for propaganda to whitewash history.

In 1947, not long after the massacre of 28 February, when Shoki was on his way home, a schoolmate from his Presbyterian Boys School days made a special trip to Hong Kong to see him and warn him not to return to Taiwan, as he might be unjustly killed. Yet Shoki held up his hope that the "enlightened and wise" leaders of the Kuomintang at the time would see the true reality and completely turn around to carry out policy that would be beneficial to Taiwan. Forty years had elapsed, yet Shoki Coe continued to see the tricky methods of Kuomintang policy in Taiwan, its consistent oppression, deception, threat, monopoly of mass media and exile of good Taiwanese intellectuals who loved their native land. Shoki had to become like an "old father" who tried every way he could to promote harmony among different racial and ethnic groups, that all might build a new country together. He was also conscious that his life would come to an end eventually. Seventy years was a life span, so he made all effort to uphold the dignity of Taiwanese people and sought the fruit of a harmonious existence with China and the world. Yet alas, he was not able to see it come to fruition. This was one of his deep regrets, a "m̄-kam-goān."

Shoki Coe's health was on the decline. Taiwanese in the United States, particularly in the New York area, invited Shoki to come to New York for a last trip. On 20 March, a big party was set up to welcome him, with more than two hundred guests on hand and 25 tables set for a sumptuous feast. Shoki felt grateful as he returned to London, still absorbing the honour he received.

Between the months of April and October, Shoki stayed put at home to write what he recollected and thought of. Just as his eldest son, David, had said, he was racing with time. He did not take any more trips but continued to receive visitors. He was very sad, for the health of his lifetime companion,

Winifred, was worse than his, and she had turned totally blind. They had come to rely on each other very much.

In early October, when the United Formosan Foundation in Southern California heard the bad news of Shoki's deteriorating health, there were great concerns about his life and condition. So Lîm Tiat-hiông, So˙ Kok-hiông, and Ông Phêng-hun took up the responsibility to raise funds and urged Ô˙ Tiong-sìn, the representative reporter of Bîn-chìn Chiu-khan (Democratic Progressive Weekly) in Los Angeles, to go to England to see Shoki to bring back firsthand information. Before his departure to England, Phê ͫ Bêng-bín and Khò˙ Sìn-liông each had special dinners to send him off and asked him to convey their special greetings. Shoki Coe received radiation therapy of Cobalt 60 to prevent the cancer from spreading further, but it destroyed the function of making new blood, and there were traces of blood when he coughed. According to the report of ˙ Tiong-sìn, he said, "When I arrived in London, Shoki Coe was in fact only having his last breaths. Inasmuch as not to affect his condition too much, I used the method of question and answer to record the frequent visits. Because Shoki's condition of spitting out blood, I could only visit him for about three or four hours each day. When he was resting, I was able to look into some of his files, and then spent some time sightseeing.[9]"

Other than immediate family, the last ones to see Shoki were Ko Lí Lē-tin, the wife of Shoki's former student at Tainan Theological College Ko Chùn-bêng, and Dr David Landsborough, who was born in the same year and in the same town as Shoki Coe. On the evening of 15 October, Ko Lí Lē-tin flew from the venue of the Executive Council of the World Alliance of Reformed Churches in Northern Ireland to London and hurriedly went to David Landsborough's home to stay overnight. The next morning, David drove Lē-tin to Seaford to see Shoki at the hospital there. The following is a section from Ko Lí Lē-tin's report that appeared in the *Tâi-ôan Kàu-hōe Kong-pò* (*Taiwan Church News*)[10] with an attached photograph, "the last photograph of Shoki Coe" taken by David Landsborough. At the visit, Shoki had just received a transfusion, so he looked in quite good shape:

> Lying on his bed, the Rev. Coe was very pleased to receive our visit. He was much thinner, and he looked pale; but he was very concerned about his wife. He told us that she was very weak nowadays, in need of his care of her, but he was now confined in the hospital, so he could not be home to care for her. He felt very sorry. The doctor and his children told him that he would feel better after the transfusion, and that he himself hoped that after the transfusion he would have more energy. He was suffering from side effects of radiation

therapy, his blood vessels had become weaker, so that whenever he coughed, some vessels would break to cause bleeding. His body was weak but his spirit remained high. He talked with us for two and a half hours. We were afraid that it might not be good for him to talk for a long time. However, the doctor said that it was all right for him to talk. He talked about many things related to the church in Taiwan, the future of Taiwan, and asked about my husband's (Ko Chùn-bêng's) retirement.

He hoped that our church would continue to study and think about the three statements the church had made, and also carefully teach our church members to know and understand their meaning. Concerning the future of Taiwan, the people were not quite sure of the meaning or implication of unification and/or independence. He hoped that the authorities would allow more discussion and dialogue between those holding the opinion of unification and those of independence. Both sides would have to say how, or what method to take, that the goal may be attained, carefully look into what benefits and what unfavorable effects they may bring, and all come together to discuss and to think, and then present them for all to vote. Do not forget that the future of Taiwan is to be determined by all people of Taiwan (all who identify themselves as Taiwanese, regardless of whether they are natives of Taiwan, or other places, or plains dwellers or original inhabitants of the island). They all have the right to make that decision. That is the essence of the three statements.

He was very keen to keep on speaking. The time was getting late. We were concerned that he would be overtired. So we said good-bye to him at about six o'clock. Before we departed, he particularly wanted me to convey his good wishes to (Lîm) Bûn-tin, (Tiuⁿ) Chhian-hūi, the Rev. Ong (Siu-kiong), Moderator Iûⁿ (Khé-siū), the Rev. Nĝ Bú-tong, my husband, and all brethren and sisters of Taiwan.

After we left the hospital, we went to the Rev. Coe's home to visit Mrs. Coe. She knew that we were coming, and had been waiting for us in the living room. She looked very thin. She said that her back was not hurting much any longer. But she was weak and frail. Fortunately the youngest son Andrew was home to accompany her—Andrew is a pediatric doctor, and has two children. In the evening, Eileen came to take his place. If none of her children were able to come, there would be a special nurse to come to give care. After a pleasant visit with both son and daughter for about one hour, very reluctantly and somewhat sadly we bid goodbye, and we prayed in our heart for God's mercy to lessen the pain and suffering of the Rev. and Mrs. Coe.

Nevertheless, he has departed from this world so soon, and went to the bosom of our Heavenly Father. Rest in peace, our beloved Rev. Coe. May

God remember the good work you have done for God. What you have done for us with your blood and sweat will not be in vain. We will faithfully follow your beautiful steps courageously, and press forward...and my ears keep on hearing his deep emotionally charged sighs, "Whenever I think about things related to Taiwan, my heart pains. I would like to do more for Taiwan, but...ah...it is your turn now."

According to Ko Lí Lē-tin, she flew from London on the evening of 27 October 1988 and arrived in Taipei shortly after 9:00 p.m. She was met by her daughter and son-in-law, and their first words to her were, "The Rev. Shoki Coe is gone." She said, "No, no! It is not possible, I cannot believe it. Only a couple of days ago I saw him; even though he was lying down on the bed and receiving a transfusion, he was in good spirits, and he talked to me a lot....How could it be so quick?"[11]

7

The Significance of Shoki Coe to Taiwan

Shoki Coe is a rare and precious person who can rightly be claimed as a "national treasure" in the history of Taiwan. Shoki was "the first" in many areas in the history of Taiwan. He was the first Taiwanese to become the head of a theological college. Prior to Shoki's installation as the principal of Tainan Theological College, all former theological college principals were missionaries from either Great Britain or North America.

He was the first person who did not study theology in any theological college in Taiwan to be qualified as a full-fledged "candidate for ministry," and he was the first person who had not gone through the process of being a licensed preacher of the Presbyterian Church in Taiwan to be ordained as a minister. In fact he was classified as a "qualified candidate for ministry awaiting a call and ordination" by the Presbytery of South London when he graduated from Westminster College in Cambridge in 1941. If he had ever been called to be a pastor in a church of the Presbyterian Church of England, he would have been ordained. However, he did not have that opportunity between 1941 and 1947. Even after his return to Taiwan, he waited for two years before he was finally ordained by the Presbyterian Church in Taiwan, and installed as principal of Tainan Theological College.

Shoki was the first Taiwanese to receive regular government university education, to graduate and then after studies of the regular theology course at a foreign theological college, to join the ministerial team of the church in Taiwan. Shoki Coe most likely was the first Taiwanese minister to be married to a foreign woman, although since he was engaged in the educational profession, his wife did not have a chance to experience the taste of the life of "a minister's wife" in Taiwan. Shoki Coe was the first to admit women students in the department of theological studies while he was principal of the college. The first four women students were all graduates of Tióng-êng Lú-tiong (Presbyterian Girls School). One of them was Shoki's own half-sister Nĝ Siok-hūi.

Due to the demands of the time, as a minister Shoki was deeply involved in church politics. Even up to now nobody has broken his records—and will not likely in the near future—to be elected as moderator of the General Assembly in two different years, at the most important times of the church. The first time was at the fourth General Assembly in 1957; though fourth was in reality the first truly unified Assembly, when the two Synods, North and South, joined together and at the time decided to hold one General Assembly every year. The second time happened in 1965. It was the year when the Presbyterian Church in Taiwan celebrated its One Hundredth Anniversary and the fruits of the "Doubling the Church" mission initiative. In fact, it could be called the golden year of the church.

By an unusual twist of the destiny and history of Taiwan, perhaps he was a very rare example of a person with no less than three legal names: (1) Shoki Ko; (2) Chang-hui Hwang; (3) Shoki Coe. There was a fourth name which has been well known in Taiwan, Nĝ Chiong-hui, although nobody knows whether he had ever used it as a legal name or not.[1] Fortunately, his name in Han ideograph remained the same.

Although Shoki Coe worked hard to build up an institution that was compatible to international standards, and even received internationally acclaimed fame, under the educational system of post-WWII Taiwan, Tainan Theological College still remains an "unlicensed" institution.

Although its students could not take licensing or qualifying examinations, or serve in government and public agencies, the theological college did provide education of genuine quality with pride and confidence. Shoki often proudly said, "Tainan Theological College is the best in the areas of English, (Biblical) Greek, philosophy, dogmatics, New Testament studies, (church) music, and religious education in Taiwan and throughout Southeast Asia." However, he also often emphasized that the purpose of the theological college was to train ministers who could serve local churches and communities, so as to build up a wholesome Presbyterian Church in Taiwan. In his opinion, there must not be a theological college that teaches only "knowledge for the sake of knowledge." To him, a theological college should serve the church to carry out the proclamation of the Christian message. When he was in office in Tainan, he prepared people for future teaching responsibility at the Theological College but did not consider his students taking up leadership positions in Asia or the worldwide church. It is probable that he thought that if a person was highly educated in theology, the person would naturally have opportunities and ability to take on leadership positions in different situations. He did not anticipate the "brain drain" from Taiwan, resulting in not enough people to meet the demands of guiding theological education in Taiwan nor to provide leadership for the ecumenical church.

In the nick of time, Shoki Coe was able to escape to study in England. Had he stayed in Taiwan, he would have been drafted into military service and thus been part of the Japanese militarist invasion forces in Asia and the Pacific. Fortunately, Shoki left Taiwan for England before it was under the grip of total Japanese control in 1937. He had already received education under a more free and democratic educational system in Japan and had acquired the highest language skills and thinking that Japan offered at the time as testified in his degree and diploma from Tokyo University. For this very reason, Shoki was able to stand on higher ground with a wider perspective and critical eyes to view the period of Japanese militarism.

For his first two years in England, 1937–1939, Shoki Coe was able to immerse himself in the free atmosphere of English society to engage in his studies. From 1939, when war began between Germany and Britain, until he completed his formal theological education in the next two years, his life and study environment at the theological college was relatively peaceful. From the time of Britain's involvement in the war in the Pacific (December 1941) until the end of that war (August 1945) and through about one and a half years of struggling to recover from the war (spring of 1947), Shoki Coe was given the best time for "awaiting the opportunity." He taught Japanese language and Chinese language (Hokkien/Taiwanese) and was accorded the opportunity to learn Mandarin (Chinese). In addition to his ability in multiple languages, Shoki Coe had experience in teaching at a school of international standing. When he returned home to Taiwan, although still young, he was a very capable, equipped and experienced person—already qualified to be considered a "national treasure."

Shoki Coe could not only communicate in several languages, he was able to communicate to people a worldview that was wide and open to future possibilities. Shoki Coe expected and taught Taiwanese to have a worldview that would not only look at their own culture with a Taiwanese perspective but would look at their own culture—and the future development of their country—from a world perspective. In looking at the future, Shoki emphasized that people should not base their judgment of opportunities and shortcomings of Taiwan on one incidence of "right" or "wrong" but should apply a long-range view, to allow the expression of the full potential of Taiwanese, to look forward to a brighter and better future of Taiwan. He often reminded people in Taiwan that we should not limit ourselves to the confines of the island but consider the Taiwanese as citizens of the world and let the world see the culture of this land of Taiwan. The achievement of Taiwan should be not only for people in Taiwan but also extend to the world and give witness to the world of the beauty and goodness of the spirit of Taiwan.

One of the greatest contributions of Shoki Coe to Taiwan was helping to make Taiwanese an "authorized" language. In German history, Martin Luther translated the whole Bible, Old and New Testaments, into German in the mid-sixteenth century. That version of the Bible occupies an important classical status and is considered a major contributor to the evolution of the German language before the dawning of modern printing techniques that popularized the language. In the seventeenth century, King James of England gathered a group of scholars to translate the Bible into standard English, which also had a huge impact on how English is written and spoken even today.

Until the early twentieth century, the phrases and vocabulary of the commonly used language in Taiwan, *Hoklo*,[2] had not been put into a collection. But the founder of Tainan Theological College, Thomas Barclay, set up a printing shop and took advantage of using Roman letters to spell out Taiwanese language to popularize it. His great contribution was the publication of the "Romanized Amoy Vernacular Version" of the Bible in the late 1920s, widely used by Christians in the Presbyterian Church in Taiwan ever since. However, it was Shoki Coe who resolutely made the reopened Tainan Theological College the only institution of higher learning in Taiwan to use Taiwanese as the main official language for instruction. Principal Coe used Taiwanese daily to express the wide range of theological thinking and vigorously trained students to use that language to articulate academic theories and thoughts and to apply them in daily interaction as well as worship and preaching. Shoki put Taiwanese as expressed in romanized written form as a requirement for graduation. All students must pass a standard test of this language to graduate. Thus, Tainan Theological College may well be said to be a precious reservoir of Hoklo Taiwanese language. And in turn it will help forge a Taiwanese spirit that will be one essential cradle and source of the future nation of Taiwan.

Acknowledgements

After reading Shoki Coe's *Recollections and Reflections*, I was very much moved by his deep and genuine love of his homeland Taiwan and also his confidence in Taiwanese people. This feeling has raised my respect and admiration of this teacher to whom I owe so much. Since there have been few records written about his life and his thoughts, I decided to collect documentation and resource materials about him, beginning in Japan. That was in 1988 when I was about to complete my missionary service there. On the one hand, six years of time passed so fast, and on the other, I had no expertise in writing. It was impossible to present a piece of good work with sufficient content. Now I am very pleased to present this biography of Shoki Coe.

I lack the skill of a writer, have been wandering abroad from home for over forty years and was required to use a not-so-familiar language—Chinese—to write. Of course I had a lot of help from friends. During the process of collecting source materials, many rendered their invaluable assistance. In order to make this writing accurate, readable and in good format, I must give special thanks to Chiúⁿ Tiong-san, Tân Khoan-tî, Tiuⁿ Chhun-liông, Ông Ài-lân, Gūi Sūi-bêng, and Nḡ Chùn-tek. Special thanks go also to my classmate at Taichung First Middle School, Mr. Lōa Phek-hong, who read my manuscript many times over and made valuable suggestions and corrections.

Through my research, I collected a great number of photographs and historical documents, printed in the earlier editions of this book. First of all, with the help of the Director of Tokyo University YMCA Hostel, Toshihiko Tokuhisa, the journal records of the daily morning devotions of the Hostel were found. And later, a fellow student, Toshikazu Miwa, who stayed at the YMCA Hostel at the same time as Shoki Coe, was found. Quite unexpectedly, with great surprise and joy, he provided more than ten photographs. In Taiwan, I was able to meet the only surviving son of the Rev. Nḡ Lêng-Lêng-kiàt, Mr. Nḡ Kî-chhiong and his wife, and they provided photographs of the Rev. Nḡ Lêng-kiàt in his later years and the Rev. Shoki Coe when he was of tender age. Mr. Nḡ Hôai-gī, the Rev. Shoki Coe's cousin, also supplied invaluable photographs of Shoki before he set out to study in England. A Korean artist

155

in Japan, Mr. Kim Tou Hiung, also kindly graced earlier editions of this book with two sketches of two events in the Rev. Shoki Coe's life. There are others, including Mr. Ñg Teng-hui, the Rev. Ko Chùn-bêng and Ms Tiuⁿ Chhian-hūi, who also provided invaluable information. The fifth-youngest brother of Shoki Coe, Mr. Ñg Teng-hui, has read the manuscript, checked the historical resource materials carefully, and has made valuable suggestions.

In order to consult the historical resource materials of the Foreign Missions of the Presbyterian Church of England, I made two research trips to the School of Oriental and African Studies of London University. Quite unexpectedly, I found more than 450 pieces of invaluable documents related to the Rev. Shoki Coe. In order to continue careful reading and research of these documents at home, I asked special technicians to transfer the documents from microfilm to compact disk. The Rev. Chiu Hông-gē and the East Bay Taiwanese Church generously provided financial support to digitize the resources. Mr. Tiuⁿ Hàn-têng of the East Bay Taiwanese Church provided technical assistance in the use of computer and digitalized information resources. The typing of this manuscript was done by the author's niece, Miss Niû Lē-hong. In the process of writing this book, I had to make several trips back to Taiwan, for which Mr. Tân Khoan-tî has made all necessary arrangements for lodging. Deep appreciation is due to all friends who have given their support of this project.

The author wishes to express his thanks to Dr Ching Fen Hsiao for translating this biography of Shoki Coe into English. Thanks are also expressed to the Presbyterian Church in Taiwan for claiming its ownership of the English version and leading the copublishing of this book with the World Council of Churches.

Translator's Postcript

Every translation is an interpretation of the original work. Every language has its own unique ways of expression through its syntax and vocabulary, and they carry nuances that cannot easily be expressed in another language. At times in the process of translating this book, I had to resort to using my imagination, which might be far from the intended meaning of the author. It is probably easier to write than to translate.

English is not my native language. In fact, it is the fourth language I had to learn. Neither is the original writing my native language. This fact in reality indicates that I must translate at least two times in my mind, from one foreign language to my own and then into another foreign language. It constitutes a double jeopardy. I have tried my best to be faithful to the original text, even to the degree of keeping the style of the original writing. Undoubtedly, there will be readers who find discrepancies between the original text and the translation, for which I wish to apologize in advance.

This is the world we live in, a multilingual and multicultural world in which we seek to communicate, to find a common ground that transcends this "multiplicity." It is my hope and prayer that the readers of this doubly translated work will find something meaningful that speaks to their hearts, that we—the readers and the translator—may find that all share some common feeling of being in one world and share the agony and joy in all its multiplicity and complexity.

I feel deeply in debt to the main subject of this book, Shoki Coe. I consider Shoki Coe my greatest mentor and thus feel it a great honour to translate this work about his life. Shoki's path and my path crossed many times. I was baptized as an infant by Shoki's father. Shoki was my teacher and mentor. I was not one of Shoki's chosen ones to teach at the school Shoki had built up and loved so much, yet I ended up not only teaching there but also becoming one of Shoki's successors to head the school for nearly as long as Shoki did, even though I could live only on the reputation my predecessors had already established for the school. God did indeed work and will continue to work with "his left hand" to carry out his purpose in spite of human frailty and the inability to perceive God's handiwork in the meantime, as Shoki might say.

I met Shoki Coe abroad at least once each year after his exile from Taiwan, so I had the good fortune of hearing many stories of his experiences in this book firsthand. Every meeting and conversation with him was an inspirational experience. I am grateful that the author had the audacity to put these stories in writing, which I could not do. Much of what Shoki taught and said to me will definitely stick in my mind as a lifelong tribute to this person—a great prophetic trailblazer for theological education in Southeast Asia and developing countries—and also for the self-determination of Taiwanese people.

Much gratitude is due to the Taiwanese Presbyterian Church in Livingston, New Jersey—where I serve as minister—for granting three months leave of absence to make this translation possible, and also to Peggy Hsiao, my spouse, who did the initial reading and editing of the transcript.

Above all I wish to express my most sincere thanks to the Rev. Dr Peyton Craighill, formerly a colleague of Shoki, who read and corrected the transcript carefully and made valuable suggestions before it was given back to the author to handle arrangements for publication.

Siau Chheng-hun
(Ching-fen Hsiao)

Appendix 1
Favourite Quotations of Shoki Coe

Shoki Coe's life was one of constant running, traveling, consulting and giving lectures, often missing meals or lacking sleep, just like when he joined
the soccer team in his university prep school, becoming a dynamic team
leader that constantly drew cheering shouts of "Ooh!" and "Aah!" from the
spectators. In order to enlarge his own knowledge and perspective, he often
had to read or prepare his speeches or reports through the whole night. He
had an abundance of ideas, vision and inspiration. However, he did not have
enough time to put them in writing, nor did he have a travel partner to record
his thoughts and statements. What he left were short articles, correspondence
and annual reports from when he served as staff and director of the Theological Education Fund. After he retired from his position, he still stayed active
and used his spare time to work diligently for the Taiwanese democratization
movement. Only after he was urgently persuaded by his friends and students
did he begin to work on his memoir.

What follows are some of Shoki's sayings that I remember from my student
days that I would like to share:

Quotation from Different Sources
Sometimes he mentioned their source, but not always.
"When a bird is dying, its sounds are sad, when a person is about to die, his
words are good." (Niáu chi chiong sú ki bêng iā ai ek; jîn chi chiong sú ki giân
iā siān ek.)

"When the sea dries, its bottom will be revealed, yet when a person dies, no
one can see his mind." (Hái ko˙ chiong kiàn tí, jîn sú put ti sim.)

He often referred to these two quotations, to the difficulty of knowing a person's mind, and human's intention of striving for goodness. They are almost
like Psalm 8, which prompts human beings to ponder the mystery of life and
provokes a response.

"Continuity in discontinuity, and discontinuity in continuity."
(Hui liân-siòk-sèng ê liân-siòk, liân-siòk ê hui liân-siòk.)

Shoki Coe liked to use these words to speak of the relationship between the Old and New Testaments and also of the relation of Christ and culture and history. When he left his position as the director of the Theological Education Fund, he used these words to explain the intricate relationship of the old Theological Education Fund and the newly emerged Programme for Theological Education: "Not united, yet not separated" (Put chek put lī.). He used this expression to speak of the duality of humanity, such as human mind and human action.

Shoki Coe quoted Lord Acton's famous dictum—"All power corrupts, absolute power corrupts absolutely"—to speak of ethics in politics considering that Christ is the Lord of politics and history. Whether it was Hitler or Chiang Kai-sek, they were all true examples of making power absolute. His explanation was more theological, rather than naming the politicians directly: "Where there is life, there is hope. Where there is hope, there is life."[1]

Shoki Coe's Own Words

"Water" and "tears of a mother"—although both consist of water, their qualities of life are totally different, and they just cannot be put beside each other for comparison. This was how Shoki used to compare human body and human spirit. The instability of the Italian government (in early 1950s, when a prime minister organized a new government, which fell in a few short months) was given as an example to show the price that democracy had to pay and the path that it had to go through.

When one preaches, he should be like "nailing a nail by hammering at the right spot repeatedly," that is, to make the main point, main message, clear and stick in the mind of the hearers. This was advice he liked to give to seniors who preached their senior sermon.

On the Miracle of "Five Loaves and Two Fishes"

"It is far more miraculous to change a stone-hard heart into a living heart than what chemical changes or mathematical multiplying can ever make. This is the power of God."

Shoki believed in the miracle of the loaves and fishes, but he considered the biggest miracle the change of human heart and mind. By the miracle of Jesus and the willing heart of a small child, selfish and greedy hearts were turned into hearts of love and sharing with Jesus and others so that all were fed and more than enough was left over. And there was also a much better result—many believed in Jesus because of what he said and did.

On Jesus' Unwillingness to Turn Stones into Bread (Matt. 5:3-4; Luke 4:3-4)

This is God's way of dealing with the socioeconomic and human situation. Nothing can be detached from human relation with God and interdependent relations of human and human.

On Jesus "Not Being Able to Save Himself from the Cross" (Matt. 27:42; Mark 15:30)

"This is God's mighty power," or in other words, "the power of the mighty love of God." There are too many "great shows of mighty powers" in the world, aiming to conquer, to subdue, to silence others who are different or who hold different opinions. But God, who was in Christ, limited himself to be the same as humans.

On Søren Kierkegaard

Shoki often referred to Kierkegaard's story, "The love story of the prince and the young girl." There was so much difference in their background—the understanding of life, thoughts, power and environment—between the prince and the peasant girl. But the prince, in the process of befriending, conversing and expressing himself, was very careful and considerate, mindful of his love and care for the girl so as not to dare in any manner, in his spoken words, interaction, or even clothes, to show off the glory and beauty that might surprise the girl. He only patiently waited until his relationship with the girl, their mutual understandings, mutual trust and feeling matured. He waited until that happy moment when he could bring her to live in the palace.

On the contents of the book *Fear and Trembling*, Shoki pointed out the inner struggle of "Abraham as a model of faith" and "Abraham as a murderer" as an expression of a deep-rooted faith. Faith, he said, was a rage that "cut through" all criminal motivation. It was not blind but, on the contrary, had clear sight of the "deep-rooted sin" in one's own self.

"Wretched man that I am! Who will rescue me from this body of death?" (Rom. 7:24) and "As it is written, there is no one who is righteous, not even one" (Rom. 3:10).

Shoki loved to quote these two verses to express the human situation, that is, how humans are under the total control of sin. To him this is the presupposition of Christian faith and salvation. Whenever he quoted these, he used the

Taiwanese version of translation in which the word "who" ("is to rescue me") stands out distinctively with clear designation.

On Martin Buber's I and Thou

These words frequently were quoted and applied in Shoki Coe's speeches. He regarded these words as a unique expression of what human relations are or should be. If a human being is regarded as "it," a human being is demeaned and becomes a "thing," a great insult to the person. He used the following as an example: There was a tall and handsome, well-dressed, uniformed guard at the entrance to the British Museum. He stood there not even making a slight motion that could be seen. He looked almost like a sculpture or wax man, so much so that visitors often mistook him for a display item and commented about his appearance, treating him as an object—"it." But that seemingly immovable sculpture began to move, to show that he was a living person, which immediately made these visitors realize that a person just could not be regarded as a "thing." It was not right to treat a person as an "it." Human relations must always be "I and thou" rather than "I and it."

"United We Stand, Divided We Fall"

This was the theme of the World Christian Youth Conference in Amsterdam. This dictum was quoted by Shoki Coe for the first time at the Synod meeting of the South Synod of the Presbyterian Church in Taiwan when it was held on 1 August 1948. He used it to advocate the necessity of the unity of the church in Taiwan. He was particularly pleading for the cooperation of theological colleges. He was of the opinion that Tainan Theological College should not restart its operation separately.

And at the 1948 Taiwan Christian Youth Rally/Conference in Tamsui, Shoki used this theme to appeal to the youth of the church to press forward to organize a united church, beginning with organizing an all-Taiwan united youth association. This appeal to the church indeed bore fruit—a Taiwan Christian Youth Association (TKC) was formed.[2]

"Text and Context"

Shoki Coe's unique and creative theological thinking is now identified as "contextual" theology. "Contextualization" is now widely deployed. When the author was a student at Tainan Theological College, this word was yet to be coined. However, during class lectures the author often heard him saying that in the course of history, the church had been greatly dictated by what he called "non-theological factors." His interpretation was that "there was no pure moral justice in the world" just as there was no pure or naked "text" without "context." Logos needs to become flesh or to appear in context in order to manifest the essence of Logos. This is why "the Word became flesh and dwelt among us." All we can do is allow that "Word" to become "flesh" in our concrete situation or context.[3]

"God's Left Hand Is at Work, Yet I Do Not See"

This quotation is derived from Job 23:9. Shoki used this Bible verse to speak of God's acts of grace that often are hidden from our eyes. He credited this to a sermon he heard from the minister at the church in Redhill, a suburb of London. When I was a student at Tainan Theological College, I heard Shoki quote it on several occasions. He used it to interpret the developments in history, in confusing and complex situations, in which God works his purpose out by giving quietly and abundantly his grace and power to the weak who do not yield to struggles.[4]

This quotation has been engraved on our hearts as the center of Shoki's teaching. In the section discussing "mission" during the 1954 WCC General Assembly, when Christians were discouraged about missionaries being kicked out of China, many thought the mission in China had failed. But Shoki used this verse from Scripture to pose a challenge to the church's world mission. He also pointed out there was a North Korea and a South Korea, a North Vietnam and South Vietnam; if there is a China, there will be a Taiwan as a challenge to our mission. After the WCC Assembly, the chair of that section, Dr D. T. Niles (of Sri Lanka) in his writing on mission theology mentioned Shoki Coe's "One China One Taiwan" challenge and the quotation of Job 23:9.[5]

Chickens and People

In responding to the question to Shoki Coe, "Why are you so effective in finding the source of funds and the funds to support your theological college?" he answered, "If you are a chicken, you must scratch hard, if you are a person you must be able to search around" (Chòe ke tiòh chhéng, chòe lâng tiòh péng). A chicken must use its claws to scratch to find food; a person must be diligent to look all over to find resources to do what is needed.[6]

Appendix 2
Record of Matins Led by Shoki Coe
at the To Dai YMCA Hostel

Wednesday, April 25, 1934
Hymn 264[1]
Scripture: John 2:1
Hymn 450

Reflection (by Shoki Coe)

The thirty years of struggle of Jesus Christ gave a ray of light to humanity who was spiritually bankrupt and on the verge of death. The blood he shed on the cross was infused abundantly into us, the sick and weak, so that we could respond to this love with gratitude, and be empowered. Having been "planted" in the heart of John who experienced this abundant love, how could he not sing praises like a living spring coming out from his heart? However, what kind of world scene do we see nowadays! The mighty and powerful, with unreserved energy, are looking for the weak to swallow, sweeping away faithfulness, justice and love, always keeping watchful eyes to wait for every opportunity to destroy. In the present situation the existing religions, although not willing to follow suit, nevertheless turn themselves into a defensive posture, busying themselves in external matters, regarding religion as something to provide peace of mind for themselves or techniques of self-edification. Do we see some of this tendency in some Christian denominations? If so, it is unusual and it should not be so! I believe Christianity's original aims must be pro-active, and creative. I think the blood of Christians must always be full of the will to destruct with creative spirit. I also believe that Christian action is to work toward the fulfillment of "IDEA." Whatever obstacle we encounter, we must strive to remove it. Although Jesus was willing to be crucified on the cross, he never gave up his fight with social evil and spiritual pollution! Alas, my spirit always falls asleep and is weak, and seems to be defeated by the evil power of this world, always on the verge of los-ing my idea. I often wish that I had forty days and nights like our Lord in the wilderness for quiet meditation! Since I came to live in this hostel, I have always felt very grateful that we have this time of morning prayers. My purpose of living in this hostel is not only for the sake of self-edification in fellowship with God, but also to quietly prepare for that very moment to come, that is, the moment the fire in my heart be lighted and explodes! I feel that morning prayer in the last three months is like the period of time for meditation and preparation of our Lord in the wilderness.

Saturday, May 12, 1934
Hymn 2
Scriptures: Revelation 13
Hymn 513

Monday, May 21, 1934
Hymn 54
Scriptures: Revelation 20
Hymn 528

Short Homily (by Shoki Coe)

"I shall pour out my Spirit to all...your young shall see visions" (Acts 2:17). Yesterday was Pentecost Sunday. The Holy Spirit must come upon us all. It was on this day that the companions of Jesus who were scattered by the wind of timidity and fear, were suddenly awakened and stood up to their sense of mission. It reminds us of ourselves as a small group of people, who were once ignorant and discouraged by what we did, and it would not be hard for us to imagine what we, the Christians, might do today to face all difficulties our society is encountering. Each one of us must first discern our own vision in order to move from a passive and inactive mode of life into being a proactive Christian. The Christians in the founding era of the church are like kindling fire. They were fires that could not be removed. No, they were not the fires that could not kindle other fires. Their "burning fire" was the most powerful source of their being; it was the point of departure of Christianity; it is what makes a religion a religion. As we reflect on the status of Christianity, how may we compare with them?

We have splendid church buildings where we may hear sermons of love preached, hymns of angelic voices sung, gracefully translated scriptures read in attractive tones. They are all but beautiful decorative lights, giving light to whoever and whatever remains in there. They are only lights, lights wrapped up in decorative glass cases. They may shine, but not kindle any fire. They are only convenient and useful things to have. Is this the only raison d'être of a religion? If so, there are more academic and concrete ethics and more moral theories than religions in the world, so why bother to hold on to religion?

Nowadays we have an unprecedented number of atheists. Before we look into the root cause, I feel it is necessary for us to painfully examine our static and conceptualized religion. All over our society today people are facing dead-end streets or they are in the bind of a dilemma. However, people are in search of help and salvation from quarters other than religion. What does this say to us? Before we blame our contemporaries for being "too secular" or "this-worldly," we must be critical of "conceptualized" religion. If I am allowed to use my own way of expression, I will say, "The religion of fire that will kindle and bring forth other fire has now been replaced by encased electric light. The living religion of life has been turned into religion of a conceptualized system." What kind of vision shall we hope for and look for in this Pentecostal season? It must be a vision that will "convert the concept of love into the practice of love."

Tuesday, May 29, 1934
Hymn 228
Scripture: John 5
Hymn 529

Thursday, June 7, 1934
Hymn 559
Scripture: John 13
Hymn 225

September 11, 1934
Hymn 322
Scripture: Acts 5
Hymn 513

Thursday, October 11, 1934
Scripture: Psalm 11
Prayer
Hymn 451

November 26, 1934
Hymn 2
Psalm 4
Prayer
Hymn 513
Silent Prayer

On Church and the Individual

Since the World War (WWI), there has been plenty of desire for self-examination in the areas of philosophy, theology and other fields. Anything that is not good has been forced to come down from the top of the ivory tower. Emphasis has been placed on the independent, individual aspect of humanity. When it reaches its apex, it also exposes its worst and meanest end. This must revert back to a more humane domain. It is natural, that the Christianity that has been resolved into this type of secular culture will not be able to avoid the same destiny. Is the reason that the church, consciously or otherwise, falls into the state of "powerlessness" because it has eaten the forbidden fruit? It must be the liberalism of the church that has become the mother of the concept of "non-church"! To understand religion as the basis of individualism, and to seek God through an individual manner eventually leads to the loss of true human existence and the meaning of the gospel of Jesus Christ.

Without you and I both there will be no way of "knowing." Without me, "you" are only a name without substance. "Human exists in responsibility." It is here in this relationship that there is love. There is no love within the same substance, such as there is no love between the same electrons. Only when there are different substances can there be a relationship of love.

Outwardly speaking, church is one form of society. What is seemingly a society, church is in reality established as a result of anti-society, a society that has been separated yet remains a part of it. Church is a society given by the revelation of God through Jesus. This church that is established by Jesus does not reject society just because Jesus was in that society, church. No, both societies belong to the same body.

An abstract individual, as long as it is an abstract concept, remains a mere concept. We have regarded the conceptual individual as a real individual; that is why the church has been misunderstood, and thus, it is powerless. If a person leaves the church, he is still called a Christian, but he is no more an appropriate disciple of Jesus, he is only a believer of modern thought. I can say it aloud that our church today is far away from what it ought to mean to be a church. I am not afraid to confess that our church today does not mean anything to me. But I cannot leave the church; if I leave the church it amounts to meaning that I have lost myself. This means that if the church does not exist, I as an individual do not exist either. The denial of one existence is based on the denial of the other. Rejecting the church is rejecting oneself. Our self-contradiction is also the self-contradiction of the church. Similarly, one's own uplifting and leaping forward is also the uplifting and leaping of the church. It is illogical to tighten steel cable on one side of the suspension bridge and let it loose on the other side.

The church and the individual are tied together in unity. This does not mean to be constantly changing. One must hold on tightly to the revelation of Jesus; carefully review one's own existence and life; consider carefully about the future image of the church. This is the task I have been given. I speak in this manner not intended as criticism of others, but as a way to review and to criticize myself.

Friday, November 30, 1934
Hymn 240
Psalm: 47
Prayer
Hymn 510
Silent Prayer

Thursday, December 6, 1934
Hymn 50
Psalm: 52-53
Prayer
Hymn 450

Tuesday, April 9, 1935
Hymn 506
Scripture: Isaiah 1

Love is our Logos, prayer is our weapon. Whom do we have to be afraid of? We pray that his record book will be the record of our spiritual journey.

Friday, April 12, 1935
Hymn 534
Scripture: Isaiah 3
Prayer
Hymn 322

Shoki Coe's short comments

Recently I read Kenichi Tsuchida's book on "Toyohiko Kagawa" until midnight. When I looked into my own life through a great saintly person's life, I found my own weakness, my insensibility to sins; I must be contrite to repent of my sins. In confronting an absolute death, everything is relative. Let us look at Toyohiko Kagawa, who has leaped over the line of demarcation of death! Everything that he encountered became merely a possible idea. Everything in life to him, it seemed that he must continue to bore through with absolute love without stopping. I do not believe that he did and would only follow the arguments of fanatic believers of "only relying on faith alone." When a person only emphasizes the theory of "Logos," he is like holding on to the spirit as the only essence, and falling into the dualism of spirit and "flesh" in which the Logos has taken form. This person's religion will become dogmatic idealism. I certainly realized that idealist religion is something that looks like truth yet in reality is false. It is like an emasculated religion, an escape from society, not true Christian religion.

April 18, 1935
Hymn 2
Scripture: Isaiah 8
Hymn 299
Silent Prayer

Sunday, April 21, 1935
Weather: Sunshine
Left the hostel at 6:30 a.m. to go to the Botanical Garden for a joint worship service and have breakfast of "rice-balls"

Wednesday, May 1, 1935
Hymn 506
Scripture: Isaiah 18
Prayer
Hymn 508

Monday, May 6, 1935
Hymn 506
Scripture: Isaiah 22
Hymn 505
Silent Prayer

Friday, May 10, 1935
Hymn 118
Scripture: Isaiah 26
Prayer
Hymn 228
Silent Prayer

Short Message by Shoki Coe

Language is an instrument to express human existence. Therefore, language acquires its being at the very moment when "I and Thou" are connected. But sometimes the language shows its demonic nature, showing forth the conflicting existence of the object and self. In like manner, language often carries this double nature, revealing the true nature of humanity, expressing and experiencing the conflicting reality of love and freedom, and we all have the experience of using the words of love and freedom very lightly, as we are all human. But if we push further and ask, "what is love" or "what is freedom," we will find it very difficult to have satisfactory answers. If the essential meaning of Christian religion is love, at this time of crisis for Christian religion, I think, we must all use our being to experience this love. At this time, when freedom is under threat all over, if one says that we must have freedom, then where can we find a new light that will lead us to find freedom?

May 15, 1935
Hymn 294
Bible: Isaiah 30
Prayer
Hymn 311
Silent Prayer

May 20, 1935
Hymn 322
Bible: Isaiah 34
Prayer
Hymn 320
The Lord's Prayer

Friday, May 24, 1935
Hymn 322
Bible: Isaiah 38
Prayer
Hymn 208
Silent Prayer

Thursday, May 30, 1935
Hymn 506
Bible: Isaiah 41

Prayer
Hymn 505
Silent Prayer

Tuesday, June 4, 1935
Hymn 510
Bible: Isaiah 45
Prayer
Hymn 450
Silent Prayer

Saturday, June 8, 1935
Hymn 509
Bible: Isaiah 49
Prayer
Hymn 525
Silent Prayer

Thursday, June 13, 1935
Hymn 529
Bible: Isaiah 53
Prayer
Hymn 450
Silent Prayer

Tuesday, June 18, 1935
Hymn 253
Bible: Isaiah 57
Prayer
Hymn 322

Wednesday, July 3, 193
Hymn 450
Bible: Psalm 51
Prayer
Hymn 322
Silent Prayer

Friday, July 5, 1935
Leader: Hiroshi Karigawa
Hymn 10
Bible: Jeremiah 4
Prayer
Hymn 568
Silent Prayer

The worship leader put the following on the record book:

A few days ago Kenji Ishido went back home; there were only three "villagers" in our village (i.e., Hiroshi Karigawa, Kiyoshi Takemoto, and Shoki Coe). I hope this record book will not stop and remain in somebody's hand. Please make note that it will continue to circulate among the "villagers," to read, and to add more in it.

Appendix 3
Chronology of the Reverend Shoki Coe

1914 August 20. Born in Chiong-hòa, Taiwan
1915 January 1. Baptized by the Rev. Campbell Moody
     April. Accompanies his father, Ng Sū-bēng, who serves for a year as pastor of Kiâm-chúi-káng Church
1916 April. Joins the whole family to move to the dormitory Tióng-êng Boys School. Father becomes a Bible teacher and dormitory warden
1922 Enters the public primary school affiliated with Tainan Teachers' School
1925 Fall. Big fight with Japanese children
1926 January. Younger brother Éng-hui dies
     Summer. Mother, Lîm Kim, dies
1927 January. Grandfather, Ng Lêng-kiàt, dies
     April 14. Enters Presbyterian Boys Middle School
     December 11. Confirmed by the Rev. Duncan MacLeod
1930 March. Transfers to Aoyama Middle School, Tokyo, as fourth-year student
1931 April. Passes exams, enters Taiwan High School, Taipei
1934 March. Enters Tokyo Imperial University Philosophy Department, lives at Todai YMCA Hostel
1936 Moves from Todai YMCA Hostel, lives with sister, Siok-êng, and cousin, Lîm Sūi-hûn, at a house in Nakano, Tokyo (bought by his father Ng Sū-bēng)
1937 March. Graduates from Tokyo Imperial University, Philosophy Department; meets his younger brother, Bêng-hui, on board a Japanese liner; brother punished for speaking Taiwanese with him
     July 7. Sino-Japanese War begins
     August 11. Boards the Kashima Maru to leave Taiwan for England
     September 21. Arrives in England
     September 22. Arrives in Birmingham to begin studies at Selly Oak
     December. Guest of the Landsboroughs in Redhill for the first time, meets young David, who is the same age as Shoki and was born in the same town, Chiong-hòa
1938 September. Enters Westminster College, Cambridge
1939 July–August. Attends World Christian Youth Conference, Amsterdam, Holland
1940 September. Enters Westminster College, Cambridge, as third-year student

175

1941   June. Graduates from Westminster College, Cambridge
       Granted status as candidate for ministry, awaits call and ordination by
       South London Presbytery, Presbyterian Church of England; commis-
       sioned as Mission Educator by the Overseas Missions of the Presbyte-
       rian Church of England, itinerating among different churches
       December 8. Japan declares war with Britain and the United States after
       Japan's attack on Pearl Harbor; as a colonial subject of Japan, Shoki
       becomes an enemy alien and his movement is restricted
1942   February 21. Granted special permission for freedom of movement within
       England by order of the British Home Office; begins Chinese Mandarin
       language course at School of Oriental and African Studies (SOAS)
1943   Introduced by Overseas Missions Committee of the Presbyterian Church
       of England to teach British military officers Japanese language at SOAS
1944   August 12. Married to Winifred Sounders, a missionary of the Women's
       Missionary Society, the Presbyterian Church of England, at Redhill Church
       September. Appointed a fulltime teacher at SOAS for three-year term,
       teaching Japanese and Hokkien Chinese
1945   February 9. German V-2 rocket hits the Offices of the Presbyterian
       Church of England; Secretary of Overseas Missions, the Rev. Douglas
       James dies, building and historical documents destroyed
       May 8. Germany surrenders to the Allied Forces
       August 15. Japan surrenders to the Allied Forces
       August. Eldest son David born
1946   October 17. Decides to resign from SOAS to return to church work
1947   February 28. Massacres in Taiwan
       July 22–August 1. Attends World Conference of Christian Youth and
       World Christian Education Conference in Oslo, Norway
       August 10. Boards SS Empress of Scotland in Liverpool to leave Eng-
       land, his home for ten years, with wife Winifred, son David; on the
       same ship are newlyweds David and Jean Landsborough
       September 1–5. Ship makes port call at Singapore
       September 9. Ship calls at Hong Kong to stay for six days
       September 15. Boards "Wing Song" to head for Keelung; September 17.
       Arrives in Keelung; reaches home in Tainan by train on September 23.
       September 29. Begins as a Bible and English teacher at Tiong-êng Mid-
       dle School
1948   February. The Ninth South Synod of the Presbyterian Church in Tai-
       wan meets at Táu-la̍k; Shoki advocates a united church to combine
       South and North synods, to continue working together in theological

education; the South Synod votes to reopen Tainan Theological College April 1. Reopening of and Thanksgiving for Tainan Theological College August. All Taiwan Christian Youth Conference meets in Tamsui

1949   May 3. Second son, Michael, born in Tainan; August 22. Ordained, takes the office of principal of Tainan Theological College

1950   April 16. The Rev. Ñg Sū-bēng (Shoki Coe's father) dies

1951   March 5. South and North Synods join to form the General Assembly of the Presbyterian Church in Taiwan; decides to hold stated meeting every two years; also votes to join the World Presbyterian Alliance and the World Council of Churches

July. Visits the Office of WCC in Geneva, Switzerland, and attends WCC Ecumenical Institute in Bossey. Negotiates for formal membership in WCC for the Presbyterian Church in Taiwan

September–November. Stanley Smith and Frank Cartwright visit Tainan Theological College

November 20. Daughter Eileen born

1952   September. Revises the curriculum of Tainan Theological College to a "Five Year Curriculum System"

Establishes Department of Religious Education

Initiates Refresher Course for ministers in the field

Visit of Secretary for Asia, United Presbyterian Church, USA, Dr Charles Leber; discussion with Shoki Coe on establishing a Christian university in Taiwan

1953   Visit of Dr Frank Cartwright, Executive Secretary of the Nanking Theological Seminary Board of Founders, its trustee, Bishop Ralph Ward, and others to Tainan

August. Invited to Bossey and Geneva to join the Preparatory Committee of the WCC General Assembly to be held the following year; visits England on the way to Geneva

November. US Vice-President Richard Nixon lays the foundation of Tunghai University

Serves, with Ñg Bú-tong, Tân Bêng-chheng and others as the first trustees of the Board of Tunghai University

1954   February 22–27. "Consultation of Mission Strategy" held at Tainan Theological College; "Doubling the Church Movement" formed, strategy sent to WCC for reference

June 20 and for the next six months. With assistance provided by Overseas Missions of the Presbyterian Church of England, wife Winifred and three children have sabbatical leave in Seaford, England

July–September. Visits Union Theological Seminary, New York; meets Reinhold Niebuhr and others

Visits Yale Divinity School

Visits Princeton and Princeton Theological Seminary; attends the General Council of World Presbyterian Alliance as a representative of the Presbyterian Church in Taiwan;

Attends the assembly of WCC in Evanston, Illinois, representing the Presbyterian Church in Taiwan

1955 Rebuilds the main hall of Tainan Theological College (now Barclay Hall) Builds a new administration building (now houses student union, lounge, faculty lounge) and library (now language centre and classroom No. 9)

June 8. Third son, Andrew, born in Tainan

1956 September. Revises the Theology Department into a "Six Year Curriculum System"; initiates a new Curriculum for university and college graduates

1957 Construction of new College Chapel, "New Hall Dormitory" (now women's residence and married student quarters, and one faculty residence) Elected moderator of the Fourth General Assembly of the Presbyterian Church in Taiwan (Ng̍ Bú-tong elected general secretary); GA becomes a yearly assembly

1957–1958 December to January. Invited to the International Missionary Council meeting at Accra, Ghana; Theological Education Fund established

1959 Invited to serve as Chair of the Advisory Committee of Missions, United Presbyterian Church, USA

October–June, 1960. Participates in PARS (Programs for Advanced Religious Studies; designed for leaders of younger churches) of Union Theological Seminary, New York, as its leader

1960 April. Awarded Honorary Doctor of Divinity by Knox College, Toronto, Canada

June–August. Joins family in England on his way home from New York

1961 December. Attends the assembly of WCC in New Delhi, India, as representative of the Presbyterian Church in Taiwan

1963 Construction of Research Centre building of Tainan Theological College (library) and a duplex faculty residence, and the official residence of the principal

1964 Construction of kindergarten classrooms for practice teaching; a pipe organ installed at the Chapel; construction of the Centenary Hall, residence hall of ten units of faculty housing at Tainan Theological College

1965   March. Granted honorary D.D. by Tokyo Union Theological Seminary
       June 16. Leads the One Hundredth Anniversary Celebration of the
       Presbyterian Church in Taiwan as the moderator of that year (Twelfth
       General Assembly)
       June-August. Wife Winifred and youngest son Andrew (nine) join him
       from England for the centenary events
       Becomes associate director of Theological Education Fund, WCC, with
       office set up in Bromley, Kent, England
1966   June. Granted multiple entry permits to Britain
1967   June. Granted British citizenship
1969   September. Receives invitation by the Executive Council of the World
       Presbyterian Alliance to apply for the position of general secretary of
       the World Presbyterian Alliance at the suggestion of president of Princ-
       eton Theological Seminary, James I. McCord; but he declines invitation
1971   August. Becomes the director of the Theological Education Fund, WCC
       December 29. The Presbyterian Church in Taiwan issues "Statement on
       Our National Fate"
1972   March. The Rev. Daniel Beeby becomes "persona non grata" and is
       deported from Taiwan
1973   December 25. Initiates "Taiwanese for Self-Determination," cospon-
       sored by Ňg Bú-tong, Lîm Chong-gī, and Sòng Chôan-sēng
       March 20. As one of the initiators, joins with 21 other persons, holds
       a press conference at Washington Press Club in Washington, D.C., to
       issue the "Declaration of Taiwanese Self-Determination Movement"
1974   March. Joins Taiwanese gathered in Wuppertal-Barmen to found Euro-
       pean Chapter of Taiwanese Self-Determination Movement
1975   November. The Presbyterian Church in Taiwan issues the statement
       "Our Appeal"
1976   February. Joined by the Rev. Tiō Iú-gôan to visit Brazil to organize Tai-
       wanese Self-Determination Movement Brazil Chapter
       March 7. Appears with Sòng Chôan-sēng, Tiō Iú-gôan, Daniel Beeby,
       and Boris Anderson before British Parliament to discuss the issues on
       Taiwan
1977   July 31. Theological Education Fund completes its tasks and evolves
       into a new agency, Programme for Theological Education; office in
       Bromley closed; office removed to Geneva; new director takes office
       August 1; Shoki becomes consultant to the new agency, PTE
       August 16. The Presbyterian Church in Taiwan issues "Declaration of
       Human Rights"

1979 August. Retires from position of consultant of PTE

1980 April 18. The Rev. Ko Chùn-bêng (C. M. Kao), General Secretary of the Presbyterian Church in Taiwan, arrested; Shoki Coe appeals to world church for prayers and concerns for Ko and the church in Taiwan
Joins Phêⁿ Bêng-bín and other Taiwanese abroad to organize and promote "Formosan Association on Public Affairs" (FAPA)

1982 July 10. Makes a special trip to New York to officiate the wedding ceremony of Ông Ài- lân and Ông Kìn-it at Newtown Church

1984 April. Conducts Mrs. Margaret Landsborough's One Hundredth Birthday Thanksgiving service at Redhill United Reformed Church where Shoki and Winifred were married

1987 July 29–31. Welcomed along with delegates of Taiwanese Church abroad at the Mission Consultation held at Sin-tek Presbyterian Bible School
August 2. Attends the Thanksgiving service for the homecoming of distinguished alumni of Tióng-êng Tiong-ha̍k (Presbyterian Boys Middle School)
August 3. Awarded honorary D.D. by Tainan Theological College—first visit after 22 years of involuntary exile from Taiwan

1988 March 20. Attends a special dinner in his honour at Taiwanese Hall, New York City, given by Taiwanese living in the eastern United States; a special fund in his honour set up
Final entry in his memoir.
October 28. Dies about 7:00 pm. in Seaford, Sussex, England, age 74
November 4. Funeral service held for him at the United Reformed Church in Seaford
December 3. Mrs. Winifred Coe, Shoki's wife, dies in her hometown of Seaford, Sussex
December 13. Memorial Service for Shoki and Winifred Coe held at Tainan Theological College

1991 *Recollections and Reflections* published after careful editing by Boris Anderson

Notes

Introduction

1. Shoki Coe, *Recollections and Reflections*, ed. Boris Anderson, 2nd ed., Formosan Christians for Self-Determination, 1993.

1. Country and Family: A History of Struggle and Faith

1. *The Historical Annals of Taiwan* (in its Annex, 20) contains the following entries:

According to the opinion expressed by Yongcheng Emperor of the Ching Dynasty on nineteenth day of the eighth month in 1723: "Since ancient time Taiwan has not been civilized. From old Taiwan was not a part of China (Chungkuo). His late Majesty Emperor Kang Hsi, using only a small military force incorporated it into the Empire." (*Yongzheng Chao Tonghua Lu 1*, {*Records East China of the Yongcheng Reign*}).

"The history of the development of Taiwanfu" in Vol. 271 of *Ta Ching Yi Tong Chi* [*Records of Unified Rule of the Great Ching*] by Chen Hui Hua, etc. published in 1774: "Since ancient times, Taiwan has been an uncultivated, desolate land. It is not in communication with China. It was named Tong Fan [Eastern Barbarian Land]. During the reign of Tianchi of the Ming Dynasty, it was occupied by the Red-haired Barbarian Dutch. It belongs to Japan." In Vol. 473 of the 1882 Edition, however, the line that reads "It belongs to Japan" was deleted.

2. *The Historical Annals of Taiwan* (in its Annex, 12) has this entry:

In fear of attack by the forces of Koxinga, the Han people were prepared to flee. The leaders of the Han secretly informed the Dutch that even though Koxinga might not be able to attack and occupy Taiwan, in order to provision the troops he brought in his fleet he might order them to plunder the land, robbing great quantities of food, domesticated animals etc. Looking, we find that even as early as the time of the Dutch occupation, the Han (Chinese), like the Dutch, were ready to rob Taiwan, take booty with them and flee. (*The Forgotten Taiwan*)

3. *Draft Records of the History of the Province of Taiwan.*

4. *Historical Annals of Taiwan*, 24.

5. For the long-time residents of Taiwan, the island became "the land with Tang (Han) male ancestors without Tang female ancestors."

6. The descendents of Ñg Lêng-kiat believed that Tong Liông Keng Temple was his professional base of operation.

7. To seek for a god who could bring offspring to the married couple was one of

the reasons people switched their religion in those days. Another major reason for switching religion was to get cured of a "terminal disease" that a family member had.

8. Translator's note: The old name of the city is Tá^n-káu.

9. *Kàu-hōe Kong-pò* (*Taiwan Church News*), October 1886.

10. Translator's note: Shoki Coe, *Recollections and Reflections*, ed. Boris Anderson, 2nd ed., Formosan Christians for Self-Determination, 1993.

11. The Japanese began to set up a "Domicile Registration System" in 1900. In the registration, N̂g Lêng-kiat was the head of the household, while N̂g Sū-bēng was listed as N̂g Lêng-kiat's eldest son.

12. Edward Band, *Barclay of Formosa*, Tokyo: Christian Literature Society, 1936, 77-78.

13. Coe, *Recollections and Reflections*, 24.

14. The father of Tiō Thian-chû, the first Taiwanese principal of the "Presbyterian High School."

15. This term is a direct quotation from his own written resume; the meaning is not quite clear.

16. The resume is collected in Series 5 of Prof. Lōa Éng-siông's *Stories of Taiwan Church History—Tâi-ôan Kàu-hō Sú-ōe*.

17. *Far Horizon* (October, 1940): 78-79.

18. The year when N̂g Sū-bēng enrolled at that school, the school was granted accreditation by the Japanese Governor's Office as "Su-lip Tâi-lâm Tiú^n-ló Kàu-hōe Ko-téng Hak-hāu" (Private Tainan High School of the Presbyterian Church), commonly called "Tióng Tiong."

19. Translator's note: The meaning of "hui" is "ray (of sunshine)" or its derivative meaning "glory." So the literal meaning of Chiong-hui (shoki) is "Ray or Glory of Chiong-hòa."

20. Translator's note: Han language and literature would be known today as "Chinese." The written form of Chinese was developed into maturity during the Han Dynasty (third century BC to third century AD) of the Middle Kingdom (China). The people and the language were both named "Han." This form of writing has been adopted as well as adapted by other people in East Asia, most notably Korea and Japan. The ruling dynasty of China changed through the ages. Sometimes non-Han (non-Chinese) were in power who had their own language, such as the Ching (Manchurian) Dynasty. Thus Han language and literature is a general term for classic Chinese that has been in use since the Han Dynasty. Even up to today, the Japanese refer to the Chinese characters or ideographs they use as "Kanji," that is, the written letter of the Han (people and/or nation).

21. Cf. Iû^n Sū-ióng, *Biography of Famous Persons of Faith in Taiwan (Tâi-ôan Sìng-gióng Bêng-jîn Tōan)* Vol. 2, pp. 83-86, and Iû^n Sū-ióng, *Biography of Famous Persons of Faith,* revised and edited by Lîm Sìn-kian, p. 85.

22. A "minister" is a consecrated vocational title given by the Christian church. A scholar or a person of religious conviction and profession is not necessarily a "minister."

However, a minister has a vocational responsibility to nurture the spiritual life of a group of people, to be a guide for their daily living, and to care for their welfare.

2. Early Years (1916–1937): Education against the Odds

1. Shoki Coe, *Recollections and Reflections*, ed. Boris Anderson, 2nd ed., Formosan Christians for Self-Determination, 1993,10-11.

2. Translator's note: This term is used here to refer to the literature and writing system developed during the Han Dynasty of the Middle Kingdom (known as China today), which spanned about 450 years between about 200 BC to 240 AD. The term "Han" has been used by the Japanese and by countries and areas under the cultural influence of the Middle Kingdom to refer to anything—literature, medicine and otherwise—that was supposed to have come from there.

3. The name of the school has gone through several changes:

1885: Tiúⁿ-ló-kàu Tiong-hak (Presbyterian Middle School).

1906: Tâi-lâm Tiúⁿ-ló Kàu-hōe Ko-téng Hak-hāu (Tainan Presbyterian Church High School), also called Tâi-lâm Tiúⁿ-ló-kàu Ko-téng Hak-hāu (Tainan Presbyterian High School).

1912: Tiúⁿ-ló-kàu Tiong-hak (Presbyterian Middle School).

1922: Su-lip Tâi-lâm Tiúⁿ-ló-kàu Tiong-hak (Private Tainan Presbyterian Middle School).

1939: Su-lip Tâi-lâm Tióng-êng Tiong-hak (Private Tainan Cho-ei Middle School).

1949: Si-li Taiwan-sheng Tainan-shi Changjung Middle School (Private Changjung Middle School, Tainan Municipality, Taiwan Province).

4. The media, controlled by the government, attacked the leadership of the school since (1) it was headed by an English Presbyterian and not a Japanese, (2) Less than half the trustees were Japanese and the school should not be lead by Taiwanese, 3) Christian principles should be supplanted by the national educational guidelines and (3) Taiwanese culture and language should be forbidden in any educational institution.

5. Coe, *Recollections and Reflections*, 51.

6. In 1931 Abe became the dean of the Theology Division, and subsequently in 1933 he became the chancellor of Aoyama Gakuin College. By 1939 Abe was appointed by the Overseas Mission of the American Methodist Church to become the sixth bishop of the Japan Methodist Church. Thus he became the top leader of the Methodist Church in Japan at a time when Protestant denominations were under government pressure to unify. In the end, he became the president of the Association of Protestant Churches in Japan, and when momentum led to the organization of the United Church of Christ in Japan (Nippon Kirisuto Kyodan), Abe became its moderator. In 1941 he, by instigation of the Japanese government, became the chairman of "Great Union of Religions in Japan," assuming the role of "religious diplomat" to carry out appropriate activities in the territories in China occupied by Japan until the end of the war. He did what was conscionable, under

the pressure of militarism, to carry out his role in international and human relations, and he did his share in the work of God's Kingdom.

7. Translator's note: It was a custom in Taiwan at the time that if someone who was a close family friend and was born in the same year and in the same town as a parent (father), he would honorifically be addressed "Tâng-nî-pa" ("same-year father") and his wife "Tâng-nî-bó" ("same-year mother").

8. After World War II, in 1949 when Aoyama Gakuin started a University Division, these two buildings of the Middle School and High School were converted for use by the University.

9. In his memoir, Shoki says it was Mr Tanaka. However, on the roster of history teachers, he was listed as Tetsui Tsumuda.

10. *Chancellors' Reports, 1930–1931.*

11. Translator's note: The school system in Japan and Taiwan was similar to the European system. There were six years of primary school, five years of middle school and then for academic study, there was high school, like Gymnasium or "Prep-school," in order to go to university. Otherwise, there were technological or vocational types of high schools beyond middle school.

12. Coe, *Recollections and Reflections*, 43.

13. Ibid., 49.

14. Ibid.

15. Ibid., 60.

16. The record of Matins has been faithfully kept by the hostel. For a record of the services led by Shoki Coe, including his homilies, see appendix 2.

17. In 1929 Yanaihara published *Taiwan under Japanese Empire*. In 1934, the year Shoki entered To-Dai, Yanaihara published *Manshu Issues*. The Japanese government immediately issued an order to suspend publication of these books on Taiwan and Manshu. In the year of Shoki's graduation from To-Dai, 1939, the professor's article "Ideal of a Nation," to be published in the journal *Chuo Koron*, was entirely deleted. Finally, the professor was stripped of his professorship on 4 November 1939.

18. This issue was shown to the author in 1999 when he visited the To-Dai Y and met with the current director, Toshihiko Tokuhisa. Unfortunately, half of the essay has been lost.

19. Translator's note: The Japanese word *fu-an*, here translated mostly as "unrest," can be understood variously according to the context and situation. It may mean civil "unrest," "disturbance," or "restlessness" or "anxiety" in one's heart or conscience, similar to *angst* or simply "uncomfortable," not feeling at ease.

20. Translator's note: This section is taken verbatim from Shoki Coe's *Recollections and Reflections*, 242-44. A Taiwanese word that is used in the title, "m̄-gōan," appears several times in his autobiography. It is an expression of a deep feeling or emotion evoked by a gross injustice being perpetrated, and it carries the meaning of "unacceptability" or a sense of an "unvindicated grudge."

21. Translator's note: NYK stands for Nippon Yusen Kaisha, Japan Postal Shipping Corporation.

3. England (1937–1947): A New World for Learning

1. Translator's note: This temple is like a "cathedral" of the local religious community.

2. Translator's note: Shoki's memoir says the ship was Kashimura Maru, a four-thousand-ton cargo ship.

3. Translator's note: Shoki's memoir puts the date as some time after 15 August. Therefore, the dates of subsequent port calls at different places may differ from what is stated here.

4. Translator's note: The original text in Chinese ideograph mistakenly puts it as Kuala Lumpur, although the English notation is correct.

5. *The Christian Advocate*, April 1938, 202.

6. *Overseas Missions Committee Minutes*, vol. xii, 1935–1938.

7. Translator's note: A place near Madras, India. The original text gives a different name.

8. When Shoki Coe was in Taiwan High School (Wan-ko), he became an active member of the Japan Student Christian Movement, led by the Rev. Hugh Macmillan. He must have been excited and glad to meet a number of old friends and colleagues at the conference.

9. Shoki's friend, the Rev. George Hood, also asserted that Shoki Coe obtained the endorsement of the Presbyterian Church of England to participate in the conference, because the Church had this outstanding mission product to contribute to the worldwide church. Translator's note: George Hood, one time Executive Secretary for the Council for World Mission, was a missionary of the Presbyterian Church of England to South China, Singapore and Malaysia, and classmate of Shoki Coe at Westminster College, Cambridge, 1938-41.

10. Report of the Japan YWCA, *Young Women* (Journal) 1940.

11. Kiyoko Takeda shared her recollections with the author in the late 1990s.

12. Sasaki was a friend and ministerial colleague of the author.

13. Japan YWCA, *Young Women*, 1940.

14. Translator's note: the Principal of Tainan Theological College at that time.

15. Both Shoki Coe and George Hood entered Westminster College in the same year, 1938. Both also were at the SOAS, Hood preparing to go to China as a missionary and Shoki as a Japanese teacher. With the consent of the Overseas Missions Committee, George Hood was ordained and assigned to be a pastor at Wellyn Garden Church, Marlly Hill. On weekdays he continued his course at the SOAS. Shoki preached in his church several times, as did Boris Anderson. Hood's father-in-law was Rev. Douglas James. In May 1945 Hood left London via Calcutta and flew over Burma to Kunming, China, as a missionary. In November of the same year, his wife Elizabeth took the same route to fly to Kunming. They then went through Hong Kong to Sòaⁿ-thâu to assume their missionary work. This was to continue the line

of his wife's grandparents and parents who did their missionary work in the same place. In 1948 they used their vacation time to go to Taiwan for the first time to visit Shoki and Winifred.

16. Translator's note: In Taiwanese custom, the groom's family is to pay a gift of money to the bride's family, something like betrothal money. At times, this gift is considered mandatory, even though it is generally understood as a show of good-will. This gift is called "phèng-kim" in Taiwanese language.

17. In March 2002, the author visited the church in Redhill where Shoki and Winifred were married, accompanied by Dr David Landsborough and Professor Kathleen Moody. Much of the sanctuary remains the same as it was in 1944, with the addition of a brass plaque placed on the right side of the sanctuary, in memory of James Taylor Gillespie, the young pastor who conducted their wedding, who died in a traffic accident not long after the event. There is, however, no record of their marriage at the church in Redhill, possibly because Mr Gillespie died before he put it on record. No doubt, however, that a record exists at the city hall. Those who witnessed the wedding are in no doubt that the marriage took place. The simple reception for the couple and fifty well-wishers was held in the fellowship hall behind the sanctuary, Prof. Moody said, in an atmosphere of celebration and abundant good wishes. Among the well-wishers was Dorothy Edwards, the immediate superior of Shoki at the SOAS and chief instructor to Winifred, George Hood, and Boris Anderson who made an impressive speech of congratulation and best wishes to the bride and groom.

4. Return to Taiwan (1947–1965): National Identity and International Outlook

1. Translator's note: The term also known in the Western world as the "Nationalist"—in contrast to the "Communist"—government on the Chinese mainland.

2. On 27 February 1947, an incident in which Chinese Kuomintang officials confiscated the goods and money of a woman selling cigarettes on the street sparked a strike in Taipai the following day and an anti-Nationalist revolt that spread around the island. Kuomintang troops were sent in, killing an estimated 18,000 people.

3. Translator's note: Better known as Chung Chi-an, among those in the international YMCA circle.

4. Coe, *Recollections and Reflections*, 123.

5. Translator's note: At the height of World War II, the college refused the Japanese government's order to name a Japanese to be the principal of the college, so it was ordered to close and merge with the theological college in Taipei.

6. Translator's note: The words used to describe "selfhood", though three in number, are different from what is known as the Three-Self Movement of the church in China. The first term in Taiwanese is "chū-chú" and carries deeper and more varied meanings than what is commonly meant by "self governing." It means "self-hood," taking initiative to make responsible decisions. The second term "chū-iȯk" emphasizes using native personnel for educational and nurturing responsibilities

rather than relying on the traditional sources of European and American missionary teachers.

7. Translator's note: It is known today as the United Church of Christ in Japan. It originated out of a forced merger by the Japanese Government of all Protestant denominations existing at that time, including Anglican/Episcopalian, Congregationalist, Holiness, Methodist, Reformed, Presbyterian, etc. After the war, except for the Episcopal/Anglicans, nearly all denominations decided to continue together as a united church.

8. Translator's note: The school, after going through several mergers, is now Tokyo Union Theological Seminary, called in Japanese the Tokyo Shingaku Daigaku in Japan.

9. Translator's note: The compound was an English Presbyterian Mission compound, with multi-story buildings. The compound had been removed to this new location from a much older one, so the name meant the "New Multi-Story Building Compound." Even today, this name remains to refer to this neighborhood of the city, although all the old "New Buildings" are all gone and replaced with modern facilities.

10. This meant, for instance, that the assets of the Tainan Presbyterian High School's Founders Fund which was $200,000 in 1936 in Japanese Yen, melted down to be worth only $5 in New Taiwan dollars.

11. Translator's note: The Overseas Missions Committee of the Presbyterian Church of England was related to the South Synod, and the Foreign Missions of the Presbyterian Church of Canada was related to the North Synod. The Presbyterian Church in southern Taiwan was the result of the missionary work of the Overseas Missions of the Presbyterian Church of England and in northern Taiwan of the Presbyterian Church of Canada.

12. Translator's note: This organization has been rechartered in the State of New York as the Foundation for Theological Education in South East Asia so that it may carry out its mission to a wider area in Asia.

13. Translator's note: The translator assumes that this programme was the so-called PARS (Programme for Advanced Religious Studies).

14. Translator's note: This is a pun in Taiwanese as there is no distinction between the sounds "L" and "R" in Taiwanese.

15. During Shoki Coe's absent years in England, his domicile registration followed his father's household to move to Ôan-lîm, and then move back to Tainan at the address of No.7 Sub-cross-lane 1, Chheng-liân Road. This designation of address was subsequently changed to No. 22, Lane 1 of Phok-ài Road. However, nobody knew how his registration was separated from his father's household to form a new household as head of the Tainan Theological College.

16. According to Ñg Teng-hui (the fifth son of Ñg Sū-bēng), when the household registration was removed from Ôan-lîm to Tainan, a mistake was made. Teng-hui's name was not removed from the registration in Ôan-lîm, and later was charged

by the Chiong-hòa County of "evading the draft to mandatory military service" (a draft dodger). An outstanding warrant was issued, and eventually he was prosecuted at Taichung District Court.

17. Coe, *Recollections and Reflections*, 237.

18. Ibid., 238.

19. Ibid., 153.

20. Translator's note: This Board was later renamed United Board for Christian Higher Education in Asia.

21. Following Daniel Beeby's report, planning for a university began in 1954 and in 1955 the decision was reached to establish Tunghai University.

22. See page 63 of this volume.

23. Later, when Shoki Coe was director of the Theological Education Fund, he asked Prof. John Foster to write a book on church history that could be used as textbook for the Fund.

24. As a preparatory meeting for the Presbyterian Church in Taiwan for the forthcoming WCC Assembly to be held in Evanston, Illinois.

25. Coe, *Recollections and Reflections*, 198.

26. Ibid., 201.

27. Translator's note: It means literally people from the "Mountain." The phrase "Kang-san" or "rivers and mountains" (abbreviated as "mountain") refers to the domain of the Chinese "dynasty." In the modern era it is normally called "Tn̂g-soaⁿ" (the Tang Mountain)—the Tang Dynasty Domain, a dynasty in ancient China—so as not to offend the current Imperial Court. "China Town" in New York City is still call "Tn̂g-lâng-ke" (Tang-ren-jie), the "town of Tang people." In Taiwan, the people from the "Mountain"—Chinese—is used to contrast with the "Sweet Potato," native population.

28. To clarify, the "great obstacle," which was the closure of China as a huge mission field, was a human obstacle and not outside of God's providence.

29. Chou Lien-Hwa, *Memoir* (Taipei: United Literature, 1983), 270. Chou Lien-Hwa graduated from Shanghai University with a bachelor's degree in business management. In 1949 he went to United States to study and earned a doctorate from a Southern Baptist institution.

30. Ibid., 271.

31. The day American President John F. Kennedy was assassinated.

32. Chou, *Memoir*, 279-80.

33. Coe, *Recollections and Reflections*, 134.

34. Ibid., 134-35.

35. After 1965 the United Board also gave considerable support to the Fund for Theological Education of WCC for which Shoki Coe served as an executive staff.

36. Coe, *Recollections and Reflections*, 215-16.

37. Translator's note: "Ha̍k-īⁿ" is a normal designation of an academic institution that is on the level of a college or university, while "su-īⁿ" is used for a lower

level school. This meant that the Kuomintang wanted to "demote" or "demean" theological education as insignificant low-level private learning.

38. This was certainly my own experience of the military training.

39. Among the invitees was Taiwan True Jesus Church, a denomination which had a long history in Taiwan. In the initial stage, this church responded very enthusiastically, however, due to historical differences in theology and other factors, it withdrew its participation.

40. ICCC as compared with WCC is quite a different kind of organization, and much smaller than WCC. "ICCC influence in the world is limited. It is a very conservative.... organization that was split off from Presbyterians. As it is against the Presbyterians, so it holds the "anti-Presbyterian" stand. Its first target aimed at Korea, for Koreans tend to be conservative, and absolutely anti-communist, so it fit well there. The Presbyterian Church in Korea was greatly damaged by this group." Chou Lien Hwa, *Memoir*, 269.

41. The World Alliance of Reformed Churches.

42. Chou, *Memoir*, 271-72.

43. Ibid., 272-73.

44. Ibid., 274-75.

45. Ibid., 276-77.

46. C. S. Song, ed., *Self-Determination—The Case for Taiwan*, 2nd ed., 1998 (*Chhut-thâu-thiⁿ*, Documents related to Taiwanese for Self-Determination Movement), 160-61.

5. Contextualization in Action (1965–1980): Organizing Ecumenical and Political Movements

1. See Shoki Coe, the Executive Director's Report of 1977, referring to the report given at the last meeting in July 1973.

2. *Chhut-thâu-thiⁿ*,13.

3. Ibid., 20.

4. Ibid., 21-22.

5. C. S. Song, ed., *Self-Determination—The Case for Taiwan*, 2d ed., 1998 (*Chhut-thâu-thiⁿ*, Documents related to Taiwanese for Self-Determination Movement). English version, 34-36.

6. Song, *Self-Determination*, 60.

7. Ibid., 47-48.

8. *Chhut-thâu-thiⁿ*, 72.

9. Ibid., 81-83.

10. Ibid., 133.

11. Ibid ., 135-136.

12. Ibid., 137-38.

13. Translator's note: An incident happened at a rally in Kaohsiung, on International Human Rights Day, 10 December 1979, at which demonstrators were

unreasonably attacked by security forces, causing injuries. The authorities saw this as a "seditious" move, and hundreds were implicated and convicted accordingly. However, this incident marked the beginning of a long struggle for democracy and human rights in Taiwan. The term "Formosa Incident" derived from the fact that the leaders involved in this rally were mostly related to a journal, *Formosa*, which had been advocating political reform and human rights in Taiwan.

14. Translator's note: "Chhut-thâu-thiⁿ" is an expression in Taiwanese to say that a person has been relieved of or liberated from oppressive authorities. Literally, it means raising one's head above the clouds and seeing the sky.

6. Active Retirement (1980–1988): Final Reflections

1. When Chiang Ching-kuo was the sixth president of the country, Lee Teng-hui was elected to be his vice-president. At the time of Chiang Ching-kuo's death on 13 January 1988, Lee Teng-hui succeeded him as the seventh president.

2. Translator's note: The Taiwanese version of translation of the word "because" carries the meaning of "just as" which makes this concluding word of Shoki's original Taiwanese speech more powerful.

3. Ko Chùn-bêng, *The Way of the Cross*, 383.

4. Translator's note: An agency set up by the United States to act as the American representative office in Taiwan when diplomatic relations with Taiwan was severed. It may be considered the American "embassy" representing all American interests in Taiwan, although international diplomatic protocol will not allow it to be called so. The Institute was established by the US Congress, and so it was not under the direct jurisdiction of State Department.

5. Translator's note: It is a common saying in Taiwanese to mean only superficial change, or, only the form is changed not the substance. Literally, it means that only the soup is changed, the substance has not been changed, as in a multicourse Taiwanese feast, some courses are basically the same except for the soup.

6. *Pacific Times*.

7. Translator's note: Or "m̄-goān." A sense of what is totally unacceptable. See the translator's note on page 186, note 20, of this volume.

8. These two persons with the same family name, though not related, were both elected to leadership position of the Presbyterian Church in Taiwan at the same time, moderator and general secretary respectively; they were neighbors in the Sin-lâu compound in Tainan; both strived to gain membership of the Presbyterian Church in Taiwan in WCC; both worked hard to establish Tunghai University; and both were cofounders of the Taiwanese for Self-Determination Movement.

9. *Bîn-chìn Chiu-khan*, No. 89, p. 40.

10. No. 1915 (November 13, 1988).

11. *Kàu-hōe Kong-pò*, no. 1915.

7. The Significance of Shoki Coe to Taiwan

1. Translator's note: In one of the meetings I had with Shoki Coe, he expressed his wish that if and when Taiwan becomes an independent country and issues its own passport, he would like to restore his citizenship as a Taiwanese and have his name officially spelled N̂g Chiong-hui in his passport.

2. Translator's note: This form of language is one of the major forms of languages spoken in Taiwan other than the government "official" language, Mandarin Chinese. The other form is known as "Hakka." One theory of the origin of the term *Hok*lo is that this language had been used by early immigrants from *Hok*-kien Province in China, so it takes the meaning of a language of the "folks from Hokkien" in contrast with the relatively late immigrant group from Kwantong Province, who were known as *Hak*-ka—which also can mean "guest" immigrants. The other theory pertaining to the term *Hoklo* is that it was originally called *Ho-Lok*, an area in central China, most likely the place where the Han Chinese culture originated. Hoklo language linguistically speaking is likely a precursor to the later form of Chinese, such as Mandarin. Furthermore, Taiwanese *Hoklo* in its form and pronunciation is very close to the language spoken in Amoy, Hokkien, a place just across from Taiwan on the other side of the Taiwan Strait—so in its classic form it is also known as Amoy Vernacular. Many words or phrases of the Taiwanese use today have been influenced by or adapted from native Taiwanese inhabitants, (the aboriginals of Taiwan) or other countries, so that it cannot be expressed by written Han (Chinese ideograph) character. The romanized version has the advantage of straightforward sounds that can even express the fine nuances and "pun" of the language.

Appendix 1. Favourite Quotations of Shoki Coe

1. Shoki Coe, *Recollections and Reflections*, ed. Boris Anderson, 2nd ed., Formosan Christians for Self-Determination, 1993, 73.

2. Ibid., 143.

3. Ibid., 118-19.

4. Ibid., 173.

5. Ibid., 174.

6. Translator's note: This is a Taiwanese adage. The last phrase can also mean "turn over every stone to find the treasure" or "a quick mind looks around for new possibilities." This adage reflects the diligent and hard work of the early settlers in Taiwan.

Appendix 2. Record of Matins Led by Shoki Coe at the To Dai YMCA Hostel

1. The hymnal used was a pre-war Japanese hymnal, *Sanbika*.

this page intentionally left blank

this page intentionally left blank

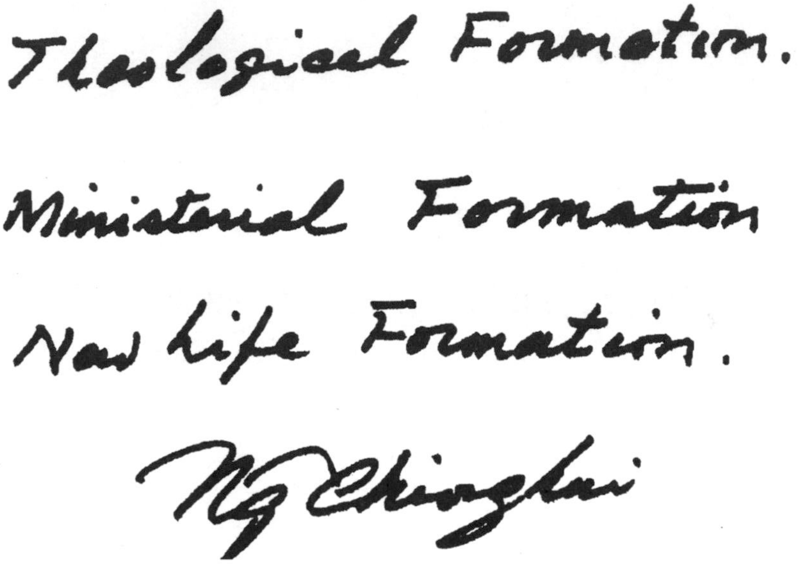

Theological Formation.

Ministerial Formation

New Life Formation.

Ng Chiong-hui

Fig. 21. Sample of Shoki Coe's thoughts and handwriting.